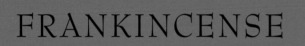

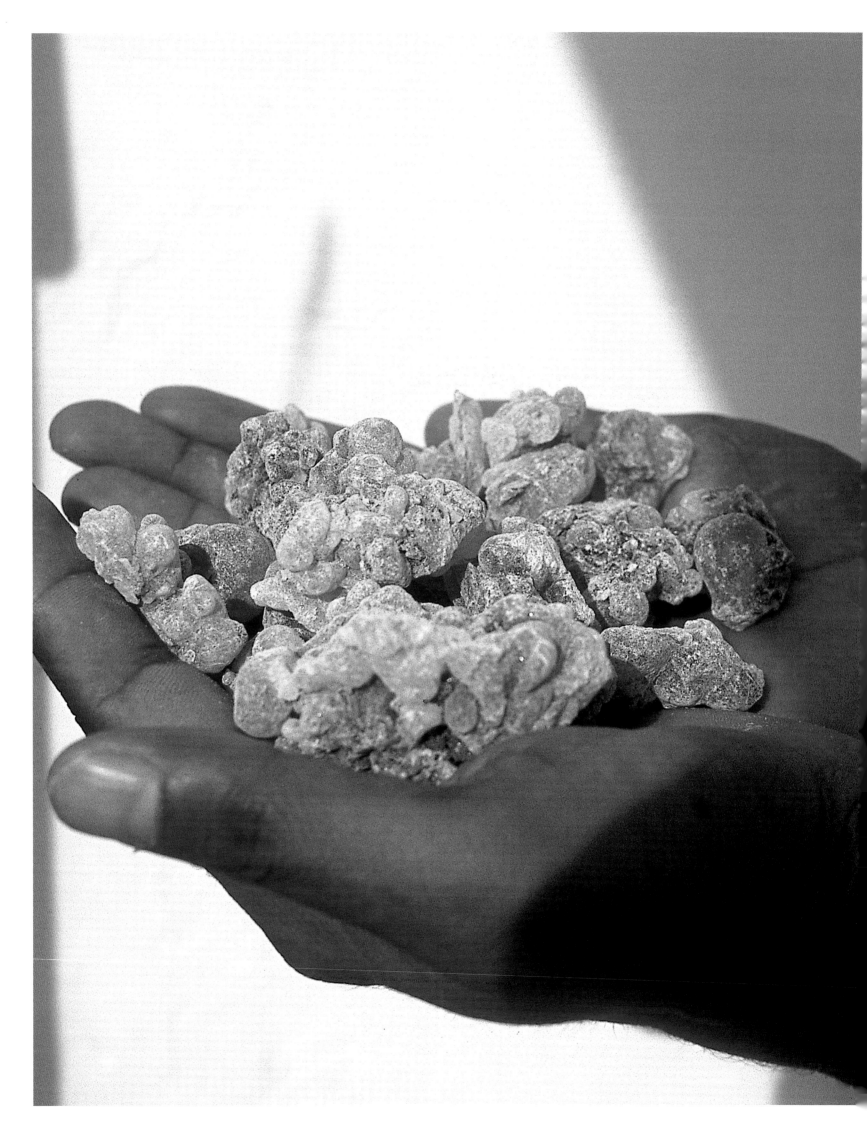

JULIET HIGHET

FRANKINCENSE

OMAN'S GIFT TO THE WORLD

PRESTEL Munich · Berlin · London · New York

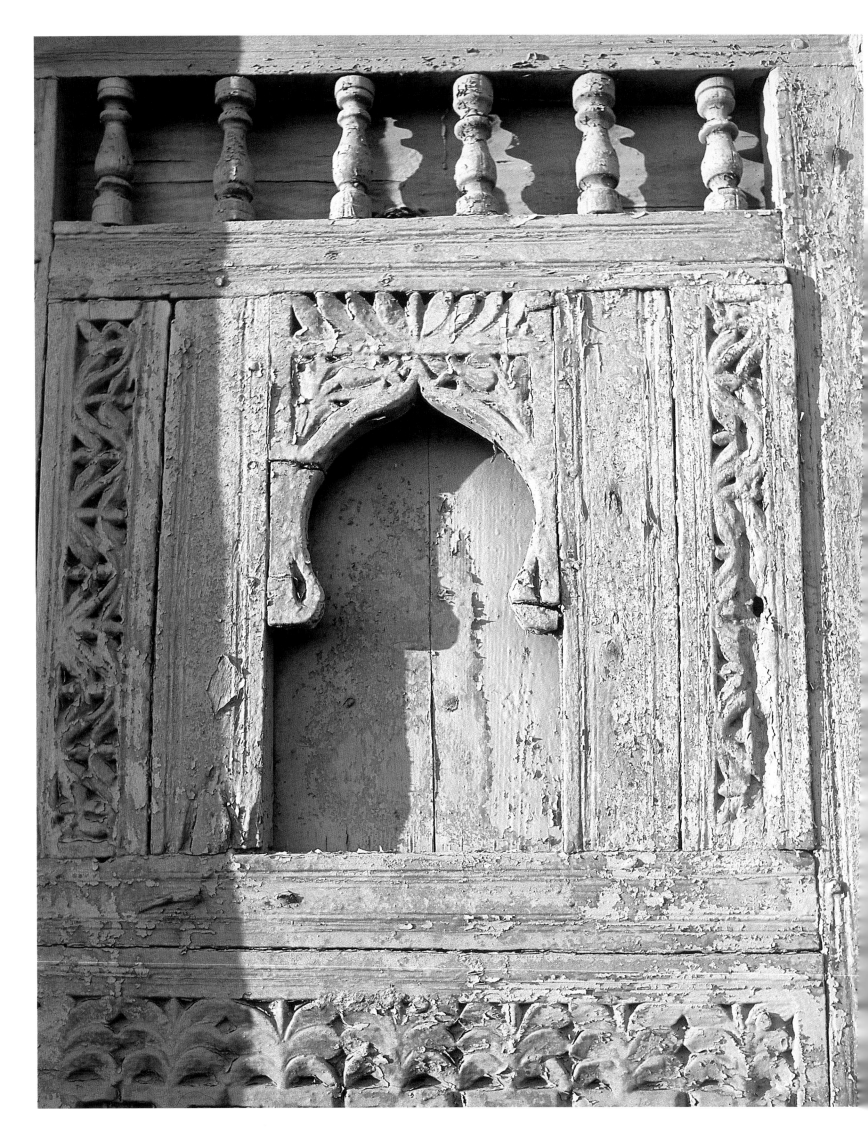

CONTENTS

PREFACE

I am very pleased that the history of frankincense has been recounted in this lively volume, which throws much light on the fascinating and mysterious past of a remarkable substance which was once worth its weight in gold. Traditional frankincense, an aromatic gum resin obtained from the *Boswellia* tree, has its home in the south-eastern area of the Arabian Peninsula, in what is now the Sultanate of Oman. The trade in frankincense was one of the most important commercial activities of the ancient and medieval worlds, and this trade led to the establishment of caravan routes and ports, as well as to exchanges and contacts between peoples. Archaeologists have found frankincense in the tombs of the Pharaohs of Egypt, and the Romans paid high prices for imported frankincense, as is mentioned in classical sources. Frankincense was exported to faraway China and Indonesia, and in return Chinese silks and porcelain as well as spices from Indonesia were imported to southern Arabia. It was used as an offering in religious ceremonies and its fragrance made everyday life more pleasant.

In 2000, the Frankincense Trail, now renamed the Land of Frankincense, in the Dhofar Province of the Sultanate of Oman, was inscribed on the World Heritage List by the World Heritage Committee. Among the 812 World Heritage Sites inscribed, four of them are located in Oman, of which the most ancient are the archaeological sites of Bat, Al-Khutm and Al-Ayn, Bronze Age sites dating from the 3rd millennium BCE. The Sultanate of Oman is to be commended for the consistent and substantial care it has given to its World Heritage sites to ensure both their preservation and their renown.

In reading about the history, travels and even poetry associated with frankincense through the ages in this enchanting and informative book, we are reminded of the importance of remembering and celebrating our World Heritage. In this particular case, I wish to acknowledge the role of His Excellency Sheikh Ghassan I. Shaker, a well-known philanthropist and humanitarian who has supported UNESCO projects in education and culture over many years. I am proud that Sheikh Shaker is the doyen of the UNESCO Goodwill Ambassadors. Even more than his generous financing of the publication of this volume, it was his inspiration and motivating energy that brought the project to completion.

KOICHIRO MATSUURA
THE DIRECTOR-GENERAL OF UNESCO

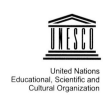

United Nations
Educational, Scientific and
Cultural Organization

FOREWORD

It was brought to my attention that a book was in preparation on frankincense. I learnt that the author and photographer had carried out extensive independent research for the text, and saw that she had taken an impressive collection of photographs over the course of fourteen years; all done because she was inspired by the historical, spiritual and practical significance of frankincense.

Long before an energy industry was even dreamt of, Oman was the major supplier to the ancient and classical world of frankincense. But how much does frankincense figure in general knowledge today, except that it was given to the infant Christ at his birth? This book brings to international attention the seminal role that it has always played in Omani and Middle Eastern society, past and present. So much is explored here, from its sacred meaning and historical associations, to functions in healthcare and modern perfumery. The work demonstrates how frankincense is still relevant to contemporary global realities.

The author has visited Oman five times to research and photograph the book, and also travelled to Europe, Yemen, Jordan, Egypt and other destinations along the frankincense routes. However, she was having no success in finding a publisher to undertake the project on a commercial basis. Nor did she meet with concrete support for publication from the various Omani local authorities she approached, although she did receive assistance from the Ministry of Information, who had faith in this effort.

I felt that such an opportunity should not be wasted for the Sultanate of Oman to capitalise on her work, and that it was an injustice that such detailed information was being ignored. In appreciation of the value of this work in presenting frankincense globally, thereby adding to the Sultanate of Oman's cultural heritage, and helping the country to assume its rightful place as a major contributor to the history of world civilisation, I took it upon myself to fully sponsor the tremendous effort by the author.

HIS EXCELLENCY SHEIKH GHASSAN SHAKER
PERSONAL ADVISOR TO HIS MAJESTY QABOOS BIN SAID,
SULTAN OF OMAN

SOUTH-EAST EUROPE,
EAST AFRICA AND
THE ARABIAN PENINSULA

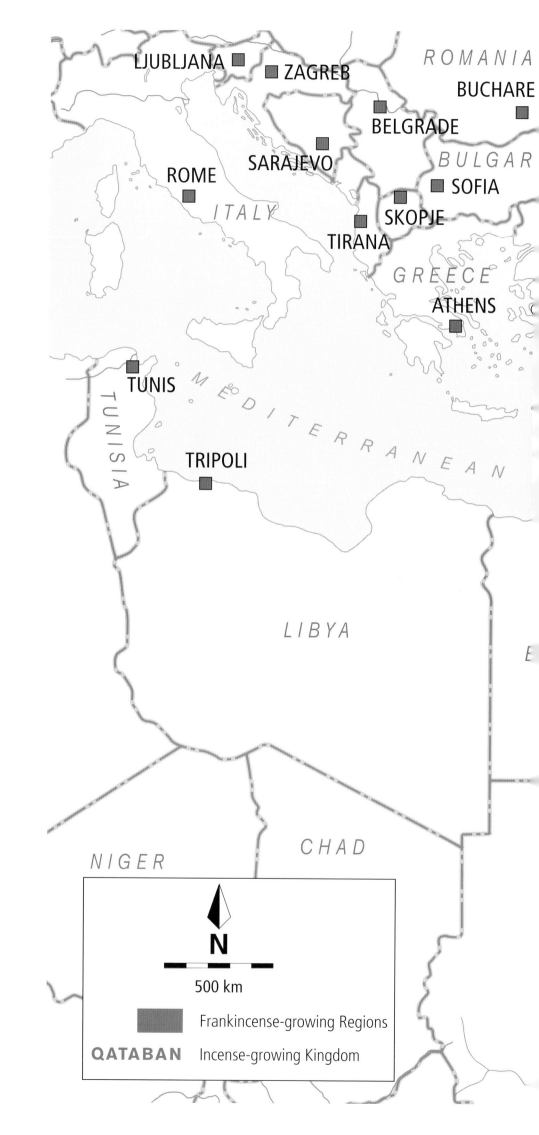

LJUBLJANA ZAGREB

ROMANIA

BUCHARE

BELGRADE

SARAJEVO

BULGAR

ROME

SOFIA

ITALY

SKOPJE

TIRANA

GREECE

ATHENS

MEDITERRANEAN

TUNIS

TUNISIA

TRIPOLI

LIBYA

CHAD

NIGER

N

500 km

Frankincense-growing Regions

QATABAN Incense-growing Kingdom

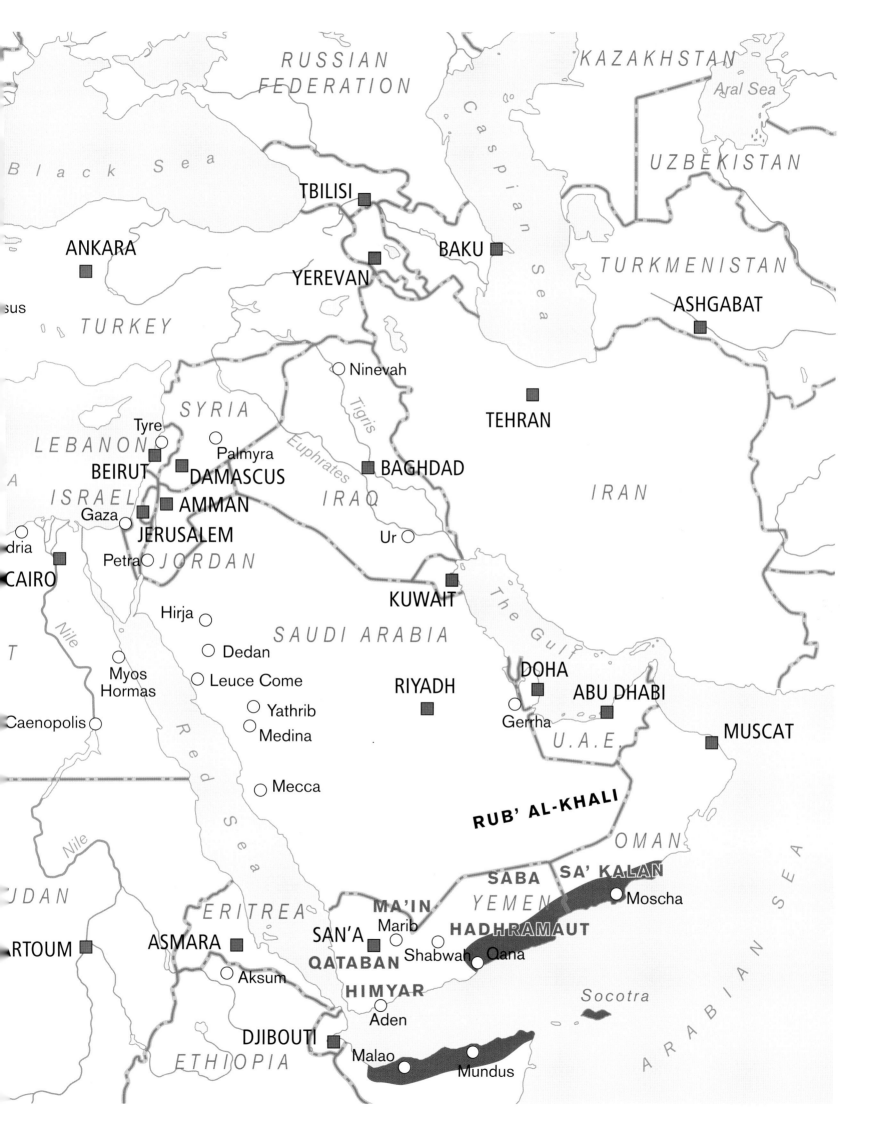

So perfumed

that the winds

were lovesick . . .

William Shakespeare,
Anthony and Cleopatra, act II, scene 2

INTRODUCTION

PATHWAY FOR PRAYER

Ever since Cleopatra sailed up the Nile to meet Antony, incense burners around her billowing forth frankincense, perfume has promised a world of exoticism, even eroticism. Yet the very fact that the Egyptian queen had chosen frankincense, which has powerful spiritual connotations, indicates its complex, many-layered dimensions. The word 'perfume' is derived from the Latin *per fumum*, meaning 'through smoke', and it was from burning frankincense that the entire history of perfume developed into the bottled fantasies of the global billion-dollar fragrance industry of today.

For at least five thousand years frankincense has been burned, its fragrant white smoke first recorded spiralling upwards in Sumerian temples some 3500 years BCE. Today its oil is used in therapeutic massage by aromatherapists and is still a constituent of modern perfumery. This gum resin, derived from strange, scrubby little trees in southern Arabia and north Africa, was one of the most prized substances in the ancient civilised world, valued as highly as gold and the gift of kings. Frankincense was and is very far from being just an alluring smell or a luxury item; nor is its legendary symbolic value confined to its healing powers, which range from treatment of psychological conditions such as stress and depression, to physical ones such as asthma and rheumatic pain.

Two thousand years ago, exactly at the time of the birth of Jesus Christ, who famously was given frankincense, as well as myrrh and gold, the incense trade was at its height, as important economically to Arabia then, as oil is now. Led by a star, the Three Magi travelled great distances to bring the three most valued products of the time to a baby in a stable. They brought with them spiritual offerings, appropriate for Christ's holy status. A tradition of gift-giving of precious perfumed oils existed in the region, the highest compliment one potentate could pay another. Frankincense symbolised divinity, myrrh indicated sacrifice and suffering, and gold implied royalty. Through its long association with religious ritual, frankincense itself was considered sacred. Its presentation to Jesus showed that, like frankincense, Christ's role was both to connect humans with God, and to be God.

Frankincense from Arabia travelled north by caravan on a long and hazardous journey to Jerusalem via one of the branches of the Incense Routes. The merchants timed their arrival there for late December, so as to arrive home in southern Arabia before the blistering heat of summer. When all the inns were full, travellers stayed in caves across the valley, as well as stables, offering their camels and donkeys

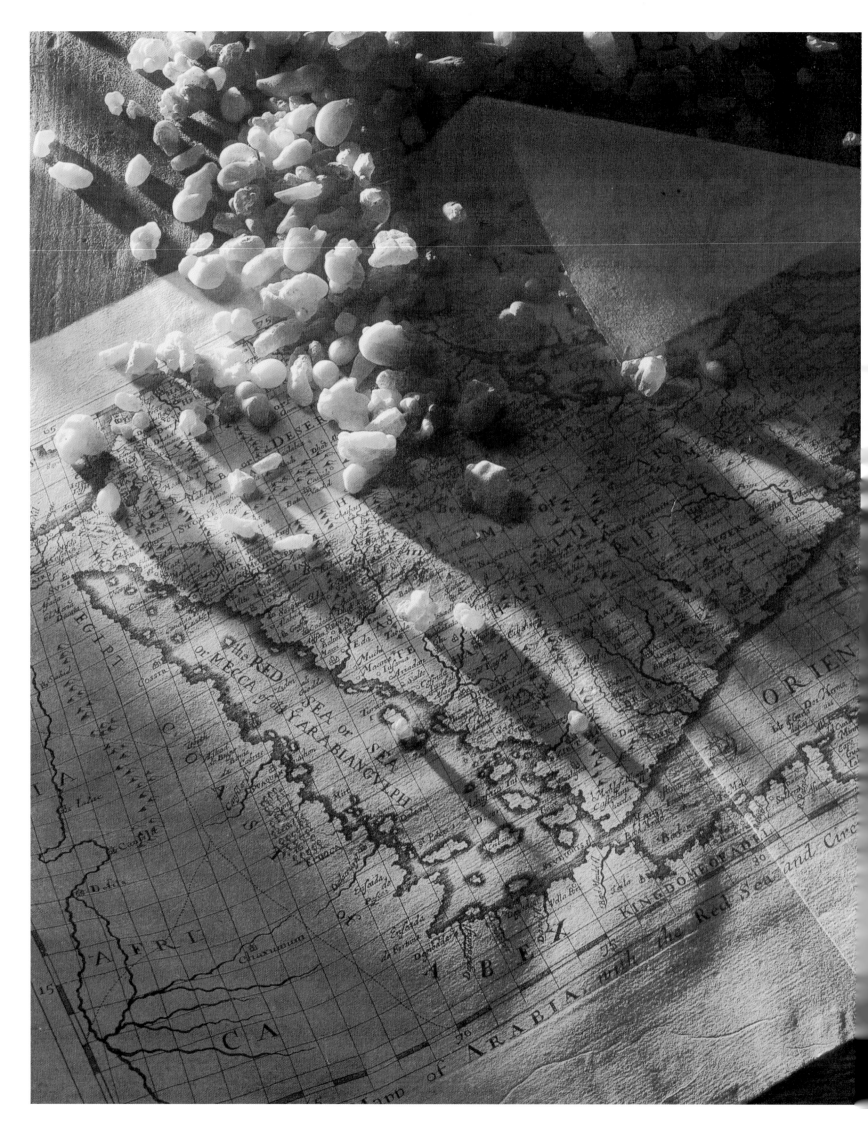

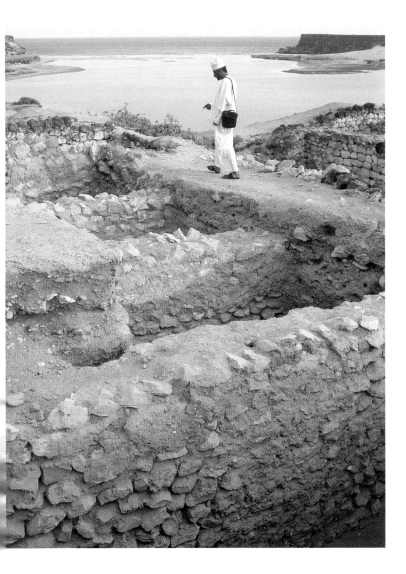

shelter from the winter weather. Arabian traders would have felt blessed if a baby had been born in their vicinity in such inhospitable circumstances, and they too might have offered tribute of frankincense.

At the apex of the trade, three thousand tons of the incense were recorded to have been exported annually to the Roman Empire alone. This frankincense came primarily from the Dhofar region of what is now southern Oman, thousands of kilometres south across mountains and the Rub' al-Khali, the vast, notorious Empty Quarter. Dhofar is where the best-quality product known as 'silver incense' is grown, described by the Roman writer Pliny as 'brilliant white and gathered at dawn in drops or tears in the shape of pearls'. Why were these 'pearls', these little pieces of resin, so prized that Alexander the Great planned to invade Arabia in order to control the trade in incense at its point of origin? Only Alexander's death prevented him from fulfilling his ambition of attaining such treasure.

Above: Storage areas for frankincense at the ancient fortress port of Sumhuram, ready for export from Khor Rori harbour beyond

Left: Frankincense crystals on an antique map of Arabia

Why would a Roman centurion be prepared to spend half his monthly salary on a pound weight of the stuff? Indeed, why did the Roman Senate send an army to colonise *Arabia Felix*—Happy Arabia, believed to be a land of unparalleled wealth—an army which got lost among the mirages of the Empty Quarter? In the first century BCE, the powerful king of today's Yemen *did* invade Oman in order to control the trade, establishing a fortified outpost there. Earlier still, in the tenth century BCE the legendary visit of the Queen of Sheba from her Sabaean kingdom in Yemen to King Solomon was ostensibly to test his wisdom, but almost certainly to secure an agreement on frankincense and myrrh advantageous to both parties. Sheba's spectacular wealth depended on control of the trade along her sector of the Incense Road.

The inimitable scent carried the fame of Arabia across three continents. The Sung dynasty in distant China sent its porcelain to Arabia to trade for it. The courts of medieval Europe complained about the amount of gold leaving their coffers, as physicians discovered the therapeutic value of frankincense as a preventative against plague; and Shakespeare's Lady Macbeth was wringing her bloodied hands, crying for the perfumes of Arabia to sweeten them.

As I write, the smoke from Omani silver incense rises beside me, and it is indeed a wonderful fragrance, warm, woody and balsamic, honeyed but not cloying, with an almost austere balancing note of pine and vetiver. Among some of the rich, heavy, floral perfumes of Arabia, it rings an unmistakably clear bell. But it is hard to understand rationally that the reason why frankincense had such status and value was

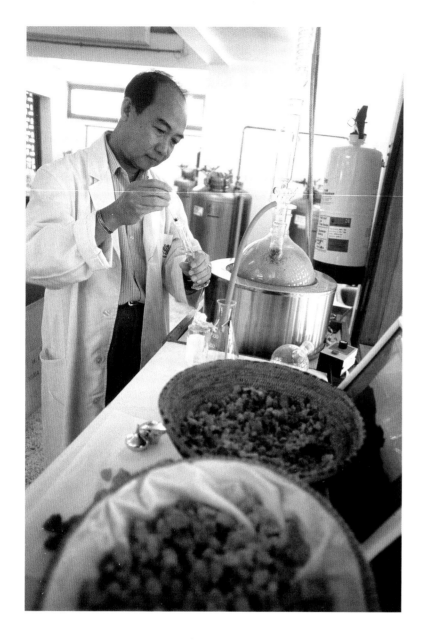

its intrinsic connection with spirituality. The answer is that the ancient world believed that frankincense pleased their gods. Since smoke rises to heaven, incense was considered the natural vehicle to carry prayers to the home of the gods, literally a pathway for prayer. As the Arab historian, Al-Tabari, wrote: 'Incense smoke reaches the heavens like no other'.

In Ancient Egypt it was 'the one who makes God known'. It was especially prized by the Egyptians for its connection to the Sun god Ra. Around 2000 BCE the use of *sntr* incense had largely been replaced by frankincense and myrrh. Egyptians believed that their souls would fly up to Ra on the wings of the smoke, which ascended every morning to honour the dawn. Holding long-handled censers called *amschirs* containing smouldering charcoal, the priests applied and re-applied frankincense while praying. As the sun rose, they would 'awaken' statues of the deities by passing the *amschirs* beneath their noses. As the smoke spiralled upwards, the solid crystals turned into perfumed clouds linking the material world below with the invisible domain of the gods above, who were inhaling the prayers. For those on earth, breathing in the sacred smoke together emphasised their oneness; and as their breathing deepened and slowed (one of the attributes of frankincense so conducive to relaxation and contemplation), they entered a collective meditative state.

The primordial symbol for Ra was the *utchat* (meaning 'all-seeing'), the sacred eye that accesses transcendent awareness. Other societies that worshipped solar deities such as Ra used frankincense for the same purpose, focusing on spiritual consciousness to attain transcendent awareness. In temples for the Babylonian Sun god Baal and the Greek Apollo, frankincense was burnt in large quantities as an alchemical substance with the power to bring devotees closer to divinity. From the Egyptian courts the Hebrews, and then the Greeks and Romans had learnt not only of the sensual delights of perfume, as well as the practical applications of essential oils in healing, but also of the inherently spiritual nature of frankincense. For the ancient Greeks, the word 'scent' itself meant 'offering to the gods'.

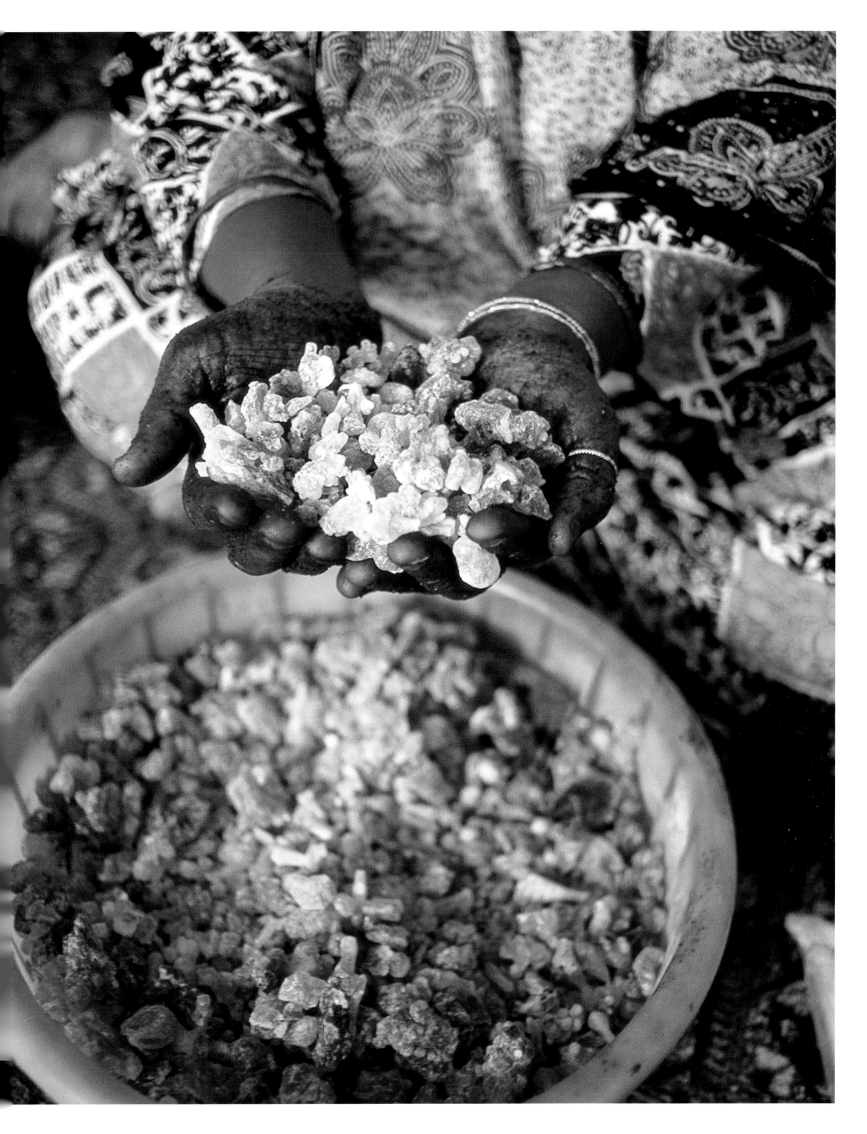

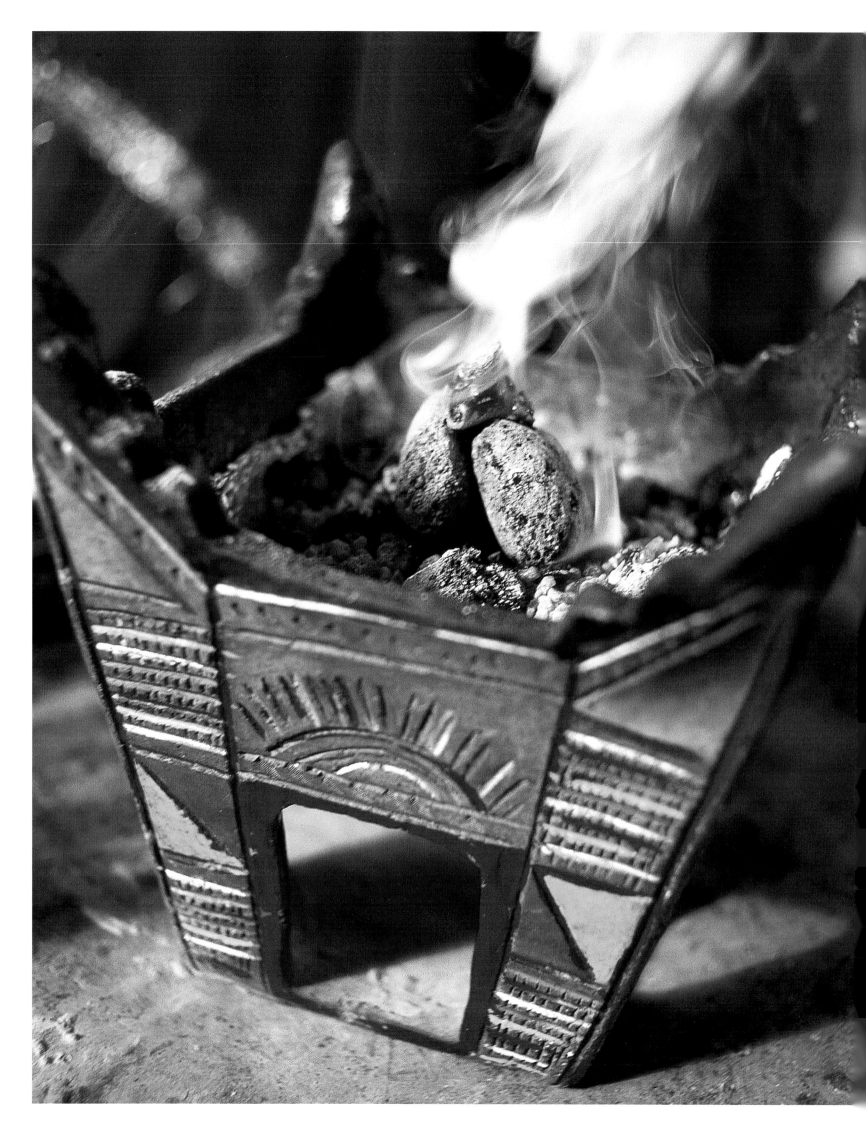

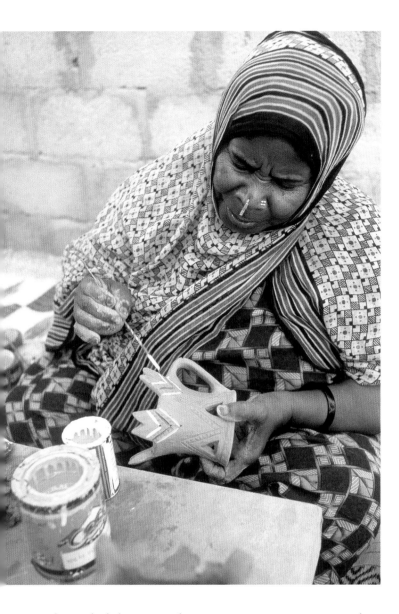

Although the infant Christ was given frankincense, the gradual growth of Christianity, and later of Islam, rang the death knell for the glory days of the incense trade. Yet a residual reverence for the transforming power of frankincense in the religious rites of these two great faiths persists. Although it is not an authorised part of Islamic ritual, frankincense is burnt at funerals to purify the atmosphere; and it often wafts around the shrines of Muslim saints. The 'odour of sanctity' is also believed to accompany many Christian saints after death, a sweet smell indicating a holy presence. Burning frankincense is an intrinsic part of Catholic, Greek and Russian Orthodox ritual, inducing a sacred transformative state in worshippers, just as it had done in ancient Egypt.

Above: Sheikah Nasser Salim painting a *mejmar* or censer made from local clay at Taqa

Left: Frankincense in a censer made at Mirbat, once a busy port for export of the resin, now a fishing village

Once collected in southern Oman, the frankincense had to be transported across thousands of kilometres of hugely inhospitable and often lethal territory to the major areas of consumption. Along the Incense Routes from Oman we will meet names reeking of history such as Ur and Damascus, Gaza and Alexandria. Over the millennia the trade in frankincense enlarged tiny villages along the routes into fabulously wealthy city-states. The Queen of Sheba's great dam at Marib irrigated a vast plain, which has since returned to desert. Shabwa, also in Yemen, was once the most feared city on the frankincense route, since all caravans had to pass through it to be taxed, on pain of death if they deviated. Today it is a sprawling ghost town, acres of abandoned history. Petra too, in modern Jordan, was once a 19-square-kilometre metropolis of heroic Nabatean architecture amid naturally sculpted caves. When the ruined 'rose-red city half as old as time' was re-discovered in the nineteenth century, it housed just a few Bedouin in the caves. The valley of Wadi Rum, south of Petra, famous for its connection with Lawrence of Arabia, is also connected to the frankincense trade: its three-thousand-year-old cave paintings depict camel caravans passing through the valley and the bandits who preyed on them. The curious, sticky sap from unprepossessing little trees has built great cities and let them fall.

But the history of frankincense has not ended; the story continues. In several areas, the 'pearls of the desert' have a healthy future, albeit often in synthesised form. It still has commercial olfactory value as a significant ingredient in the international fragrance industry. Frankincense is used in 13 per cent of high-quality female scents and three per cent of male. We shall discover how the burning of frankincense, *per fumum*, became perfume; and how by the seventh century CE the Arabs traded with areas producing fragrant materials as far as South-East Asia. Their merchant seamen sailed great distances in dhows, returning with ingredients such as sandalwood from India, aloe wood and musk from China and ambergris from Africa. Their chemists discovered the techniques of distillation, blending and fixing.

Writing about his research on medieval Arab perfume makers, Nigel Groom pinpoints the bridge in perfume history between ancient and modern times: 'Perfumery could now be seen as an art with a continuous history of development since the dawn of civilisation'.[1]

In dynastic Egypt, frankincense was used in rejuvenating facemasks and other skincare products, and today research is going on into its anti-ageing properties, with considerable commercial implications. Not only has frankincense been used in medical practice in the Arab world for millennia, it also plays a part in contemporary aromatherapy. Although this is a gentle, subtle treatment, promoting and maintaining individual physical, psychological and spiritual wellbeing, the use of frankincense essential oil travels via the olfactory nerves to affect the limbic system, which is the most primitive region of consciousness, and reaches deep into the psyche. Is it really possible for something so apparently delicate, so intangible as the sense of smell capable of affecting our emotions, triggering memories, influencing our brains and behaviour? As Daniel MacKenzie writes: 'Of all the senses, none surely is so mysterious as that of smell… its effects on the psyche are both wide and deep, at once obvious and subtle'.[2]

Of all our five senses, smell is the least appreciated, the least developed and the most repressed. Even the words 'smell' and 'odour' have a pejorative ring. Apart from the countless concoctions of the modern perfume industry, smell is largely ignored, though entire industries are devoted to taste. The human nose is capable of registering in excess of ten thousand smells, but so unused is our sense of smell, and so downplayed, that we have not developed a vocabulary capable of describing a fraction of them. The language of wine experts, who are as dependent on their sense of smell as on taste, is often pretentious, if not at times downright absurd. The 'nose' of an oenologist can be compared with that of a perfume 'nose' or creator, yet both are literally lost for words. Even the names for the fragrance families, crucially important categories in the world of scent, are vague and allude to imagery other than smell itself, for example 'Oriental', 'Fern', and 'Amber'.

Sigmund Freud maintained that once humans had assumed an upright posture, our sense of smell began to depreciate. Distanced from the earth, and forgetting how to smell it, we repressed the sense, leading to all kinds of conditions appropriate for psychoanalysis. During early space flights, when astronauts were deprived of olfactory stimuli, they suffered. For lack of anything else in that sanitised environment, they took to sniffing lemon-scented hand-wipes. Pretty soon these were no longer used for cleansing, but became coveted items, saved up for sniffing rituals. As Robert Tisserand explains in *Aromatherapy for Everyone*: 'Later flights purposely carried a variety of fragrant articles, and sometimes astronauts were given bottled reproductions of familiar smells from their own home, to help prevent home sickness.… We need odour stimulation for our aesthetic and spiritual well-being'.

The Latin word *sagax*, from which 'sagacious' or wise is derived, also means having an enhanced sense of smell. Can one accrue wisdom or 'the idea of immortality', from sniffing, as Salvador Dalí suggested? It is such an intimate action, in the sense that one is actually taking into one's being minute particles of whatever one smells; and thus it is, perhaps, that one gains insight into its intrinsic substance.

In an evolutionary context, smell and its partner, taste, are the primeval senses, the first to develop. Single-celled organisms were guided through the oceans by smell, drawn to the useful, repelled by the

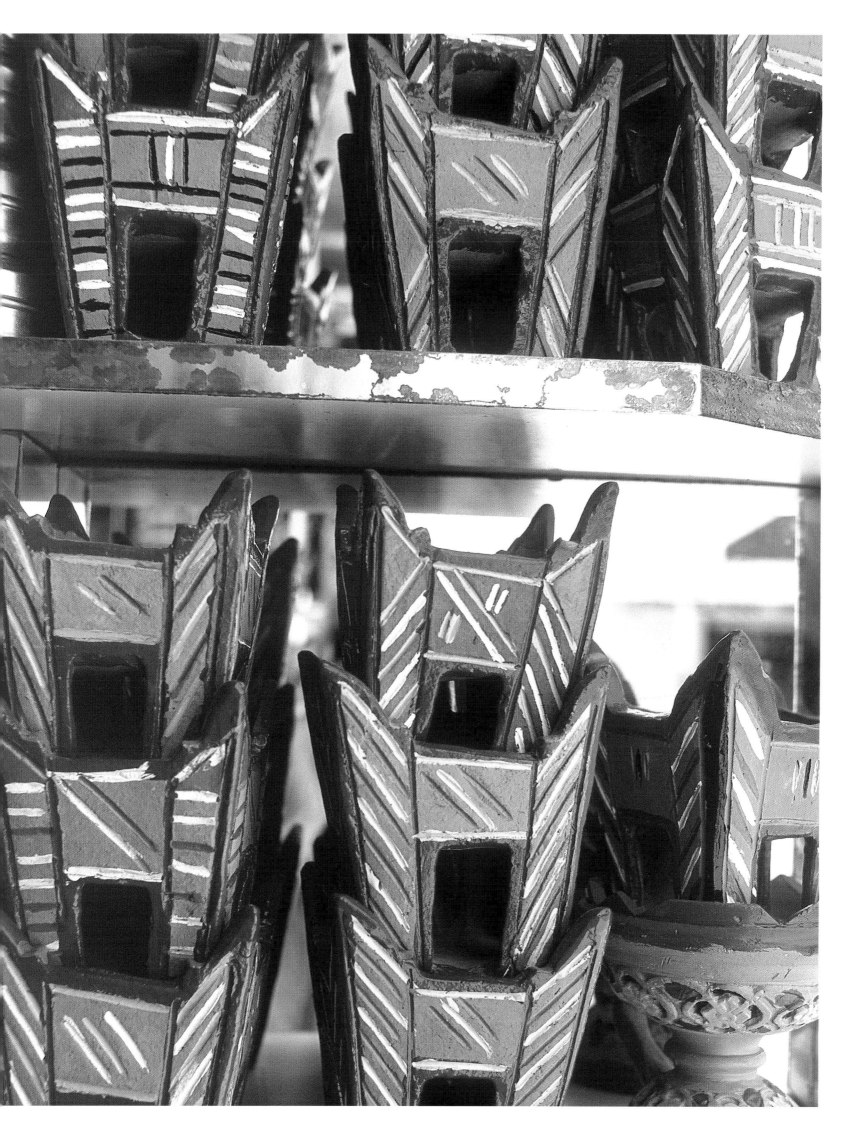

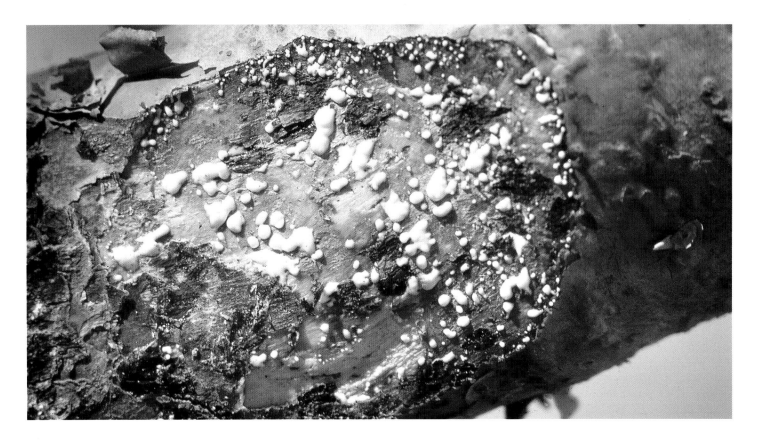

Above: 'Pearls of the Desert'—droplets of resin newly emerged from beneath bark which has just been pared away

Following double page: Frankincense National Park at Wadi Hanoon

risky. The atavistic 'hero' of Patrick Süskind's novel *Perfume* is obsessed by odour to the point of murder: 'As he fell off to sleep, he sank deeper and deeper into himself, leading the triumphant entry into his innermost fortress, where he dreamed of an odiferous banquet, a gigantic orgy with clouds of incense and fogs of myrrh, held in his own honour.'[3] That 'innermost fortress' is the limbic system. This hidden labyrinth contains the main olfactory centres, memory and emotion, and acts directly on the autonomic nervous system. It is the seat of the most primitive emotions, such as love, hate, desire and aggression, which enabled our hominid ancestors to find food and a mate, and escape danger. The limbic system still controls our most basic drives—sex, fear, repulsion and sense of security—and is linked to the hormonal and reproductive systems. The limbic system is also that part of the brain dealing with non-selective memories, and triggered by specific smells. Recollections build up into a scented memory bank. 'Smells are surer than sounds and sights to make your heart-strings crack', wrote Rudyard Kipling in his poem *Lichtenberg*. For me, the recollection of the smell of my mother's cheek powdered with Coty's *L'Aimant* triggers intense feelings of tenderness and nostalgia.

Since smell is so inextricably linked to memory and emotion, laboratory technicians call this link 'olfactory nervous stimuli', and their employers, the perfume manufacturers, are fully aware of the potency of perfume to evoke the past and cause emotional reactions. Familiar smells such as our mother's kitchen can activate feelings of happiness and security, real or imagined, which is why food smells such as vanilla are popular in fragrance construction. 'Nothing revives the past as completely as a smell', wrote Vladimir Nabokov in *Mary*.

When the nose catches a swirl of air, smell receptors in the mucous membrane at the back of the nasal cavity pass a message through the olfactory nerves to the limbic system in the cerebrum. Whether our reaction is positive or not depends on many factors, of which association is the most important. In our scented memory banks we store up the fleeting impressions, myriad moods and concrete experiences that smells have aroused. Before any other sense is fully operative, a baby's nose receives and transmits information on where its mother is and therefore the source of its food. Childhood memories are often a chain of recollected smells, such as a certain cupboard, pet or freshly ironed clothes.

These recollections in the memory bank build up, not just over the years, but also arguably over many lifetimes, sometimes accessing the 'collective unconscious', as Carl Jung called it. Certain scents, such as jasmine, rose, sandalwood and frankincense have been used for so many thousands of years and have such deep associations with romance, as well as religious experience, that scientists argue that their learned olfactory references have become ingrained in our collective memories. Sandalwood, as well as being one of the key sensual base notes for around eighty per cent of contemporary female fragrance, is the *only* wood used for *pujas* or altars in Hindu worship, and in addition has therapeutic qualities.

The first time that I saw white droplets of resin oozing out from beneath the cut bark of an Omani frankincense tree, I was catapulted into an experience of *déjà vu*. These pearls of the desert contain such an abundance of volatile oils, that they release their extraordinary fragrance straight away. It was an inherently spiritual scent that assailed me, allied with ritual, prayer, longing and peace.

Through the operations of this 'mass memory', perfumers are able to create successful fragrances with notes that strike a common chord in many people. Manufacturers of household products exploit this collective unconscious too, and are reluctant to alter the smell of some of their long-established products. Think lavender and we're transported to granny's handkerchief, or happy holiday memories of sunny Provence, the smell of the south.

Smell messages travelling to the right hemisphere of the brain stimulate what is now generally accepted as its province—intuitive, creative thought—as opposed to the left side, which deals with logical thought processes and verbalisation. Olfactory stimuli do reach the left hemisphere, but research appears to show that the right responds more. The imaginative aspect of the right side is gloriously evoked by the fourteenth-century Sufi poet, Hafiz:

> I do not feel like writing verses;
> But as I light my perfume-burner
> With myrrh, jasmine and incense,
> They suddenly burgeon from the heart,
> like flowers in a garden.

The right hemisphere of the brain, so responsive to fragrant messages, is not only associated with lateral thinking, but also with enjoyment, even euphoria. Accessing this sensation of hedonism, which can also be aesthetic pleasure, the art of the perfumer moves us deeper than the intellect; the aromatherapist evokes a sense of well-being and allays stress; and incense still promotes heightened states of consciousness in religious rituals. This is the significance of olfaction in the modern world, which comes to us directly through frankincense's original role as the pathway for prayer.

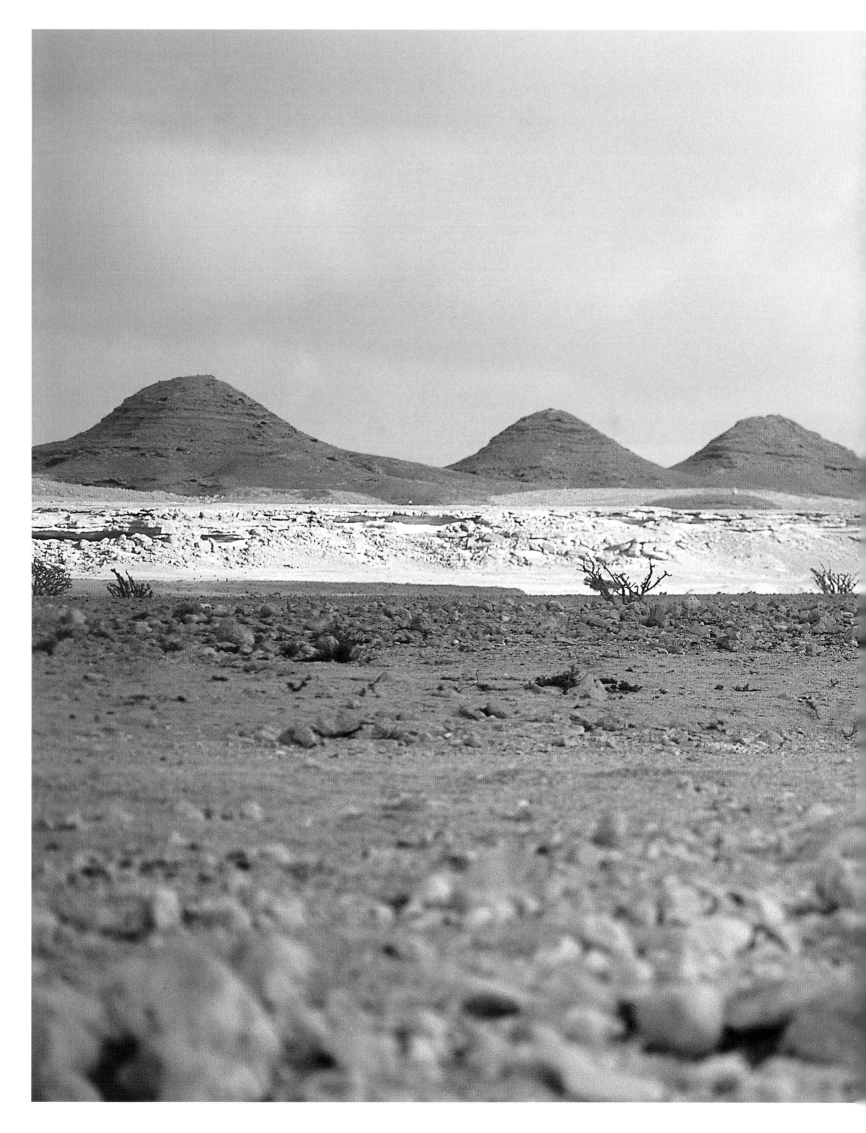

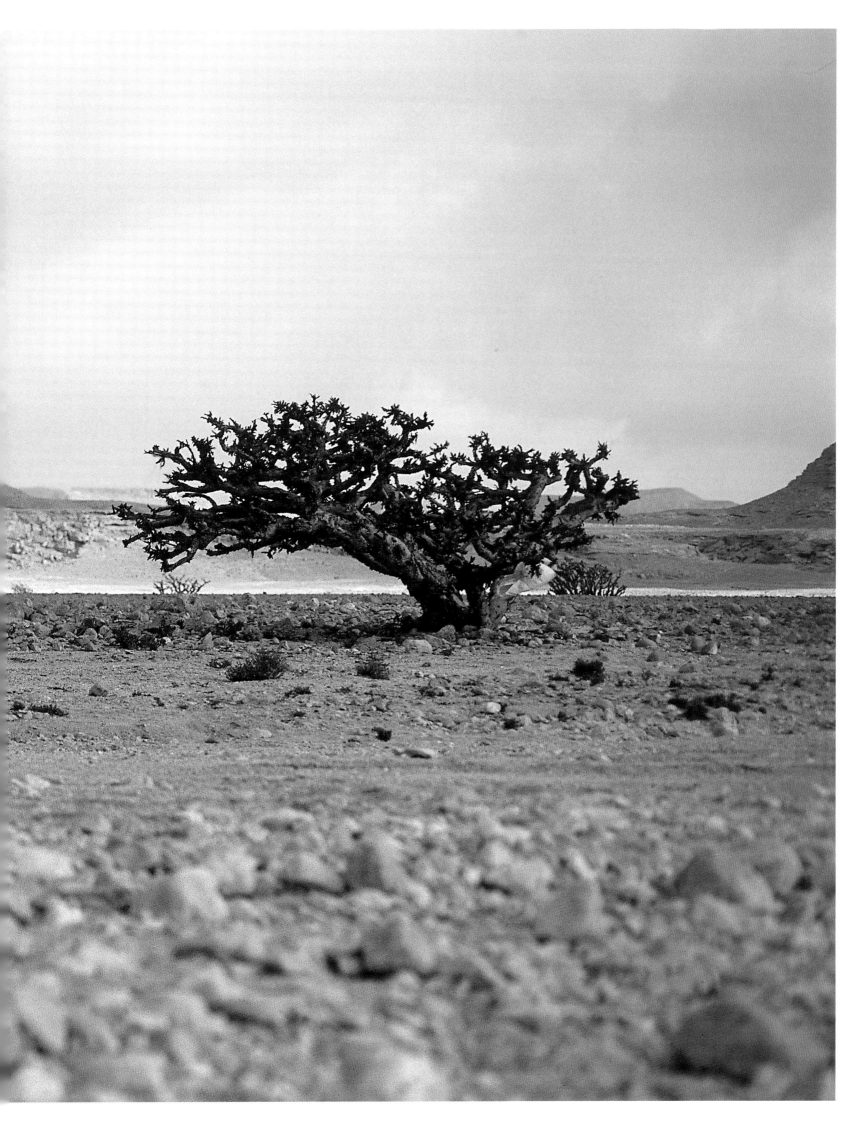

Who is this that cometh
out of the wilderness
like pillars of smoke,
perfumed with myrrh and
frankincense, with all
powders of the merchant?

Song of Solomon 3:6

CHAPTER ONE

A PERFUMED TRAIL
THROUGH HISTORY

At the beginning of his novel *Perfume*, Patrick Süskind refers to 'a domain that leaves no traces in history...the fleeting realm of scent'. Yet this is very far from the truth in the case of frankincense, which cut such a defining swathe through history, in particular the history of southern Arabia, as the region's most important trade item for thousands of years. This chapter traces the use of frankincense in sacred, medical and domestic life in great fragrance cultures, which were also the great historical civilisations of the world. Their continuous demand for incense through antiquity marked rites of passage from birth to grave, healed and purified and not least served the homely pleasures of hospitality, the scenting of rooms, of clothing—and of people. But the main purpose of frankincense historically was to serve as a sacerdotal perfume in religious and funerary rites.

MESOPOTAMIA AND SUMER

The story of incense begins at least 5000 years BCE, at the birth of urban life in the Tigris–Euphrates river basin. Archaeological excavations and other paleoclimatic/geological evidence has shown that a trade route was already in place in the sixth millennium BCE linking the Dhofar region of southern Oman with Mesopotamia.

By this time it appears that the northern city of Ubaid was importing incense from Arabia, as well as pearls and precious stones, and the earliest tangible record of incense use in the region is an incense burner found in the ruins of a temple at Tepe Gawra, near Mosul in modern Iraq, dated 3500 BCE.

Over time the Sumerian culture overtook the Ubaid. At their great city, Uruk, Sumerian bas-reliefs illustrate offerings of incense to the Sun god and his consort, and clay tablets covered with cuneiform calligraphy tell the story of the sailors and the caravaneers who brought the incense to the region. These tablets record the importance of existing trade in the region, not just in frankincense, but also in copper, precious woods, fabric, oil, dates, pearls and bronze sculptures. They are very detailed trading records, giving the weight of purchases and information on ships' cargoes. In his book *The Land of Incense*, Juris Zarins notes: 'With the invention of formal writing by 3200 B.C., the Uruk IV and III period tablets...have undergone scrutiny.... Increasing urbanisation had brought pressure to bear to maintain records for merchants' accounts, wages, inventories, shipments etc…. We know from written evidence that by the late phases of Period III, frankincense was imported into southern Mesopotamia…via the northern Gulf in Dilmun boats.'[1] (The Dilmun culture existed at present-day Bahrain.)

Zarins goes on to mention Old Akkadian and Ur III texts which record the construction and voyages of Magan boats. Northern Oman was then known as Magan, and was as famous for its copper exports as for its incense. 'By Early Dynastic times (c. 2500 BCE) extending through the early Bronze Age, sea-faring boats linked Oman with the Indus Valley, the Emirates, Bahrain, Eastern Arabia and Sumer.'[2] The implication is that Omani (Magan) boats brought copper and incense to Dilmun, from which it was shipped northwards in their boats.

Another Sumerian cuneiform tablet of 2350 BCE, confirms that the incense offered was frankincense:

Shim – incense

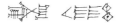

Shim.gig – frankincense

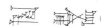

Garash.shim – merchant of aromatics

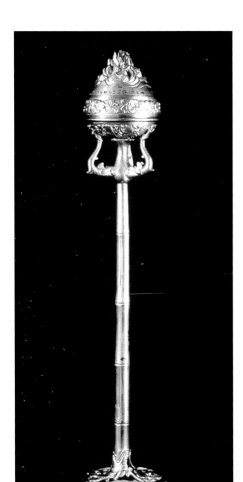

According to the Greek writer Herodotus, a thousand talents (about thirty thousand kilogrammes) of frankincense were burnt every year during the feast of Baal in Babylon. The annual consumption at the temple of Baal was a staggering two thousand kilogrammes. Basing his research largely on classical sources such as Herodotus, Nigel Groom dates the use of frankincense in the Tigris–Euphrates region or northern part of the Middle East much later: 'Fragments of jars with south Arabian lettering on them found in Eilath (or Aelana, near Gaza) are dated to the fifth or sixth century B.C., the earliest archaeological evidence for the trade.'[3]

Gradually the ritual use of frankincense as an appeal to the gods, took over the function that sacrificing animals had once fulfilled. The Sumerian epic *Gilgamesh* recounts how these deities 'smelled the sweet savour. The gods gathered like flies over the sacrificer'. Incense historian, Walter Müller, contends that throughout the Middle East frankincense was considered to have extraordinary expiatory power, paralleled by the power accrued from sacrificing animals: 'Its resin was considered to be the blood of a tree, which was taken to be animate and divine.'[4]

As well as being pleasing to the gods and providing sustenance for the ancestors, the scented smoke of aromatics was woven into the fabric of everyday life. The ancient Mesopotamians and Sumerians must have found many practical uses for

Left: Maoling censer in bronze with gold and silver gilding, Western Han dynasty, c. 206 BCE
Right: 'Throne' of Bilqis, Queen of Sheba at Marib, Yemen

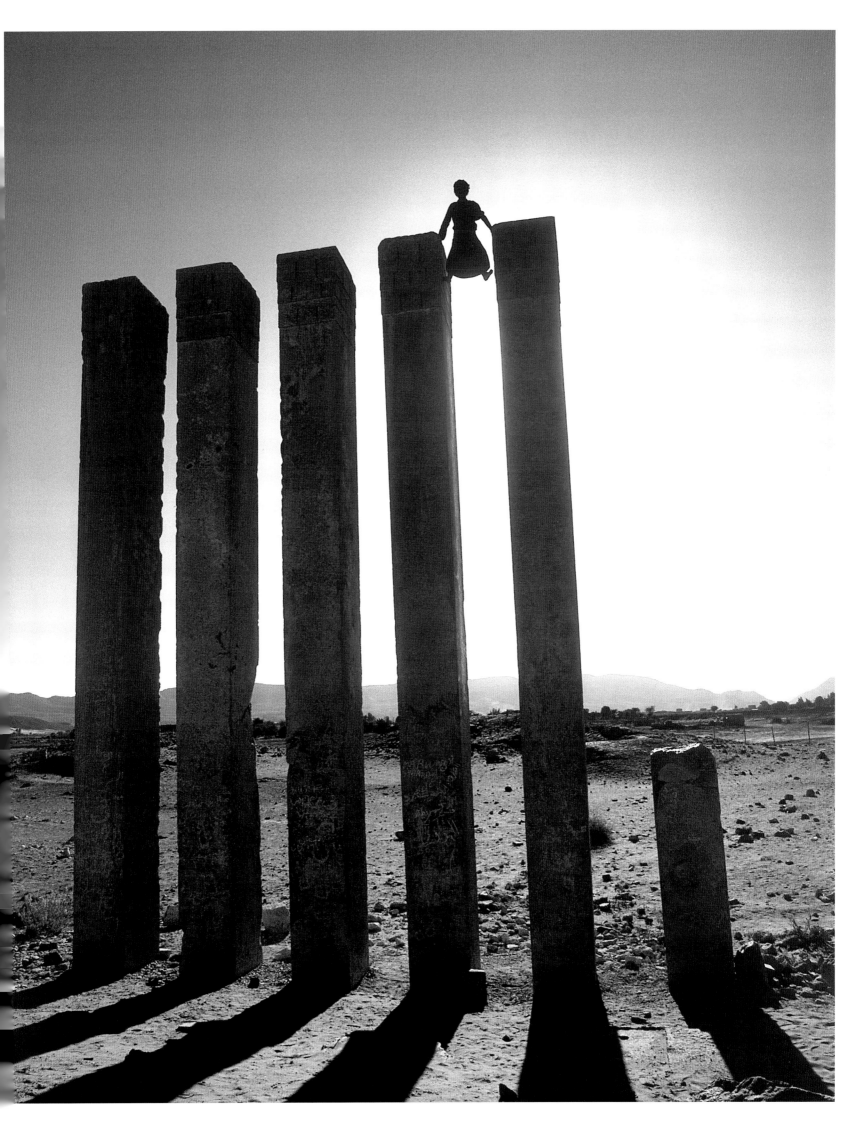

frankincense, not least of which was medical. 'The Babylonians were the first to write herbals, recording the various properties and uses of plants, and they devised the earliest system of weights and measures for light-weight items, such as those used in perfumery'.[5]

The Sumerians discovered that most aromatic plants have powerful antiseptic properties that make them effective as salves for external wounds and skin infections, and as infusions for internal ailments. Frankincense contains disinfectant phenols, powerful agents against germs and infection, and is effective as a fumigant, burnt to banish disease-bearing flies and mosquitoes.

PERSIA AND SYRIA

As one of the ancient world's most sought-after substances, frankincense enticed many suitors to Omani shores, bent on controlling output and trade. One of the more effective of these conquerors was Persia, during the reign of the Achaemenid Dynasty of kings. Darius I (522–486 BCE) was already receiving voluntary tributes of frankincense from Arabia, which so far Persia had not invaded, in recognition for assistance given during his incursion into Egypt. In listing tribute paid by the twenty 'provinces' of Persia, the industrious Herodotus notes that yearly about thirty thousand kilogrammes of frankincense were offered (recorded as one thousand Babylonian talents).

However the tide soon turned more aggressive, with parts of Oman and present-day UAE incorporated into the Achaemenid Persian Empire. From that time until about 200 CE, they were ruled by various Persian dynasties, including the Sassanian. But not long after the Sassanian invaders had made their presence felt, they were driven out of most of their coastal settlements by a migrating people known as the 'Ad, who arrived from the Hadhramaut area of today's Yemen. Apparently the 'Ad had been forced out by lack of water when the great dam at Marib, capital of Sabaea, had collapsed. The dam had originally been built by Bilqis, the Queen of Sheba (Sabaea), on profits from controlling the frankincense trade in her territory. The 'Ad settled in southern Oman, headquartered at the fabled 'lost' city of Wubar, a caravanserai for incense merchants travelling north. Recently rediscovered, subsequent excavations at Wubar have yielded Persian material remains.

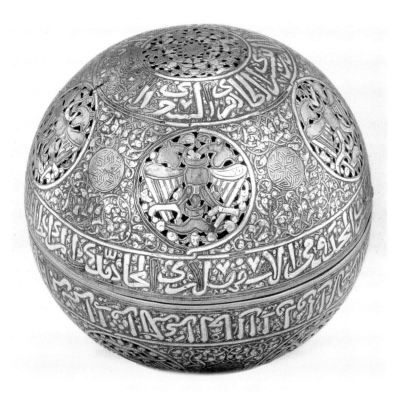

Left: Spherical Syrian incense burner, Mamluk dynasty, 1277–79 CE, brass inlaid with silver

Right: Sixth century BCE stone relief showing a priest or servant in Persian dress holding a container with offerings. From Achaemenid palace, Susa, Iran

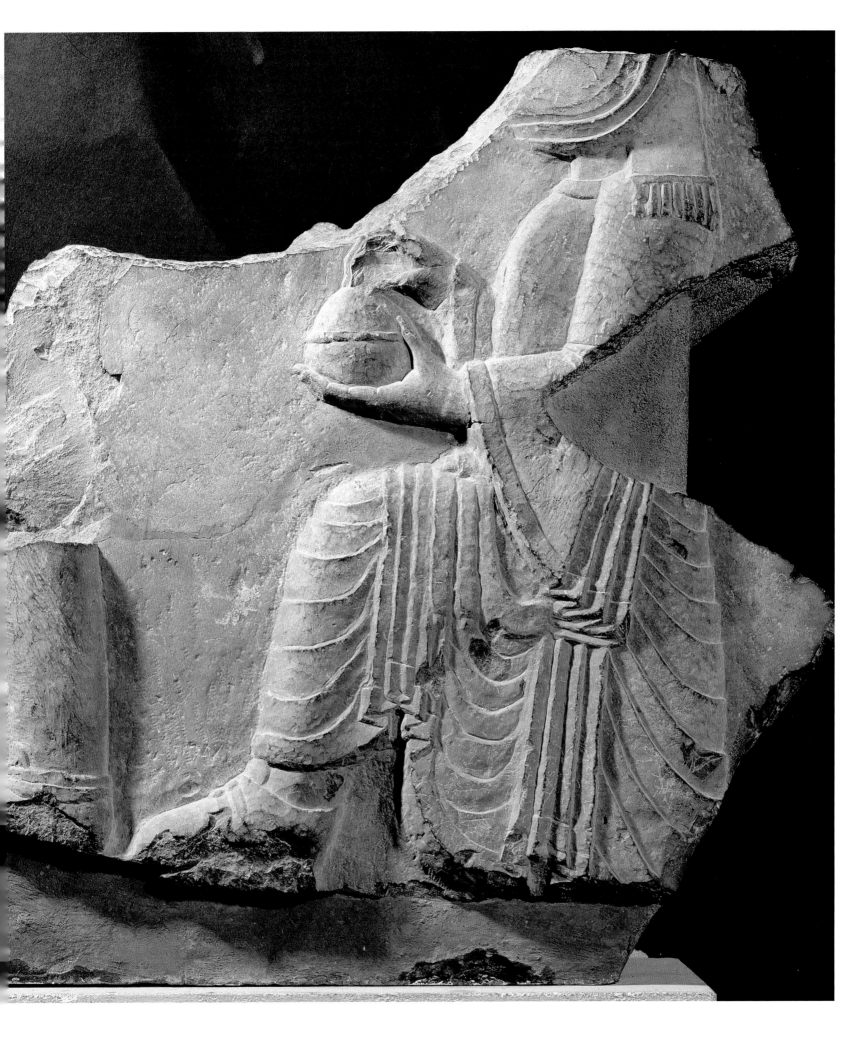

Fragments of stone reliefs found at the former Persian capitals of Persepolis and Susa depict gift-bearers, priests or servants carrying jars and covered vessels, and since frankincense was *the* prized commodity in antiquity, we may surmise that some did indeed contain it. Other monuments at Persepolis show the king himself offering incense. At ancient Gerrha in present-day UAE, a hugely important caravanserai on the eastern frankincense route, neo-Assyrian-Achaemenid-period cylinder seals with south Arabian characters have been discovered. Cuneiform texts describe both frankincense and myrrh, and date from the Middle Assyrian, neo-Assyrian and neo-Babylonian periods. Other incense-related material, highlighting its importance in this region, include thousands of four-legged incense burners of Neo-Babylonian and Achaemenid origin.

Incense, perfumed oils and cosmetics were an intrinsic aspect of Persian and Syrian lifestyle. Collections of bronze incense burners often had handles of charming realistic sculptures of animals such as the Arabian ibex. Tiny cast-bronze cosmetic containers shaped like miniature vases have been found throughout south-eastern Iran; as well as written records and perfume recipes dating to *c.* 1750 BCE, unearthed at the palace site of the Syrian city Mari. These records reveal that the Mari palace had specific accommodation for preparing scented products, that both men and women were perfume 'noses', and that their profession was an esteemed one. Although it cannot be conclusively proved at this point that Assyrian sculptures and reliefs showing incense being burned for the Sun god, and tall incense stands separating the king from the gods and his subjects, depict frankincense, the fact that it was being brought from southern Arabia in such huge quantities makes it very likely.

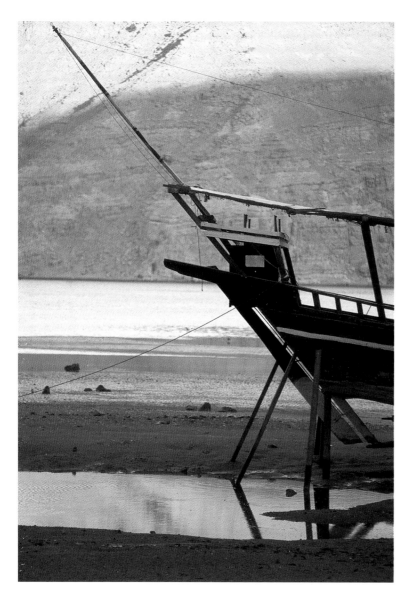

Frankincense has always had practical applications all over Arabia, including medical. Remedies using frankincense appear in *The Syriac Book of Medicine*, dating from the fourth and fifth centuries CE. In this book frankincense seems to be a 'wonder drug', a cure for all ailments, including pain, palsy, pleurisy, haemorrhage, dysentery and diseases of the liver, kidney and bladder. With its disinfectant properties, it is still used to purify drinking water, to combat harmful or unpleasant odours, and in a region always short of water, frankincense sweetens the smell of well-worn clothes and bedding, as it is wafted through them, hung on special stands. The Roman Strabo reported that frankincense was burnt after sex in Syria, for purification.

Left: Dhow at Khasab port, Musandam, Oman

Right: Dhow in a relief on the wall of Borobodur Temple, Java, indicating how far the Arabian maritime trade reached

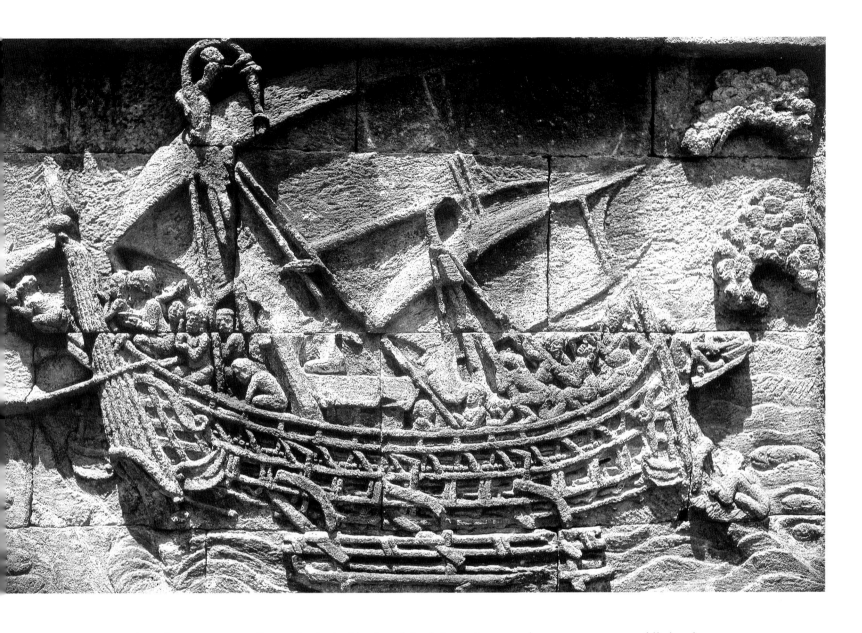

Even the ocean-going dhows which plied back and forth from Oman to three continents were filled with the fragrance of frankincense, partly to counteract the smell of stale water in the stern. An intrepid couple of nineteenth-century travellers, Theodore and Mabel Bent, journeyed to Mumbai in a dhow, along with some family silver. Mrs Bent describes how she had reason to be glad of the presence of frankincense: 'In our little cabin in the stern the smell of bilge-water was almost overpowering, and every silver thing we had turned black…. These pungent odours were relieved from time to time by burning huge chafing dishes of frankincense, a cargo of which was aboard for transport to Bombay'.[6]

ARABIA FELIX

He is crazed with the spell of far Arabia,
They have stolen his wits away.

Walter de la Mare, *Arabia*

It was the Roman Pliny the Elder who in the first century CE coined the phrase *Arabia Felix*, Arabia the Fortunate, Arabia the Blessed. Ruminating on the excesses of Empire lifestyle, he grumbles that the entire annual import quota for Rome of Arabian frankincense had been used up on one occasion for the funeral pyre of Nero's wife, Poppaea Sabina. 'It is the luxury of man,' he wrote, 'which is displayed even in the paraphernalia of death that has rendered Arabia thus happy'.

How irksome it must have been for the Greeks and Romans not to control this territory that they believed to be so fabulously fertile and wealthy, judging by the price they were forced to pay for frankincense. As it turned out, they were not only unable to conquer the source of production, they were ignorant about it too.

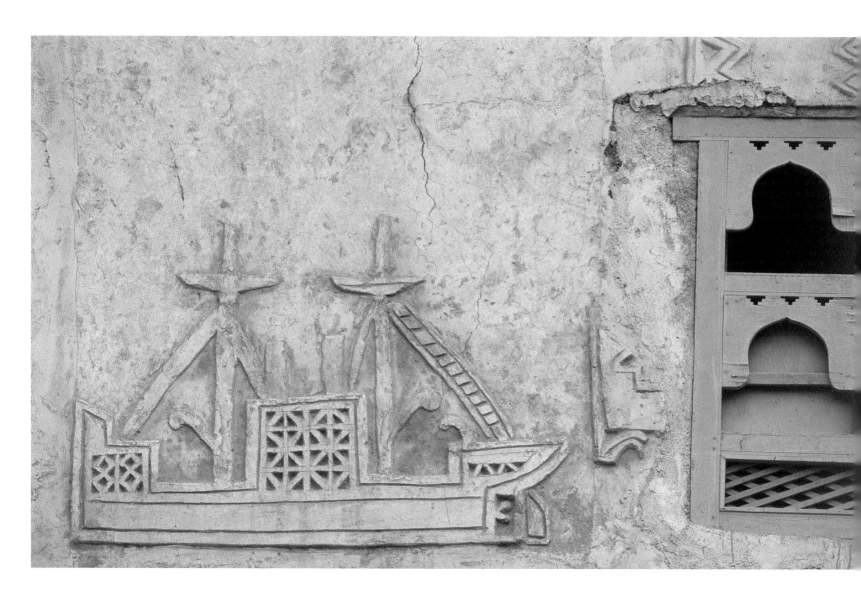

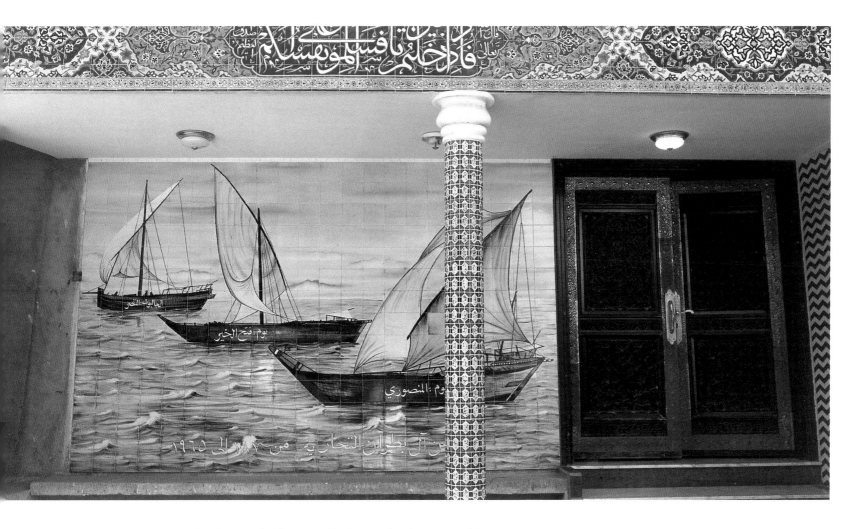

Left: Relief of a dhow on the fort at Sad'h, famous for the export of frankincense

Above: Tile mosaic of dhows on a house at Musandam

To the outside world, Arabia Felix was shrouded in mystery, synonymous with incense and inconceivably wealthy. But for the average south Arabian, life was pretty basic, a hard slog of agricultural toil. For thousands of years, Arabia baked in the sun behind closed doors, 'fiery hot and scorched', as Strabo commented, except for a freak monsoon, which covers Dhofar, the incense-growing area, with vegetation during the summer.

By the time the most sought-after commodity of the ancient world reached Greece and Rome across desert and mountain, the incense-carrying caravans had paid extortionate 'travel expenses'. Records show that a pound weight of frankincense would have cost about £1,000 ($1,800/€ 1,460) at modern-day prices. And an Italian farmer would have to pay these prices, conscious that he *had* to offer frankincense to his god to ensure a good harvest.

The myths about Arabia Felix became ever more far-fetched (and bad-tempered). Pliny comments: 'A singular thing too, one half of these almost innumerable tribes live by the pursuits of commerce, the other half by rapine: take them all in all, they are the richest nations in the world, seeing that such vast wealth flows in upon them from both the Roman and the Parthian empires; for they sell the produce of the sea or of their forests, while they purchase nothing whatever in return'. However, Pliny does make an exception to this last remark about the imbalance of trade. He goes on: 'In Arabia there is a surprising demand for foreign scents, which are imported from abroad, so soon are mortals sated with what they have of their own, and so covetous are they of what belongs to others'. Nowadays the Middle East is still such a fragrance-conscious culture, that not only does it support a hugely profitable indigenous industry, which includes importing perfume materials from abroad, but also new international scents are test-marketed there.

Between 1400 and 900 BCE four kingdoms emerged to the west of Dhofar, which despite growing some low-grade frankincense themselves, relied on southern Oman to provide the best quality in considerable quantity. Sabaea (Sheba), which controlled the main north-western incense route, nearby Ma'in, Qataban and Hadhramaut grew into prosperous city-states that traded incense, and constructed dams and irrigation channels, which fed a vastly more prolific population then than the odd pockets of habitation I saw in this area of Yemen not so long ago.

Omanis and Yemenis of the time had also harnessed the monsoon winds from India, and evolved technically sophisticated maritime navigational tools and methods. With these skills and their expertise in constructing ocean-worthy dhows, they already had a lengthy history of maritime trade as far as China and Indonesia, to which, of course, they were exporting frankincense. Far from 'purchasing nothing in return', as Pliny reported, luxury goods were flowing into Arabia—imports from China, India and the Spice Islands. Highly covetable silk, porcelain and spices were landed at ports along the coast of south Arabia, some for home consumption, but mainly for onward trade. When the Queen of Sheba went to visit King Solomon, her cavalcade was loaded with spices, and they add their flavours to Arabian cooking to this day. The coastlines of the Arabian peninsula are still littered with fragments of antique Chinese porcelain and old coins.

For centuries, the Greeks and Romans believed that the kingdoms of south Arabia, Arabia Felix, produced these oriental luxuries. The Arabians were keen to perpetuate this myth, successfully shrouding the origins of their valuable exports in mystery, in order to control the business themselves. Claudius Ptolemy called the 'Ad caravanserai of Wubar 'Omanum Emporium'—the marketplace of Oman—though he erroneously mapped it too far inland from the Dhofari coast. Classical authors speculated about the 'sweet smell' wafting from the coast of Dhofar, and one of the most evocative if fanciful descriptions (by Artemidorus) reads: 'On account of the abundance of fruits, the people are lazy and easy-going in their mode of life. Most of the populace sleep on the roots of the trees which they have to cut out of the ground. Those who live close to one another receive in continuous succession the loads of aromatics and deliver them to their next neighbours, as far as Syria and Mesopotamia; and when they are made drowsy by the sweet odours they overcome the drowsiness by inhaling the incense of asphalt and goats' beard'.

Interaction with the world beyond their shores enriched the rulers and merchants of Arabia Felix in more ways than money alone. The frankincense trade brought them into contact with people and ideas from the Mediterranean, the Levant, India and the Far East, with their cultures as well as their goods. Distinctive hybrid styles of architecture, art and calligraphy emerged, reflecting the blending of imported forms with local South Arabian. Again, Artemidorus comments: 'From their trafficking both the Sabaeans and the Gerrhaeans have become richest of all, and they have a vast equipment of both gold and silver articles, such as couches and tripods and bowls, together with drinking vessels and very costly houses; for doors and walls and ceilings are variegated with ivory and gold and silver set with precious stones'.[8]

EGYPT

*A stairway to the sky is set up for me that I may
ascend on it to the sky, and I ascend on the smoke
of the great censing.*

Pyramid text

Egyptians believed that incense was the very 'sweat of the gods', and that their souls would ascend to Ra on the wings of smoking resin. Funerary rites were therefore inconceivable without vast quantities of frankincense the 'stairway to the sky'. There were also the pleasures of personal use. So obtaining incense was a very important part of Egypt's foreign relations. It is probable that as early as 2800 BCE Egypt was receiving high-grade *Boswellia sacra* from Oman to the north-east via the Red Sea. Far more accessible, though still necessitating challenging journeys by land and sea, were the sources of low-grade frankincense, *Boswellia papyrifera* from the Land of Punt (or Pwenet), now modern-day Somalia and Eritrea. It is also possible that dynastic Egypt obtained incense much nearer home, from Nubia, the ancient land of Kush, now Sudan, about which Harkhuf writes (*c.* 2200 BCE). This is the first historical mention of incense in Egypt, during the Fifth and Sixth Dynasties. However, current botanical evidence casts doubt on the presence of frankincense trees in Sudan.

The Banquet. Fragment of a wall painting from Thebes, New Kingdom, *c.* 1400 BCE, showing incense cones worn on the head

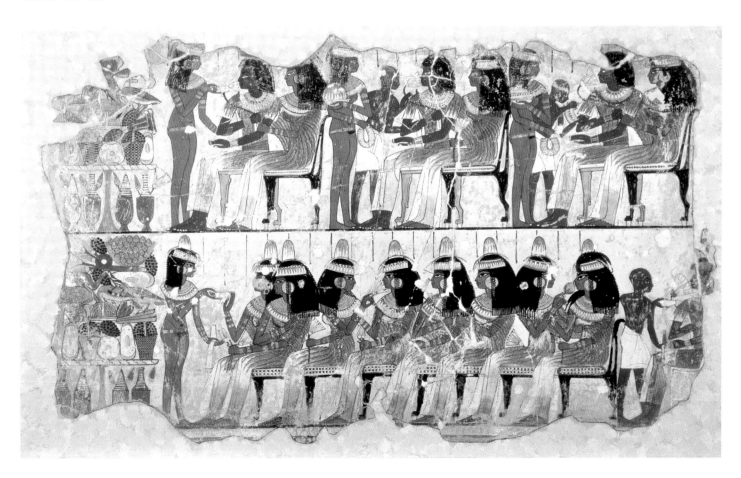

By far the most epic quest was an impressively stage-managed affair ordered by Queen Hatshepsut (r. 1478–57 BCE). The scribes who accompanied her army carefully recorded all they saw, which included giraffes, cheetahs on leashes and a woman named Eti, who was famed for her massive girth. Some of the people described are of Negroid stock, others Hamitic, which suggests Eritrea as their home.

Central to this huge piece of theatre, which Hatshepsut commissioned to show to the world that her reign could deliver the coveted incense, was a series of commemorative descriptive frescoes on the walls of the temple of Deir al-Bahari, near Thebes. Naturally, Hatshepsut herself appears, accompanied by descriptions of her fragrance: 'The best of *'ntyw* is upon all her limbs', and 'Her fragrance was a divine dew'. Apparently myrrh, rather than frankincense, was the queen's particular predilection, (the ancient Egyptian word *'ntyw* usually translated as 'myrrh'), but other authorities contend that *'ntyw* means 'frankincense'. Certainly the 31 trees depicted in the frescoes, which were dug up, root ball and all and carried back in ships, do not closely resemble frankincense trees, but neither do they look like myrrh. The description of Queen Hatshepsut's scent as 'divine dew' alludes to the fact that the pharaohs were considered sacred as well as regal. The queen's words clarify the holy mission of the expedition, which the oracle of Amon had demanded. 'I have hearkened to my father (the god Amon)…commanding me to establish for him a Punt in his house, to plant the trees of God's land beside his temple, in his garden'. In the weighing and measuring scenes, the frescoes show incense trees in tubs, ready to be planted, as well as workers gathering the resin itself in the usual way, scraping the crystals off the trees. These images also illustrate other booty: five ships piled high with treasure, over which baboons swarm,

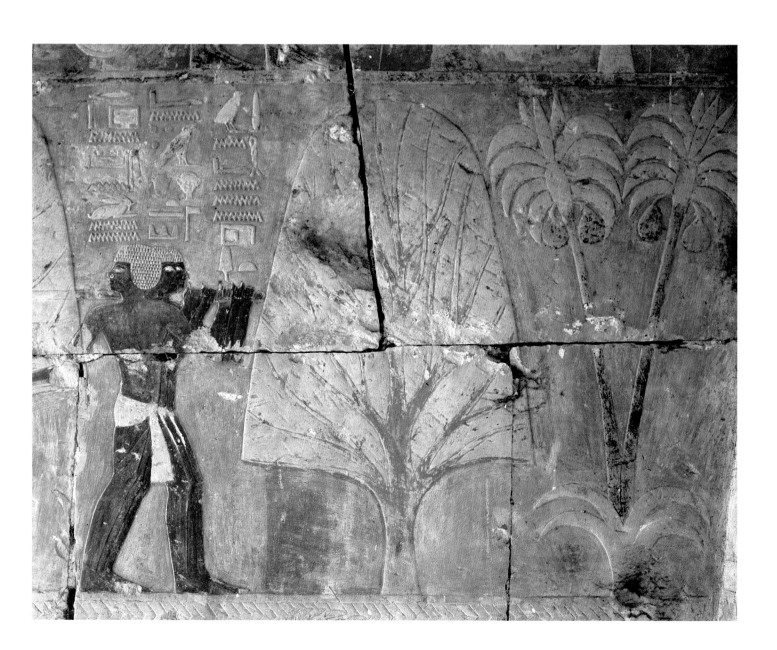

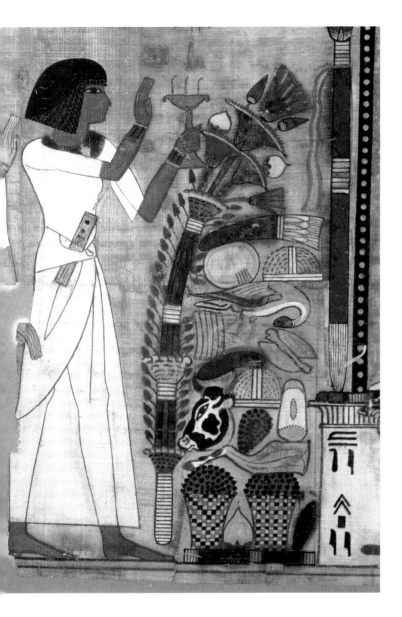

clambering over date palms. In addition we are shown a lioness and what remains of a rhinoceros or hippopotamus.

If Hatshepsut's *'ntyw* cannot be conclusively proved to be frankincense, the very first historical evidence that it was used in ancient Egypt is from the tomb of Tutankhamun (*r.* 1333–23 BCE), and other tombs created between the Eighteenth and Twentieth Dynasties. When Tutankhamun's tomb was opened over three thousand years later in 1922, a perceptible whiff of frankincense emerged from a sealed flask of unguent, and balls of it were discovered inside.

Frankincense was not used for embalming; this was the province of myrrh. But it was an intrinsic part of mortuary rituals and funerary rites. *The Book of the Dead*, the earliest written record of religious and mystical ceremonies, which Egyptians call *The Book of the Coming Forth by Day*, makes it clear that incense is far more than a ceremonial trapping: in itself it is sacred. The text instructs that at a funeral, 'thou shalt cast incense into the fire on behalf of Osiris': this is not an offering to the gods, but analogous to the gods themselves. The smoke would guide the soul of a departed one to heaven and protect it from harmful influences. To ward off enemies of the dead, the Book states that it should be burned in four clay troughs, the flame extinguished with cow's milk. This would enhance the afterlife journey of the deceased and protect it from harmful influences.

The next significant date in the history of frankincense in Egypt is *c.* 1224 BCE in the wall reliefs at Karnak temple. These show Rameses II offering incense to The Sacred Barge. Carrying a triple incense burner in his left hand, with his right he throws incense crystals onto it, the trajectory marked by a curved line of dots. In ranks of five, priests of Horus with hawk-like heads carry The Sacred Barge. This barge was dedicated to Amon, god of light and air, which crossed the Nile every ten days in a sacred procession to the other shore—to the cities of the dead on the West Bank from the temples of the living on the East Bank.

Ceremonial purification was another significant function of incense, not just for ritual purposes, but practical ones too. After the sacking of Memphis in the eighth century BCE the Pharaoh ordered the city to be censed against the risk of disease. In all the major ceremonies incense played its part, recorded in countless murals and reliefs. Usually it is the king who stands before the statue of a deity, smoking

Left: Incense trees from Punt. From a limestone relief in the Temple of Hatshepsut, Thebes. New Kingdom, 18th dynasty, *c.* 1470 BCE

Above: The Fumigation of Osiris. Page from the Book of the Dead of Neb-Qued. New Kingdom (papyrus), 19th dynasty, *c.* 1297–1185 BCE

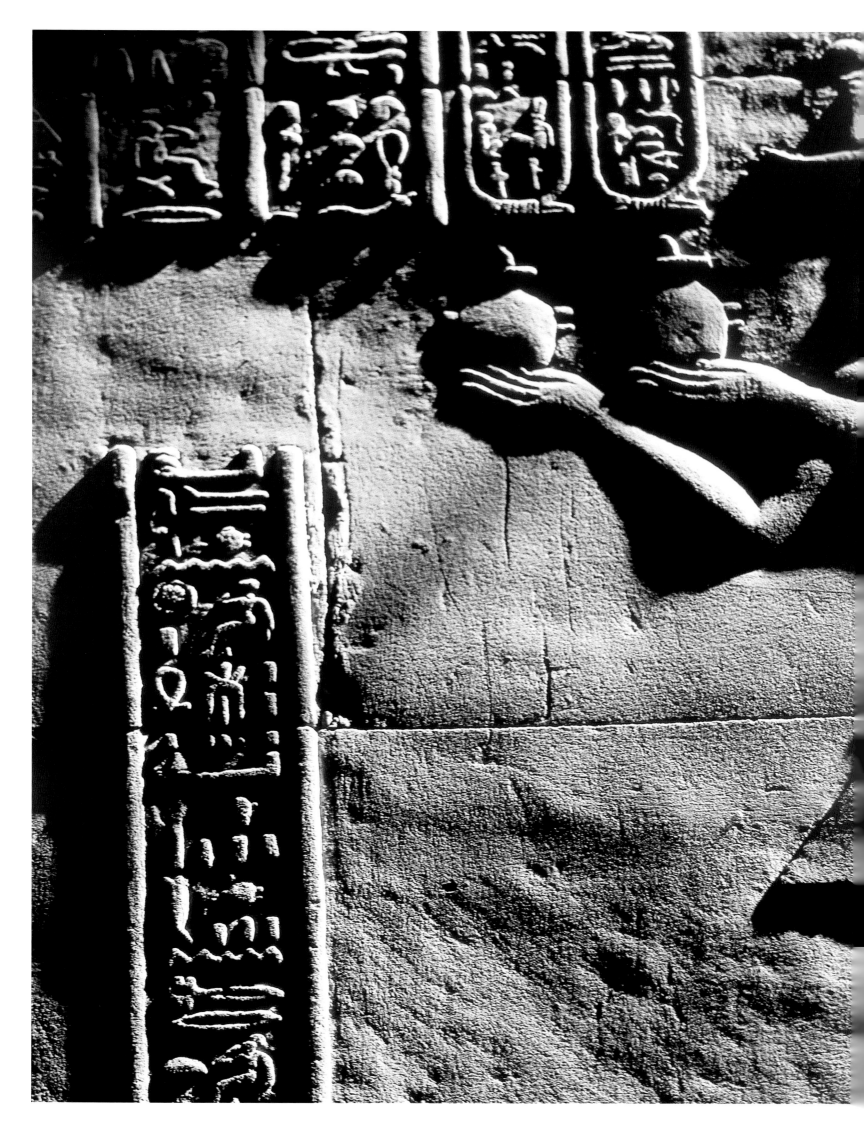

censer in hand, at the 'procession of the shrines' and after military triumphs. On other occasions, it is the priests who offer it, for example at the celebrations for a Pharaoh's coronation.

In the form of incense, frankincense was also used to fumigate sick people, not only by purifying and disinfecting the atmosphere, but by driving out the evil spirits believed to have caused the disease. In the same way, it was burnt at home as protection from malevolent forces, a custom still followed all over Arabia. References on papyrus in the reign of Khufu (c. 2800 BCE) relate to the use of infused oils and aromatic unguents in medicine. The viscous resin of frankincense was used as sticking-plaster to bind together the edges of wounds, rather than stitching them, which helped prevent or clear up infection. Robert Tisserand describes how 'a form of aromatherapy (using infused oils) was being practiced five thousand years ago, and the credit for this is probably due to an Egyptian called Imhotep (*fl. c.* 2630 BCE), who was later deified as the god of medicine and healing. The combination of aromatic oils and massage was very common in all ancient civilisations and formed a part of medical practice for some 4,000 years.'[9] Imhotep's powers in the use of frankincense were well known to the royal family: 'An Egyptian princess suffering from an eye problem after using some new makeup was taken to see Imhotep…. Inflamed eyes and ingrowing eyelashes were causing the princess great pain. Imhotep pulled out the eyelashes with tweezers, after the eyes were cleaned, he massaged them with a cream of frankincense and other ingredients.'[10]

'A day without incense is a day lost' goes an unattributed Egyptian saying, and judging by the thousands of elegant glass bottles, jars and pots unearthed, some with traces of the distilled oil from resin crystals, for many Ancient Egyptians it was an everyday affair. Glassmaking techniques, discovered in the Near East around 1400 BCE, travelled rapidly to Egypt. From the Eighteenth Dynasty onwards, along with stone and metal, glass containers held a sophisticated battery of toiletry items—lotions, ointments, pomades and perfumes—all with an oil base. Frankincense was an important ingredient in skin-rejuvenating products. Under that harsh Egyptian sun, dehydrated skin was smothered in therapeutic products such as face masks, often containing honey and milk as well as frankincense, promising to 'banish wrinkles', or to 'turn an old man into a youth'. Regular bathing was the order of the day for Ancient Egyptians, after which they applied their moisturising scented oils and unguents.

A delightful if bizarre custom noted in hieroglyphics on cartouches and painted on murals was the use of cones of ox fat permeated with aromatics such as frankincense. The wall of the burial vault of Nebenmadt (120 BCE) shows Nebenmadt and his wife being prepared by their children for a celebration in the Valley of Kings. These scented cones were worn like little crowns attached by tiny spikes to their wigs. During the course of a hot evening, the wax would melt, causing little rivulets of perfumed oil to trickle onto bare shoulders. This performed the dual function of keeping lice at bay (since human hair was used for wigs), and restoring sun-baked skin. The custom persisted among some Egyptian Bedouin people up until the early twentieth century. And today many Egyptian women still use *kohl* as an eye cosmetic, which also has therapeutic qualities, and is composed of charred, powdered frankincense.

ISRAEL

A garden enclosed is my sister, my spouse;
a spring shut up, a fountain sealed.
Thy plants are an orchard of pomegranates,
with pleasant fruits; camphire, with spikenard,
Spikenard and saffron; calamus and cinnamon,
with all trees of frankincense; myrrh and aloes,
with all the chief spices.

Song of Solomon 4:12–14

In the chapter summary introducing the beautiful verses above, the Bible makes clear that the garden—'my sister, my spouse'—refers to 'the graces of the church'. Frankincense is mentioned 22 times in the Bible: 16 times for worship, twice as tribute, and three times as a product of the royal garden of Solomon.

The Egyptians had passed on the art of perfumery and science of healing using aromatics such as frankincense to the Israelites, while the latter were enslaved in Egypt. Returning out of exile to their land, perhaps in the reign of the Egyptian King Shoshenq I, around 776 BCE, they took with them various formulae, some of which are still used to this day One of them is on record in Exodus 30:34–35. 'And the Lord said unto Moses, Take unto thee sweet spices, stacte and onycha, and galbanum; these sweet spices with pure frankincense: of each shall there be a like weight: And thou shalt make it a perfume, a confection after the art of the apothecary, tempered together, pure and holy'. Divinely revealed, these instructions for a 'perfume' refer to sacred incense and holy oil and it was at this time that frankincense became part of Jewish religious observance.

In the rituals of the Tabernacle, incense smoke was believed to veil the very presence of God. Thus it was reserved for temple use, guarded by priests, and not for public consumption. As Nicholas Clapp recounts: 'In the Great Temple of Jerusalem, frankincense alone was reserved for the worship of Yahweh; any misuse or profanation of it was punishable by death'.[11] It was stored, along with other aromatics, in a special chamber at the Great Temple. Beside the altar in the Tabernacle was a table on which every Sabbath day, frankincense and 'shew-bread' (holy bread) were offered. Advice about other Sabbath preparations is given in the Dead Sea Scrolls: 'Each person must launder their clothes and rub them with frankincense'.

With its mystical properties, incense was indispensable to early Israeli life, perceived to be as useful in governance as in ritual. During the Biblical rebellion of Korah, frankincense was used to invoke the judgement of God. The 250 rebels were ordered to bring censers of burning incense to the temple: 'And bring ye before the Lord every man his censer... And the earth opened her mouth and swallowed them up…. And there came out a fire from the Lord, and consumed the two hundred and fifty men that offered incense'.[12] Even the censers were sacred: in verse 37, the Lord says, 'take up the censers out of the burning, then scatter thou the fire yonder; for they are hallowed.'

With its volatile antiseptic phenols, frankincense has already been seen to play its part in combating disease. Now, in the role of fumigator, it arrests an outbreak of plague. Moses tells his brother Aaron,

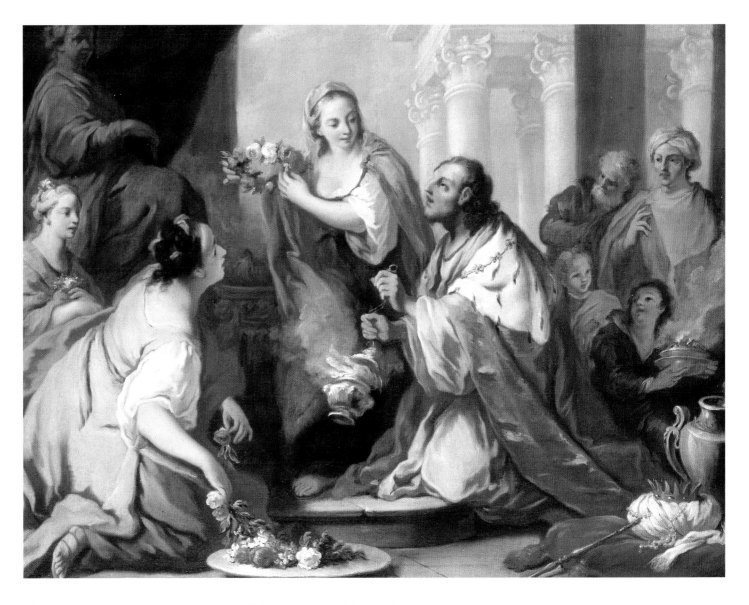

Above: Jacopo Amigoni (1682 – 1752), workshop, *Solomon's Idolatry*. Oil on canvas, 112 × 148 cm. Galleria dell'Accademia, Venice

the high priest: 'Take a censer and put fire therein from off the altar, and put on incense and go quickly unto the congregation, and make an atonement for them… And he stood between the dead and the living; and the plague was stayed'.[13]

Frankincense was not only used to create aromatic smoke, whose visible movement upwards towards heaven made it synonymous with prayer. At times it was placed on top of other offerings to give them added sanctity. In Leviticus the instruction reads: 'If thou offer a meat offering of thy first fruits unto the Lord thou shalt… lay frankincense thereon… and the priest shall burn… the beaten corn… with all the frankincense thereof: it is an offering made by fire unto the Lord'.[14]

The use of the special incense altar continues from the Old Testament into the New. This time frankincense plays its part in bringing about the conception of a baby for the priest Zacharias and his wife Elizabeth who was barren. St Luke writes: 'His lot was to burn incense when he went into the temple of the Lord. And the whole multitude of the people were praying without at the time of incense. And there appeared unto him an angel of the Lord standing on the right side of the altar of

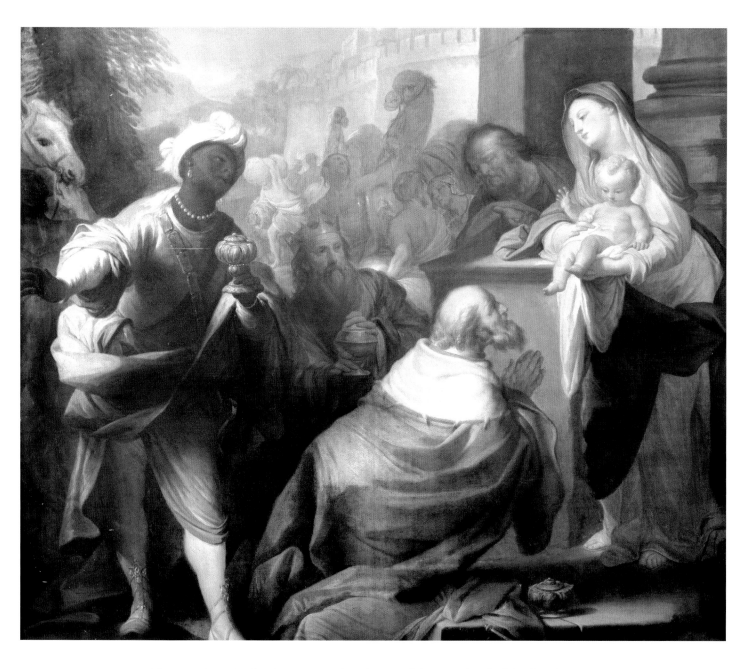

Above: Andrea Casali (1705–84), *The Adoration of the Magi*, detail of the three kings, c. 1750

incense.… But the angel said unto him, Fear not, Zacharias: for thy prayer is heard; and thy wife Elizabeth shall bear thee a son'.[15]

But the most familiar Biblical story about frankincense concerns the most famous presents in history, those given to Jesus at his birth, and endlessly celebrated in art from the second century onwards, when the Three Magi or Kings first appear in a mural in the catacomb of Santa Priscilla in Rome. There are many debates as to the origins of the travellers who were 'following a star'. They could have been Zoroastrian priests from Babylon, who were also astrologists responding to a Biblical prophecy (Micah 5:2) that a great leader would be born at astrologically a specific time and place. But it seems that two of the three 'wise men from the East' could have come from much further afield. Balthazar, the king depicted in Renaissance paintings as giving frankincense to Jesus, may indeed have travelled from Mesopotamia, though John of Hildesheim records in the fourteenth century that Balthazar was from Sabaea, where 'there groweth incense more than in all the other places of the world; and drippeth out of certain trees in the manner of gum'. This account has Melchior, sometimes called Gondopharnes, the oldest of the three, bringing gold as his offering from Arabia, though he was also reputed to be the ruler of an empire in north-west India, and the great civilisation of the Indus Valley had long been using incense. Caspar, from Africa, is frequently depicted in art as an elegant black youth, the 'tallest of person and a black Ethiope without any doubt' according to John of Hildesheim. Eritrea, until recently a region of Ethiopia, is one of the main contemporary sources of frankincense. The Kings 'from the Orient' are celebrated to this day in evocative Christmas carols, and other hymns. An early example, translated from the Latin of Prudentius, clarifies the significance of their offerings: 'Sacred gifts of mystic meaning: Incense doth their God disclose, Gold the King of Kings proclaimeth, Myrrh his sepulchre foreshows'.

King Herod, on hearing about the pilgrimage of the Three Magi, called them to him to ask them what they were seeking. The ninth-century Arab historian Al-Tabari records Herod's question: "'What is the meaning of the gold, the myrrh and the frankincense, which you are offering in preference to all other gifts?" And they said: "These are symbolic of Him, for gold is the lord of the material world, and this prophet is the lord of the people of his time; and myrrh is used to heal wounds and sores and thus God through this prophet will heal the crippled and the sick; and the smoke of incense reaches heaven as does no other smoke, and thus this prophet will be raised to God in heaven as no other prophet of his time shall be".[16]

PAKISTAN AND INDIA

Parallel to the great civilisations of Egypt and Mesopotamia, an equally advanced if much less well-known society evolved in the Indus river valley in present-day Pakistan. From around 2500 to 1500 BCE (though earlier dates are suggested too), sophisticated cities of brick were built, the two main ones being Mohenjo-daro and Harappa. Indeed the Indus Valley culture is also called the Harappan Civilisation since Harappa was discovered first.

These cities were models of advanced urban planning, laid out on a grid system, with street drainage channels, and an underground sewage network servicing the latrines in almost every one of the two-storey houses. These homes had bathrooms too, and at Mohenjo-daro, which at its height had a population of eighty thousand, there was a Great Bath. As in Egypt, where cleanliness was next to godliness, and where a remorseless sun beat down, the enlightened people of the Indus Valley applied oil-based skin-care products. Juris Zarins contends that from at least 2500 BCE sea-faring boats linked Oman with the Indus Valley. Ancient trade links undoubtedly existed, importing copper from Magan (Oman), and Harappan steatite seals depict ships, which look very much like dhows. Furthermore, terracotta representations of women have been unearthed, possibly mother-goddesses, stained with the smoke of incense. It is not beyond credibility, therefore, that the oil used in the Indus Valley civilisation was distilled from frankincense crystals.

Trade to India was facilitated around the first century BCE by the discovery of a route from Arabia via the Red Sea. However there was a much more direct route to India from ports along the Dhofari coast, which exported not only frankincense in vast quantities until 1948, but also horses. In the nine-teenth century Dr Carter, assistant surgeon to the East India Company, travelled to Dhofar to study the frankincense trade, identifying Dhofar as 'Arabia's chief lucrative spice centre'.

India has always been a hugely important and sophisticated perfume and incense culture, and grows its own low-grade frankincense (*Boswellia serrata*), which in Sanskrit is known as *kunduruka*. But for such a discerning consumer, only the best will do, and that has to be *Boswellia sacra* from Oman. Frankincense also has considerable medical applications in India: as a fumigant and to deter disease; applied locally as an astringent and to relieve swelling; and taken to promote menstruation. The Vedas list therapeutic plants and extracts which include frankincense, and the traditional system of Ayurvedic medicine has always used it for its anti-inflammatory properties.

CHINA

Clouds of incense, mists of perfume

Edward H. Schafer

'A man or woman of the upper classes lived in clouds of incense and mists of perfume. The body was perfumed, the bath was scented, the costume was hung with sachets. The home was sweet-smelling, and the office was fragrant, the temple was redolent of a thousand sweet-smelling balms and essences',[16] wrote Edward H. Schafer of the Tang Dynasty (618–906 CE). The use of incense in China would appear to be as ancient as the civilisation itself: the Shang Dynasty (*c.* 1700–1050 BCE) has bequeathed a legacy of ornate bronze incense burners. In the temples 'redolent of a thousand sweet-smelling balms and essences', the burning of incense was an intrinsic part of Buddhist worship.

Incense was originally conveyed along the Silk Route to Ancient China, laboriously wending its way north of the highest mountains in the world, and across vast tracts of desert. The Chinese called incense

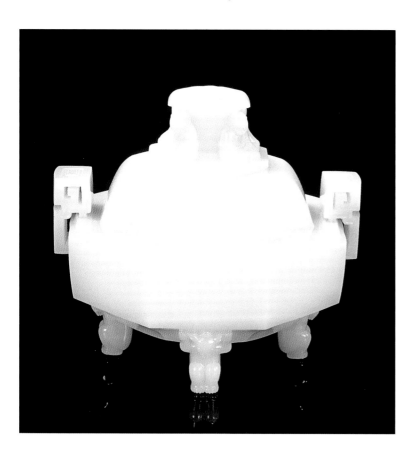

ju hsiang, meaning 'white milk': when a section of bark of the frankincense tree is pared away, the beads of resin that immediately ooze forth do indeed resemble little droplets of milk. The Chinese expression *wengxiang* elegiacally translates as 'listening to the incense'; and in the oldest Chinese pharmacopoeia, *The Book of Medicines*, aromatic remedies are *hsiang yao*. Together with *Weng*-man, the name given to Oman by Chinese travellers to Dhofar, the whiff of frankincense emerges, as in *wengxiang*.

From the first century CE ships were plying their perilous route laden with aromatics. In his ninth-century book *Silsilat al-Tawarikh* [Chain of Chronicles], the Persian Abu Zeidal Hasan describes maritime routes from the Arabian Gulf via the Maldives, Sri Lanka, the Nicobar Islands, then onwards to Canton by way of the Straits of Malacca and the South China Sea. Mastery of the seasonal monsoon winds blowing across the Indian Ocean facilitated an era of accelerating frankincense trade, enabling huge quantities of frankincense and myrrh to be landed at

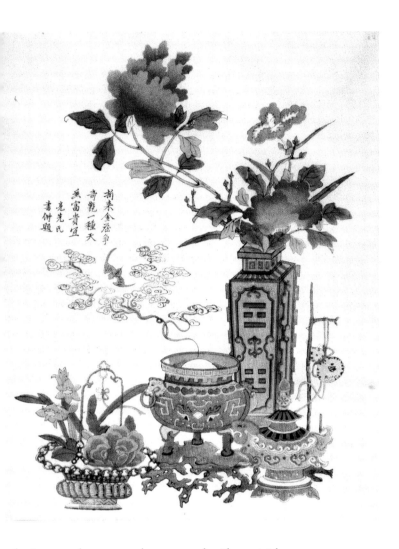

southern Chinese ports. The etymology of Hong Kong's name ('fragrant harbour') relates to the reception and processing of incense in that part of the world. By 300 CE Arab and Persian traders had been granted leave to establish settlements on the outskirts of Canton, one of the great incense markets of the world. The trade further increased in the ninth century when larger dhows enabled Muslim merchants to bring their families to settle in South-East Asia. Such voyages are described in the *Zhu Fan* chronicle, called *Records of Foreign People*, of the Southern Song period (1128–1279 CE). In 1285 that entrepreneurial traveller, Marco Polo, recorded in his journal that Al-Mansura (Al-Balid) on the coastal plain of Dhofar (which the Chinese called *Nu-fa*), was engaged in exporting both white incense and horses with China. The trade existed in both directions, as Wilfred Thesiger surmised while travelling in the region to the north of the Dhofar mountains, on the edge of the Empty Quarter, when he found a jade axe-head: 'Here I picked up a small, well-burnished, Neolithic axe-head… made of jade, which is unknown in Arabia.'[17]

The landed price of frankincense in China reflected the hazards and *longeurs* of the two-year round-trip. These included frequent attacks by pirates as well as shipwrecks. In southern China, the traders had to pay customs duties and other kickbacks appropriate to speeding up the lengthy complexity of doing business in China, then wait for seasonal winds to take them home. Such was the hike in price and the appetite for this highly desirable import, that in the thirteenth century a serious imbalance of trade rocked the Chinese economy. The aristocracy used frankincense extravagantly, even incorporating it into architecture. A certain government minister, Yang Kuo-Chung, built a gallery whose walls were plastered with frankincense and musk. Edward H. Schafer describes more conspicuous consumption: 'Feng Jo-Jang, the Haienese pirate, who lived lavishly among his Persian slaves, burned frankincense only to give light for his parties—a case of sumptuously conspicuous waste. Similarly, as a grand gesture of contempt for worldly wealth, one Ts'ao Mu-Kuang burned ten catties [over six kilos] of the precious incense in a basin, saying, "Wealth is easily obtained, but the Buddha is hard to find".'[18]

Chinese scrolls depict the 'five precious things' arranged on altars: two candleholders, two vases and an incense burner, with the burner always centre stage. Exquisite incense 'sets' were created for domestic use, too, in materials such jade, as well as bronze and openwork-carved bamboo. The incense set consisted of a vase matching the design and material of the burner. The vase held tongs for handling the smouldering crystals and a spatula, along with an elegant box in which to store the incense. Braziers in the shape of animals and birds were popular, for example unicorns, elephants and, more prosaically, ducks. Even more ornate shapes emerged, like the 'Universe Mountain', or a 'hundred-jewel' brazier, three feet high and adorned with figures of gods, devils and divine musicians, set with a prince's ransom of precious gems. This was the gift of a royal princess to a Buddhist temple. Joss-sticks (probably a Chinese corruption of the Portuguese *Deos* or God, as the Portuguese were zealous missionaries in South-East Asia) led to Chinese or Japanese temples being known as 'joss houses' for the sticks of incense burned at their shrines. The Chinese also burned incense before consulting the *I Ching*, a book of oracles still in use worldwide today.

Below: Antoine Dutry (1775–1781), Four-level incense box in the form of a tea-caddy, with Japanese laquerwork. Japan/Paris, 18th century

Right: Painting of Japanese Jizo Boddhisatva fragrancing his cloaks with incense

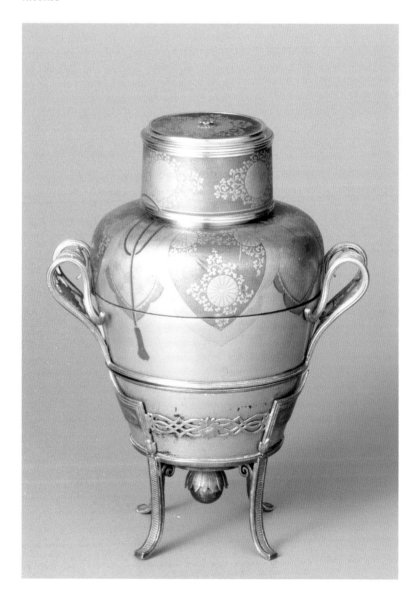

There is an ancient Chinese proverb which says 'a perfume is always a medicine', since that holistic society believed that the healing, transcendent and aphrodisiac powers of perfume were different aspects of one plant energy. They had a goddess of perfume, Shi Che. In China frankincense had therapeutic and hedonistic functions, in addition to its spiritual role as a pathway for prayer. It was used to treat leprosy and other serious medical conditions, and mentioned in *The Yellow Emperor's Book of Medicine* as useful against external ulcers and intestinal complaints. It was also an ingredient in Chinese cuisine. In powdered form it was placed in sachets tucked into sleeves or bags hung on girdles, and during the Tang Dynasty these perfumed sachets were pelted at dancers. Clothes were censed too, hung over frames above special censing baskets. In a nineteenth-century poem a young soldier is described setting off for an evening of pleasure, on a white horse, in a shirt with a phoenix pattern and 'the famous aromas of strange countries fill his sleeve with scent'.[19]

JAPAN

Itinerant monks and trade delegations introduced many of the sophisticated refinements of Chinese culture to Japan, especially during the Tang and Song Dynasties (618–906 and 960–1279 CE). The Japanese adapted these influences, creating an elegant hybrid set of rituals and adult games. Both societies offered incense in their temples, in Buddhist and Shinto worship, as well as using it in medicine, food and the home. During the Tang Dynasty, the Chinese incense clock arrived in Japan. The first of these were circular wooden seals about 33 centimetres in diameter and two and a half centimetres thick, divided into twelve segments. Each segment rep-

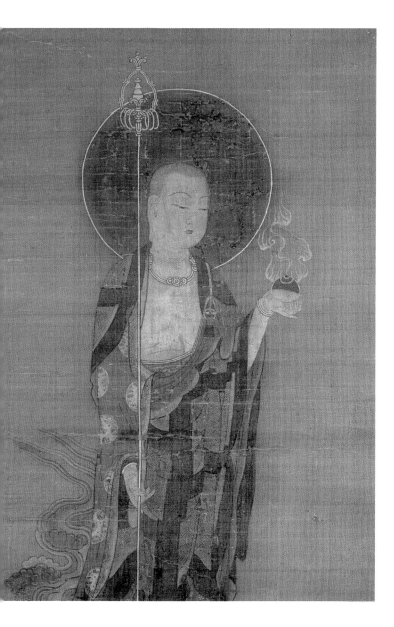

resented one *shih*, or a Chinese hour, (the equivalent of two Western hours). Within each segment was a series of interconnecting lines that subdivided the incense clock into *koh*(s), each one equivalent to thirty Western minutes. The incense mixture was invariably the same tally of components—a powdered aromatic and gum Arabic—so that when lit, it would burn for exactly 12 *shih*, making it effectively a 24-hour clock. The Japanese twist on the proceedings was to use the incense clock to calculate the amount of time a client spent with his *geisha*, by the amount of incense burnt.

Part of the ceremonial appreciation of incense the Japanese adopted from the Chinese, yet made uniquely their own, was the creation of an incense ceremony, akin to the localised tea ceremony. Savouring incense is known as *koh-do*, or 'way of scent'; while *cha-do* is the 'way of tea'. In essence, *koh-do* is a complex fragrance guessing game, using one's olfactory skill and memory. Vessels of unlabelled, scented materials, which could contain a single ingredient, or a blend, are passed around with the aim of detecting the ingredients and relating them to literary themes. Traditionally played by members of the ruling élite, it is still a refined parlour game for the Japanese. In some circles, it became an elaborate game of striptease, with risqué penalties for the losers.

Like the Chinese, the Japanese concealed sachets of aromatics in their clothes, in this context, between the layers of their kimonos. While both societies censed their clothes, the Japanese invented the *fusego*, a custom-built rack for suspending kimonos, while they became steeped with fragrant incense smoke. Diminutive lacquer boxes became an art form in Japan. These exquisite little cases named *inro*, were gilded, jewelled, embellished and treasured, suspended by a clasp on a silk cord, and secreted within the folds of a kimono. Discreetly, they contained ingredients vital to the welfare of the wearer, such as medicine, and in another section, sacredly charged frankincense.

GREECE

The town. . .heavy with a mingled burden of sounds and smells, of groans and hymns and incense.

Sophocles, *Oedipus Rex, c.* 425 BCE

Minoan society on present-day Crete, (*fl. c.* 3000 to 1100 BCE), maintained contacts with Egypt and Cyprus, and luxury goods such as aromatics were imported by ship to the island. Minoan graves have yielded up ritual incense burners, and at Paphos in Cyprus, where there was a temple to the Greek goddess Aphrodite, an incense altar was described by Homer (*c.* 850 BCE). Lively Minoan frescoes depict a sophisticated, perfume-using culture, recalling Ancient Egypt in its penchant for bathing, shaving and use of fragrant oils. An inscription on a *stela* from 2000 BCE reads: 'The lily carved here is the scented symbol of Seka, who in life emanated only perfume'.

Pockets of perfume culture grew up on mainland Greece, whose elegance, creativity, interest in athletic bodies and skincare products enriched with regenerative frankincense were disrupted by three hundred years of continuous warfare. With its disinfectant phenols and holy connotations, frankincense was

Below: Fort Qaytbay and Eastern Harbour, Alexandria, where frankincense was processed before final delivery to the ancient Greek and Roman empires

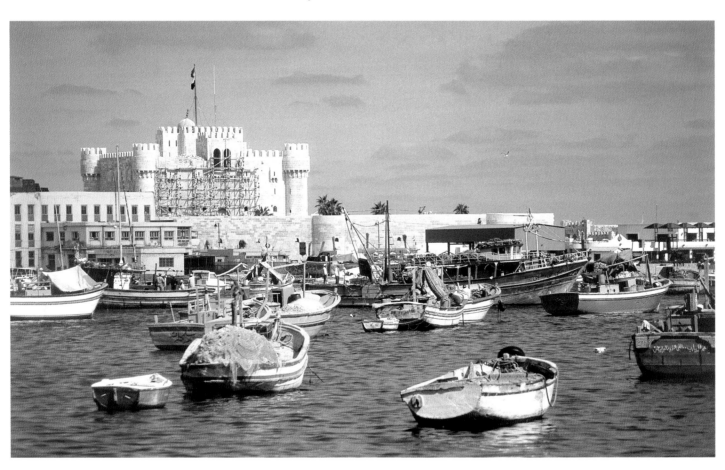

burnt in cities sacked by the Ancient Greeks, as it had been by other conquering cultures, and used to purify after pestilence. At the beginning of Sophocles's play, Oedipus describes the plague-stricken city of Thebes: 'The very air of Thebes is thick with the smoke/Of frankincense and prayers and hymns to God/And frightful lamentation.'

By the sixth century BCE the city-states of Athens and Corinth were once again blending and exporting perfumed oils. Indeed Corinth had its own industrial production line of terra-cotta perfume containers. Although it would appear that in very ancient Greek society, incense was not used ritually, by the sixth century incense had replaced animal sacrifices as an offering to the deities. Aristophanes alludes to the practice of sprinkling incense for a sacrifice with the thumb and two fingers. By the fifth century BCE the Greeks were importing frankincense from Syria, (although the Persians had been obtaining it from southern Arabia before this time), and soon afterwards, they started going straight to the source, with a few intrepid Greek mariners sailing down from the Gulf of Suez to southern Arabia.

Herodotus (485–425 BCE), had only travelled through northern Arabia (as well as Egypt, Africa and the Greek empire of his day), but from his wide learning he knew that frankincense came from further south. He was the first classical author to provide this evidence gleaned from other travellers' tales, but obviously realised that they may have grown in the telling. He recounts some of the hazards endured by people collecting the resin: 'When they gather frankincense they burn storax…in order to raise a smoke to drive off the flying snakes; these snakes…are small in size and of various colours and great numbers of them keep guard over all the trees which bear the frankincense'.

During the fifth century BCE the export of frankincense from southern Arabia had become substantial. The trade was to gather pace and volume in Greece, and then Rome, up to the time of its maximum consumption, in the first century CE. Unless you were a slave, soldier or peasant in Ancient Greece, your life would have been scented from the first dab on the wrist to the funeral pyre. Apollonius is credited with initiating the application of perfume to pulse points on the body, saying: 'Perfumes are sweetest when the scent comes from the wrist'. At banquets, a flock of doves might be released, whose wings had been saturated with scent. Not every Greek approved of such extravagant perfumed habits, however. The Athenian statesman Solon tried to ban the use of fragrance, alleging that it typified the decadent lifestyle of Persia, Greece's traditional enemy.

Persian influence grew stronger after the army of Alexander the Great had conquered the Achaemenid Persian Empire in the fourth century BCE. This brought a greater knowledge of exotic fragrant plants, and Alexander himself sent seeds and cuttings of Persian plants to the philosopher Theophrastus (372–287 BCE), who created a botanical garden and wrote the world's first treatise on scent, *Concerning Odours*. The text included an inventory of all the Greek and imported aromatic plants known at the time, with a section on frankincense and myrrh. It also discussed the ways in which aromatics could be blended by the perfumer.

Like Herodotus, Theophrastus depended for his information on southern Arabia, from the tales of Greek sailors who provided eyewitness accounts of incense trees growing there. It was the first time in classical works that the South Arabian peoples and their customs are recorded, along with their incense kingdoms, although the majority of the trees grew to the east, in the Omani incense kingdom of Sa'kalan, which shipped the resin to other kingdoms in and around present-day Yemen for its journey northwards. On home ground, Theophrastus noted that frankincense was used as an antidote to hemlock poisoning; and later on, Dioscorides included frankincense in his list of *Materia Medica* (*c.* 65 CE). Much earlier, around

400 BCE, Hippocrates, the 'father of medicine', had recommended frankincense as a treatment for ulcers. As in other ancient civilisations, it was extensively used for treating sores and wounds.

Yet another thread runs through the history of frankincense in Ancient Greece, and that is its persistent, potent function in ceremony, ritual and religion. We have already seen that by the sixth century BCE incense had replaced animal sacrifice to the gods in Israel, and elsewhere. The concept of *sacrifice* involved offering something—or someone—of great worth in order to propitiate the deities, to thank them or pray for a change in fortune. As animal sacrifice gradually fell into disfavour, incense was placed on top of the meat or other food to be offered, and then in time became a complete substitute. It was kept in a small box, which sometimes doubled up as a censer. In some Greek sacrificial ceremonies a virgin carried the incense in a basket on her head, along with flowers and a knife. The altar, the sacrificer and the victim would be garlanded, and for bloodless sacrifices the altar would be inside the temple on which the incense would be burnt. Frankincense was also offered on tripods or in portable censers in a variety of shapes. At home, where sacrifices were made to household spirits, the incense would often be placed in a brazier. An inscription from the third century BCE recounts how Seleukos II of Syria gave incense ingredients including frankincense to the temple of Apollo at Didyma. State presentations like this show how prized frankincense was. Virgins carrying baskets of it appear again at ceremonies for the oracle at Delphi, and indeed no significant festival or procession would take place without an offering of incense.

Gaza, in present-day Palestine, was of strategic importance in the ancient world, occupying a key position on trade routes from Arabia, and from Egypt via Palestine to Mesopotamia. After Alexander the Great's capture of this pivotal city, he sent the booty of warfare to friends, including five hundred talents' weight of frankincense to his former tutor, Leonidas. Plutarch tells a story about their relationship: 'Leonidas once, when sacrificing, reproved Alexander for taking incense by handfuls to throw upon the victim when it was burning on the altar. "When", he said, "you have conquered the country from which incense comes, Alexander, then you may make such rich offerings as these; but at present you must use what we have sparingly." Alexander now wrote to him: "We have sent you abundance of frankincense and myrrh, that you may no longer treat the gods so stingily"'.

Alexander was so enthralled by the prospect of owning the means of production of frankincense, that he considered adding Arabia to his conquests. He sent reconnaissance missions to gather information on inlets and ports on the long shores of western Oman, in preparation for an invasion. His admiral, Nearchos, sailed with a fleet of fifteen hundred vessels from India in 326 BCE, and in his journal, refers to Maketa on the Cape of Arabia (probably Musandam in northern Oman). He describes it as 'the emporium for the sea-borne trade in frankincense and all the other fragrant products of Arabia.' But Musandam is not an incense-growing area, so Alexander despatched further expeditions to explore the southern coast of the massive country. According to Strabo: 'Alexander alleged as the cause of the war that the Arabians were the only people on earth who did not send ambassadors to him, but in truth [he] was reaching out to be lord of all'. Arrian, in his seven-volume history of Alexander's campaigns, sheds further light on the reason for the planned invasion: 'The wealth of their country was an additional incitement—the cassia in the oases, the trees which bore frankincense and myrrh, the shrubs which yielded cinnamon, the meadows where nard (spikenard) grew wild'. But on the eve of his foray into Arabia in 323 BCE Alexander died in Babylon, of a sudden fever aged only 32. He was cremated on a pyre piled high with frankincense.

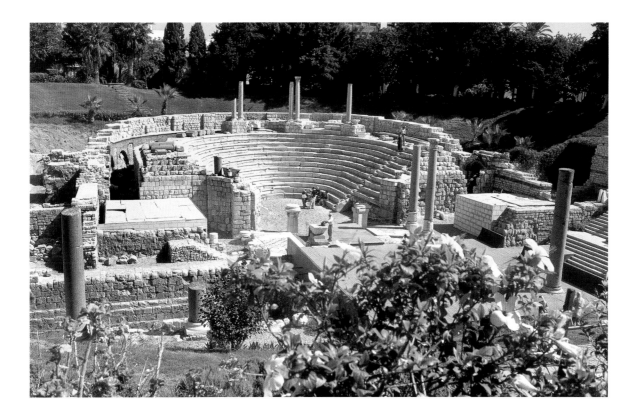

Above: Roman amphitheatre at Alexandria, home of Cleopatra, and eventually of Marc Antony and their children

ROME

'The purple sails of her barge were so saturated with perfume that the winds were lovesick…. From the barge a strange invisible perfume hits the sense of the adjacent wharfs'. Plutarch's description of Cleopatra's first journey to meet Marc Antony in 42 BCE, inspired Shakespeare with his evocative imagery. Cleopatra was the fifteenth and last of a dynasty of Ptolemy rulers of Egypt, which originated in Macedonian Greece. Through her lover, Marc Antony, a Roman senator and soldier, she planned to unite Egypt with the rising star of imperial Rome. Her dream was not to be realised, but her 'strange invisible perfume' had for a long time played an important part in Roman life.

Long before Rome had become a civilised city, the Etruscans had emerged as a sophisticated society, in the region of present-day Tuscany and Umbria. Between the eighth and third centuries BCE, they were trading not only with the Near East, but also further south. Being skilled metalworkers, they created superb, long-stemmed censers in which they burnt imported incense resins. Their perfumers blended these with local materials such as rockrose and myrtle to create aromatic oils and unguents.

A climate of rampant military expansion in the early days of the Roman republic was hardly one conducive to the 'luxuries' of incense and perfume; indeed personal fragrance was forbidden. But gradually, by the second century BCE, contacts with Greeks and Phoenicians who were by then importing frankincense from Arabia, heralded the most intensive use of frankincense in its entire history. Coils of the sweet white smoke wreathed their way around Roman temples, and appeased household gods. Soon frankincense, burnt on its own, was *the* sacred incense, an indispensable element of imperial culture for all religious and state ceremonies. The priestess of the oracle at Patras would offer incense, pray, and then look into a mirror in a sacred well to divine the oracle's message. Billowing censers were placed along processional routes.

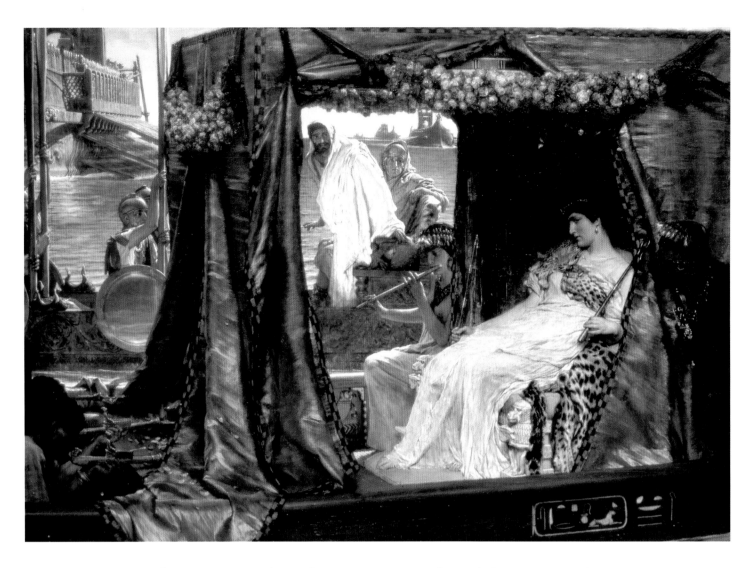

Above: Sir Lawrence Alma-Tadema (1836–1912), *Anthony and Cleopatra*, 1883. Oil on canvas

Following double page: Sir Lawrence Alma-Tadema, *Roses of Heliogabalus*, 1888. Oil on canvas, 132×214 cm. The painting depicts the excesses of the Romans use of fragrance. In Emperor Marcus Aurelius Antonius's (r. 218–222 CE) most celebrated practical joke, a canopy above released tons of rose petals suffocating his guests below. The emperor, also known as Heliogabalus, watches the spectacle from the upper table

An ill-fated expedition to invade Arabia set off in 24 BCE, with the aim of gaining control of the incense trade. Led by Aelius Gallas an entire army of 11,500 legionaries was either lost in the desert, or died at the battle of Marib in Yemen. But as Rome consolidated and expanded southwards, it annexed the Nabataean kingdom in 106 CE, including Petra in present-day Jordan, which had grown powerful and wealthy controlling the frankincense route passing through its valley city. Now a Roman fleet patrolled the Red Sea, protecting shipping from pirates; and around the Mediterranean the *pax romana* ensured secure, prosperous communities. The overall effect was a phenomenal increase in demand for luxury goods, and corresponding rise in volume of the frankincense trade. Overland camel caravans increased in size to thousands of camels, but it was the Romans who developed the frankincense sea trade, as foreign ships began to dock with increasing frequency at southern Arabian ports. In Dhofar, they used the natural harbour of Khor Rhori, now silted up, above which stood the fortress town of Moscha, later known as Sumhuram.

Alexandria became the main distribution centre for frankincense in the Mediterranean, since this Roman-controlled city in Egypt had always been the industrial heart of the Empire. It occupied a special position as the sorting and processing centre for frankincense. Whether it arrived in compacted form or as loose crystals is unclear, but at Alexandria some of it was distilled into oil. Pliny describes the precautionary methods to deter theft: 'At Alexandria where frankincense is worked up for sale, no vigilance is sufficient to guard the factories. A seal is put upon the workmen's aprons, they have to wear a mask or net with a close mesh on their heads, and before they are allowed to leave the premises they have to take off all their clothes'.

By the first century CE, between two-and-a-half and three million kilogrammes of frankincense were reported to have been exported to Rome alone, from southern Arabia. This did not take into account additional quantities sent overland to Mesopotamia, Syria and the rest of the Levant; nor the amounts sent east to India and further afield, to South-East Asia. A considerable amount was also consumed locally in Arabia.

Even before the height of the trade, Pliny was attempting to estimate the cost to Rome of their imports: 'And by their lowest reckoning India, China and the Arabian peninsula take from our empire 100 million *sesterces* every year—that is the sum which our luxuries and our women cost us' (although Roman men as well as women wore Eastern silk and ate their spices). Slightly more than half of the money leaching out of the Empire was going to Arabia Felix, that is about fifty million sestertii a year—equivalent to eleven thousand Roman pounds weight in gold. So significant was the draining away of gold bullion and balance of payments deficit, that it contributed to the eventual economic collapse of the Empire.

From the first century BCE the Romans had been expanding their empire eastward, eventually conquering most of the Middle East. But the final part of the frankincense route leading north-east was controlled by the Syrian traders of the pivotal city of Palmyra, which held out against Roman domination. For several centuries Rome was content to allow Palmyra nominal independence, due to its strategic location between the rival empires of Rome and Parthia. Palmyra, 'city of palms', known as Tadmor in the Bible and in Arabic today, played an important role in international commerce and culture. Palmyra stood at the junction of the Silk Road (which originally took frankincense to China) and the north-eastern section of the later Frankincense Route. A cultured oasis city and hospitable caravanserai, it also hosted travellers entering and leaving Mesopotamia.

In luxury-loving Rome, the Women's Senate decided on the composition and quality of perfumes. Essential oils were used in the famous Roman Baths, and the daily bath was followed by a visit to the *unctuarium*, the anointing room, where slaves massaged fortunate Romans with aromatic oils. Other slaves, called *cosmetae*, prepared skin-care products and make-up for Roman women. There were different scented unguents for each part of the body, including the soles of the feet. Perfume was integrated into the mortar of buildings, and even horses and dogs were perfumed too. The art of glass-making reached an apogee in the creation of exquisite little scent bottles.

While it is impossible to surmise how much of a part frankincense played in the composition of these perfumes, oils, unguents and cosmetics, there does seem to have been a fascinating interplay between perfume and medicine. There is evidence from Dioscorides in 65 CE, in his *De Materia Medica*, that frankincense was used for 'broken heads…and to bind bloody wounds and assuage malignant ulcers about the seat'. Remedial aromatics seem to have been the province of perfume merchants, who took on a similar role to that of dispensing chemists today.

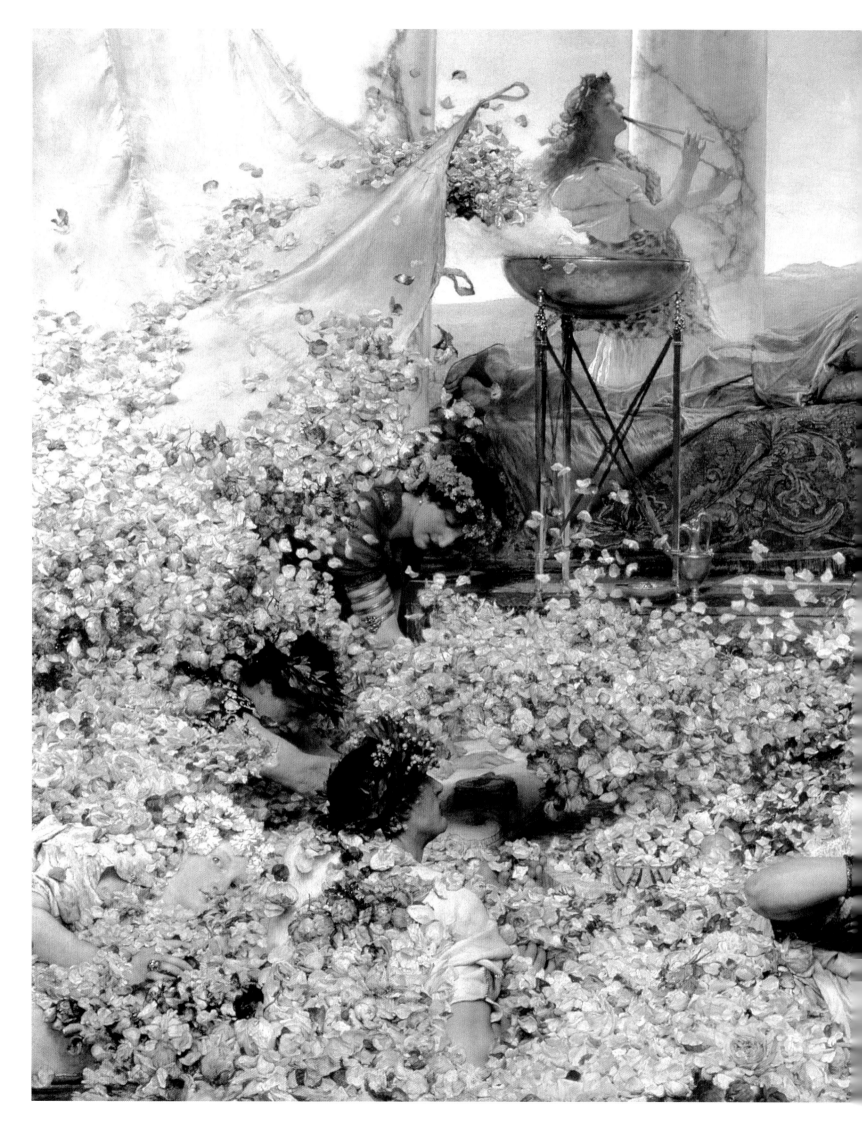

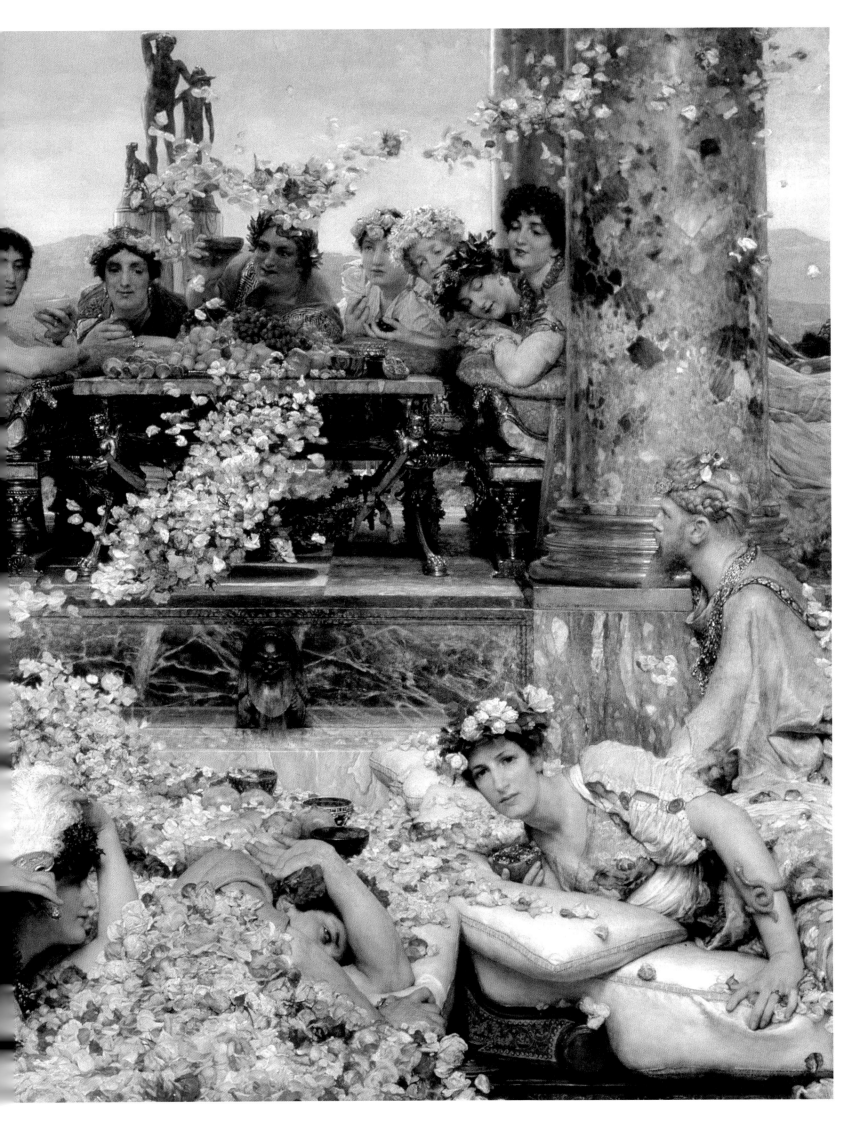

CHRISTIANITY

I have noted that [perfumes] cause changes in me, and act on my spirits according to their qualities; which makes me agree with the theory that the introduction of incense and perfume into churches . . . was for the purpose of raising our spirits, and of exciting and purifying our senses, the better to fit us for contemplation.

Michael de Montaigne, theologian (1533–92)

By the fourth century CE, the disintegration of the Roman Empire and rise of Christianity caused the incense trade to crash. Christianity became the official imperial religion, and its early leaders were appalled by the profligate consumption of frankincense in Rome. Emperor Theodosius I (347–395) forbade the 'pagan' practice of offering it to household gods. St Augustine (354–430) railed against all pleasures of the flesh, in which perfume was perceived to play a disreputable role. At the same time the economic decline of the Roman Empire caused climactic change in occupied territories. Insecurity, then strife, became evident in areas with which Rome was trading, including along the Incense Routes into southern Arabia, where the Incense Kingdoms began fighting each other. For two centuries the aromatics trade was affected profoundly, until in the sixth century pre-Islamic traders from Mecca revived the overland route. Trade by sea continued to areas outside the Roman Empire, though on a greatly reduced scale.

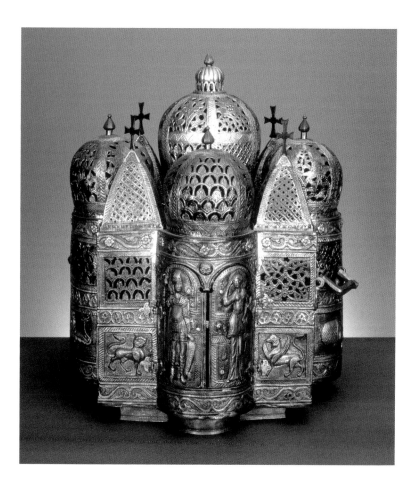

At first, as Christianity took hold in Europe, incense was completely proscribed, but it was gradually re-introduced. As early as the ninth century, the thurible, a swinging censer, hung from chains, had been invented, its openwork construction allowing clouds of sacred smoke to stream out. By the thirteenth century, censers were an integral part of church paraphernalia, in Catholic, Protestant High Church, and Orthodox services, as well as now in most Evangelical/Pentecostal African and Caribbean churches.

It seems that none of the ancient transformative power of frankincense had been lost in the translation from pagan to Christian. For example, the transubstantiation of bread and wine in Catholic services takes place by purification with frankincense, transforming them into the body and blood of Jesus Christ. The custom of burning a candle on entering a church or during prayer relates directly to the role of incense smoke forming a pathway for prayer. To this day, the most sacred aspect of the coronation of a British king or queen is their anointing with sacred

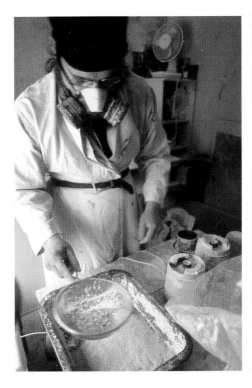 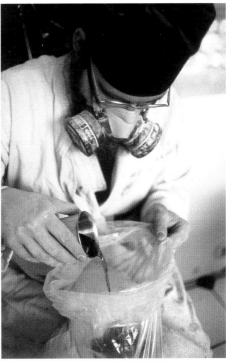 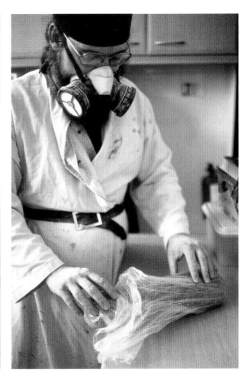

Left: Censer in the shape of a crossdome church. Georgian (?), 12th-century silversmithery. Silver, gilded and embossed. S. Marco, Tesoro, Venice

Above: Father Thomas of the St Edward Brotherhood of Russian Orthodox monks making incense:
Left: Sieving frankincense crystals out of powder after first grinding; Centre: Adding other oils to the frankincense powder; Right: The 'sausage' of powder and oils

frankincense oil. The Feast of Epiphany on 6 January, still celebrates the Three Magi. On that day in 1299 the Wardrobe Accounts of the British King Edward I record that he offered gold, frankincense and myrrh in his chapel. Queen Elizabeth II still gives an oblation of these sacred gifts in the Chapel Royal on the Feast of Epiphany.

Gradually, after the fifth century CE, the use of perfume went into sharp decline in Europe. But the skills and knowledge of the perfumers, which had always interacted with those of the medical profession and household herbalists, were somehow retained, carefully nurtured by monks and nuns in their cloistered gardens and kitchens. In the twelfth century universities were founded in some large European cities, and those which had trade links with the Middle East became repositories of knowledge about Arab science, medicine and perfumery. The first medical school in Europe opened in 1220 in Montpellier, France, later to be a great centre of perfumery on a par with neighbouring Grasse. Frankincense is mentioned in a French medical manuscript of the early thirteenth century: 'Olibanum is known as frankincense, it is hot and dry in the second degree; it has the capacity to comfort and to fortify, to bring together, and to bind. It is also good for the shutting of the eyes, toothache…soreness of the nostrils, and also indigestion and sour eructations. For the breasts, make up a powder prepared with vinegar and plaster on a sheet, and place it on the naked breasts'.

As the long period of cultural poverty and repressed sobriety of the Dark Ages receded, Europe began to welcome the fragrant influences drifting in from the East. Crusaders returning from the Middle East brought back to Europe their aromatics and reports of enhanced personal hygiene there. In 1320, a functioning distilling plant was constructed at Modena, long after the process had been developed in Alexandria in the second century CE.

Just as it had been noted that the embalmers and doctors of ancient Arabia, Egypt and Mesopotamia had not fallen prey to the diseases from which their clients had died, because they were constantly surrounded by essential oils, so during the Black Death in England, from 1665 to 1666, it was also observed that pharmacists and perfumers of the period seemed to be immune to plague. Medical professionals of both societies fumigated themselves, their clothes and their workspaces with frankincense, just as the Israelites had done. A medical writer of the time recommended preventatives such as 'spicy drugs and gums', among which he included frankincense.

Today, there is no fixed formula for the incense used in churches, though it is recommended that as much frankincense as possible should be included in its composition. In Roman Catholic services, the ingredients are usually ten out of 15 parts of frankincense, 4/15 benzoin, and 1/15 storax. In the Vatican only frankincense is burnt.

I paid a fascinating visit to the St Edward Brotherhood of Russian Orthodox monks, who have a monastery and church in Brookwood Cemetery, Surrey, last resting-place of followers of many different denominations, including Zoroastrian and Ismaeli. The Brotherhood is one of the last places in England to make incense for sacred functions, both for consumption at its own services, and for sale to Anglican and Catholic churches. Father Thomas, the Brotherhood's incense maker, is a former research scientist, and continues with his other skill of bookbinding.

Ten different incenses are created according to formulae composed by perfumers Margaret and Michael Woodrow. 'I tell them the kind of fragrance I want, and they then establish the ratios of oils and dry ingredients, of which there may be as many as 28. Then I try them out and sometimes adjust them.' Almost every incense contains frankincense, sourced from Somalia and Eritrea, 'because Omani frankincense is too fragrant', said Father Thomas. He explained how church incense is created today: 'I take the frankincense crystals and grind them to powder in a coffee grinder. Then I weigh out the powder and measure the oils according to the formula ratio. I mix them up and roll them into a large "sausage", which is kept in the refrigerator for two to three days, to help the crystals re-form. Then I chop it into four, warm the segments gently, and roll them out thinner and thinner. With scissors, I cut them into tiny pellets. These are left on trays for six months to dry out. Finally, I bag them up with clay powder, to prevent them sticking together.'

ISLAM

Perfumes are foods that reawaken the spirit, and the spirit is the camel on which man rides and has himself carried.

The prophet Muhammad

In the mind's eye, the image of the traditional world of Islam is of gardens of paradise on earth; of cherished flowers watered as if to challenge the encroaching desert beyond; of richly cloying perfumes; and woody, resinous incense smoke softening the harsh edge of life in Arabia. Incense and perfumes are still threads in the fabric of everyday life in Islamic culture. Braziers and censers billow in palace and nomadic tent; and it has always been an essential component of ceremonies for births, marriages and funerals.

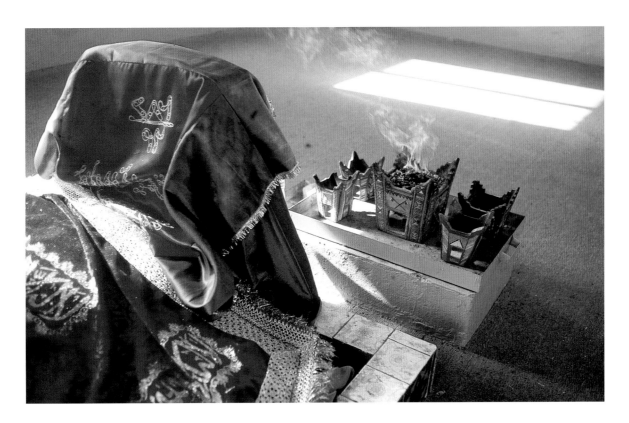

Above: Frankincense burning at Prophet Ayoub's tomb, Dhofar

Although the offering of incense is not an official part of Islamic religious rites, it is frequently burnt in mosques and at the shrines of saints in the Middle East. The Field Coordinator for Frankincense Land Sites at Dhofar, Ghanim al-Shanfari, told me: 'All of us believe both in the past and now that God loves beauty and one aspect of beauty is a beautiful smell. Whether Muslim, Christian or Jew or any other religion, no one wants to go to a place of worship which doesn't smell pure. It has to be clean and smell good, to stand before God'. This Omani, who comes from Salalah, capital of Dhofar, continued: 'We use frankincense for spiritual protection to this day here. Every morning and evening, mothers burn it to protect their children, and read some holy words from the Qur'an, wafting it round their children's heads'.

In the sixth century CE, while there was still some trade by sea, the overland frankincense route was revived by Quraish merchants from Mecca, heralding a new trading pattern. Two huge caravans, mentioned in the Qur'an (sura 106), set off each year, one in the winter bound south for Yemen, the other in the summer north to Syria. By now there was a well-organised sequence of travellers' inns for the hundreds of men guarding and guiding the procession. Medina in present-day Saudi Arabia, the second holiest city of Islam, was an important crossroads on the Incense Trail. It was here in the 620s that the prophet Muhammad established an Islamic city-state, the springboard for the spread of Islam worldwide, now the religion of more than a billion people.

'Women, children and perfumes are what I love most in the world', the Prophet said, ushering in the golden age of Arab civilisation, in which perfume making became both an advanced science and an exquisite art. As widespread conquests took place, it was said that a merchant could receive a cheque in Moorish Spain, and cash it in Canton. Traders carried home to Arabia exotic ingredients and took with them their wares, which naturally included frankincense. Muhammad himself was originally engaged in the caravan trade with Syria. Nowadays, thousands of antique incense burners appear every year at Islamic art exhibitions and auctions, some of them of delicately chased silver, others massive, ornate bronze sculptures of animals and birds.

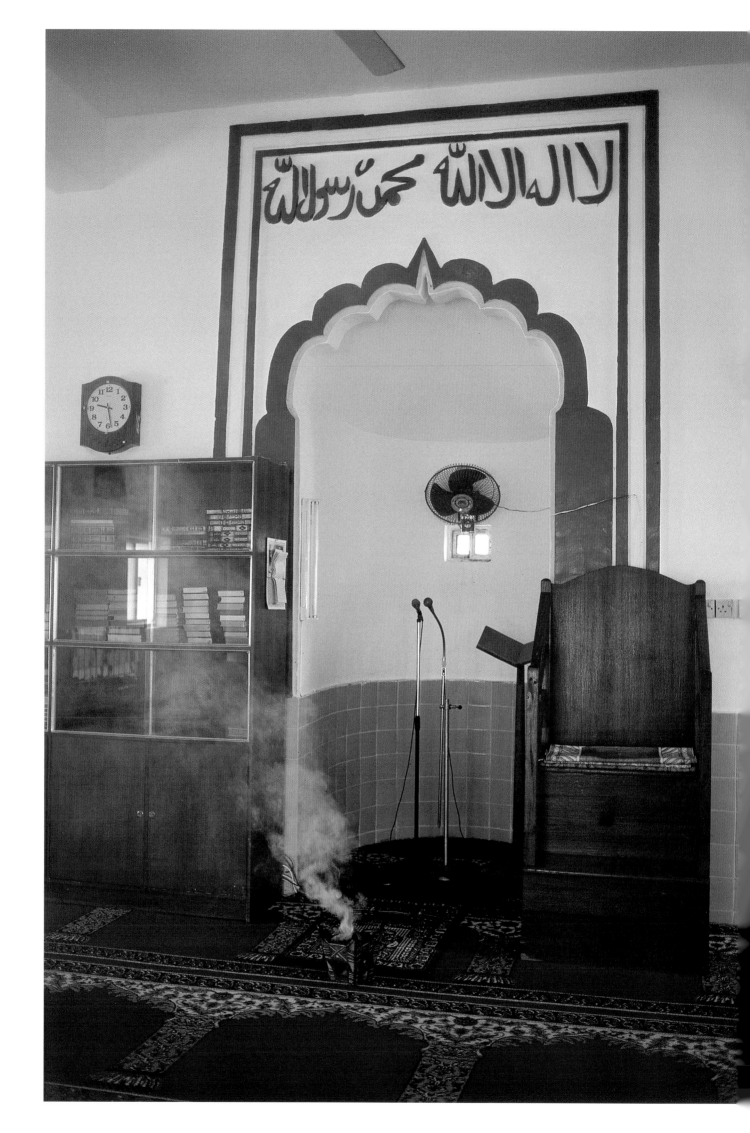

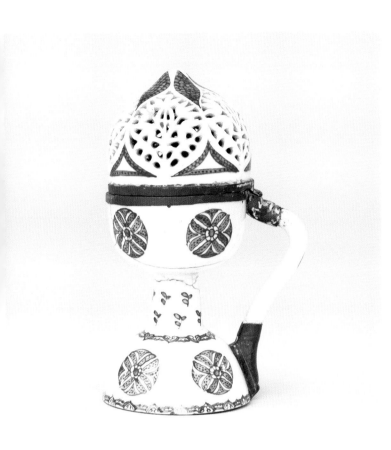

Left: Frankincense burning in a small rural mosque in Dhofar

Above: Kutahya pottery incense burner, Ottoman Anatolia, early 18th century

Both the Qur'an and the Bible recount the story of Bilqis, the Queen of Sheba (Sabaea) and her visit to King Solomon of Israel long before the time of Islam, in about 950 BCE. In sura 27 we hear about how Solomon's favourite bird, a lapwing, went missing. 'Where have you been?' 'I have come from the land of Sheba and listen to this. There I found a woman reigning over the kingdom, and she is possessed of every virtue. They don't worship God, they worship the sun'. Again, according to the Qur'an, the 'Queen of the South' lived in a land in which 'everywhere was heavy with the scent of frankincense and myrrh. Sheba was so fertile—it looked like an earthly paradise' (sura 34).

The Bible tells us that Solomon had 'strange wives, which burnt incense and sacrificed unto their gods'. (I Kings 11:8), so he must have been intrigued at the prospect of the queen arriving in Jerusalem. At this time the incense-rich kingdoms of Sabaea, Ma'in and others were in the habit of sending out ambassadors on fact-finding missions for the enlargement of trade. When the Queen arrived, she did so in truly spectacular fashion: 'She entered Jerusalem with an immense caravan of camels laden with precious stones, gold and aromatic incense, the like of which had never been seen before in Israel, and has never been seen since'.

When Solomon asked her why she had come, she replied: 'I have heard that you are the wisest man on earth and I was curious to see if this could be so…'. Her reason was actually to work out a deal to supply incense to Israel and other countries of the eastern Mediterranean, with the Israelites serving as brokers. Like everyone else outside of Arabia Felix, Solomon's knowledge of the origin of incense was vague, and Sheba was not about to enlighten him. The story goes that after asking him many questions, to all of which he replied, 'he satisfied all her desires'. The deal presumably was also satisfactorily concluded, and Sheba returned to her 'earthly paradise'.

Life in the Jahiliyyah, the four-hundred-year period in Arabian history preceding the rise of Islam, seems to have been particularly ruthless and depraved. As the prophet Muhammad began to reform his society, he preached against the cruelty and injustice of malpractices such as female infanticide, which was commonplace. He also comments in the Qur'an on the people of 'Ad, who practised it, and on their drunken, debauched lifestyle centred on the caravanserai of Wubar in southern Oman. Wubar is presumed to be Iram, which became prosperous through the frankincense trade. Preaching in Mecca in c. 640–650, Muhammad's suras describe the downfall of the wicked city, as between 300 and 500 CE Wubar, the city of the people of 'Ad, was violently destroyed overnight. The town built on frankincense sank back into the sand.

From my branches

flows the fluid to

which millions

of hearts beat on

hearing its name.

Omani proverb

CHAPTER TWO

OMANI TREE OF LIFE

In Dhofar frankincense trees are regarded as a sacred gift of God, and are therefore never planted or watered deliberately. The people on whose land they grow are considered especially blessed. Formerly known as Zufar, Dhofar was referred to in the Bible (Genesis 10:30) as Mount Sephar, marking the edge of the known world.

Covering about 100,000 square kilometres, the Dhofar region is the southernmost province of Oman. It borders Yemen to the west and Saudi Arabia to the north; from its southern coast dhows sailed across the Arabian Sea. Three different zones lie virtually parallel to the shore: the narrow coastal plain; the Dhofar or Jebel Mountains peaking at 1,700 metres; and the semi-desert areas to the north leading into the Rub' al-Khali desert, the forbiddingly named Empty Quarter. Here, on the northern slopes of the three mountains forming a four-hundred-kilometre-long crescent around the Bay of Salalah, the world's best frankincense, *Boswellia sacra*, grows. On Jebel Samhan, Jebel Al-Awsat and Jebel Al-Qamar, conditions are ideal for the trees: steady, scorching sun, limestone soil with deposits of calcium bicarbonate and cooling winds from the monsoon peculiar to this part of Arabia.

The Dhofar Mountains have a unique microclimate. From mid-June to mid-September, while the rest of Oman is sizzling in temperatures around forty-five degrees Celsius, the coastal plain is cooled by drizzling rain, clouds and fog. The temperature can drop to 22 degrees Celsius, as the Indian Ocean is stirred up by strong winds and cooled by deep-sea currents. A much lighter north-east monsoon arrives intermittently between November and April. Yet the rain only falls on the south-facing slopes of the mountains, never crossing over the top. Extraordinarily, it is in the valleys of the north-facing slopes, which remain forever dry, from which the purest yield of silver frankincense is obtained, 'beyond the reach of the monsoon rain, but within reach of the cool winds which blow steadily during the (monsoon) season.'[1]

Whatever the geographical, climatic or geological conditions, the trees survive, though they do seem to need limestone soil. Although they grow equally as prolifically on the southern slopes of the Jebels, and less so in pockets of the coastal plains, it seems that the quality of the oleoresin is affected by rainfall—the less, the better.

Right: Frankincense trees at Dhofar in apparently arid, stony land

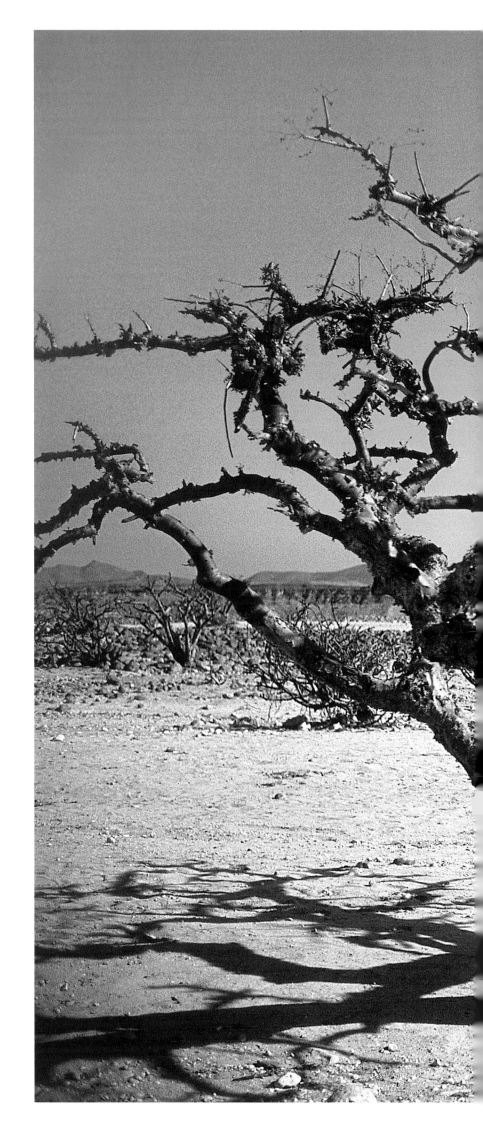

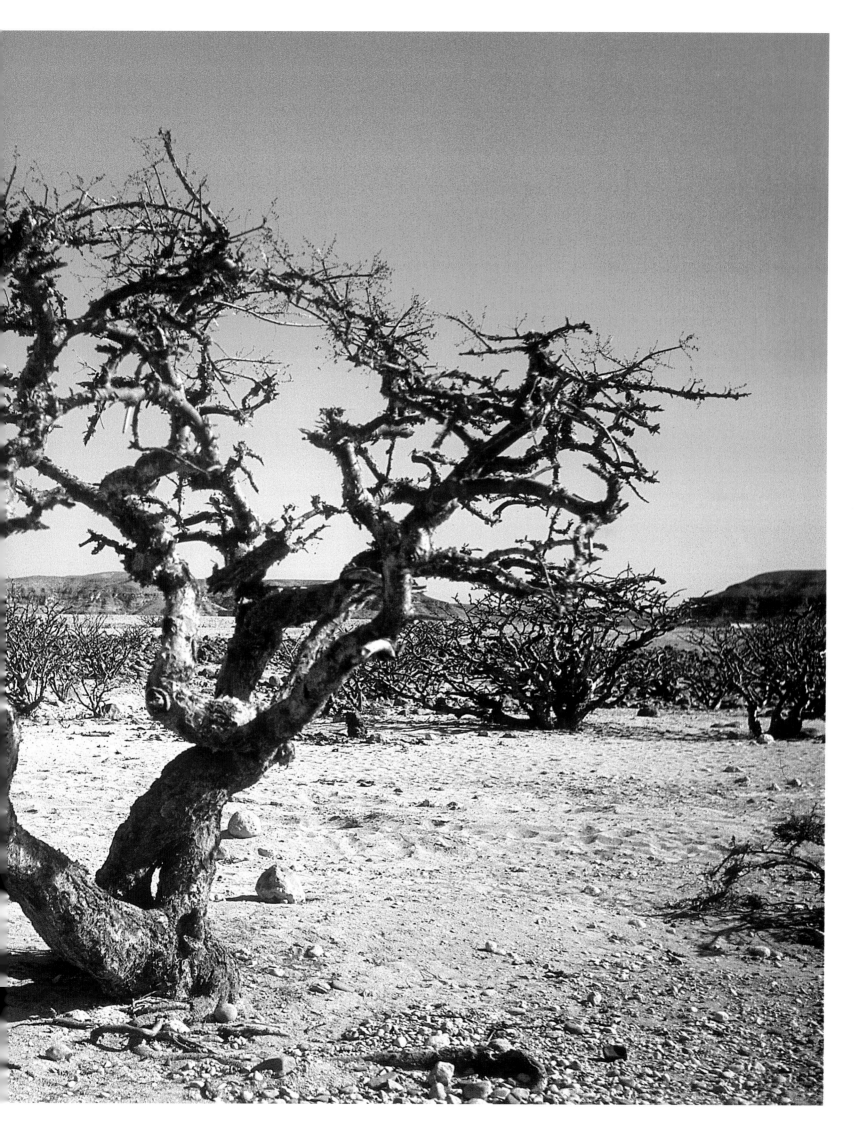

Until the day break, and the shadows flee away
I will get me to the mountain of myrrh,
and to the hill of frankincense

Song of Solomon, 4:6

As well as in the Dhofar region, frankincense trees grow elsewhere in Arabia, principally in the east Hadhramaut region and in the hinterlands of Mukalla, in Yemen. Freya Stark wrote: 'Incense still grows in the Hadhramaut valleys; I found it used all over the country … both in small earthenware braziers and floating on drinking water "to make it pure" and always locally grown'.[2]

Most of the resin exported today originates in Somalia, Eritrea, the island of Socotra, and a small amount is found in India. Though these trees are often more imposing in size than the unprepossessing, scrubby little ones of the Dhofar Mountains, no other trees produce the same pure, exalted fragrance.

In Dhofar the area in which frankincense trees grow wild and untended is surprisingly small. As usual, there have been disagreements in the past which continue today as to which particular part of the mountains produces the highest grade of frankincense. Most contend that it is *nejdi* from the Nejd (meaning 'plateau') to the north of Jebel Al-Awsat. These central highlands rise across the plain north of Salalah, capital of Dhofar. *Nejdi* is known among the women traders of Salalah's frankincense souk as *fusus*, meaning 'gems'. Shaped like teardrops, most are silvery, but some have opalescent tinges of pale rose or green. Some local Dhofaris argue that even more superior trees grow further to the east, in Wadi Andhur, surrounding Andhur Oasis, and their resin is known as *hujari*. As long ago as the fourteenth century, the Moroccan traveller, Ibn Battuta, (1325–54), described it as the best *luban*.[3] Once called 'royal' incense, *hujari* was formerly only available to the Sultan's family. It has a fresh, lemony scent, warmed by the characteristic woody, sensual note. Another illustrious resin, called *hasiki*, comes from within and above the three wadis (river beds) around Hasik, a port surrounded on all sides by the Samhan range of mountains. To the east of these, no more incense trees grow. *Hasiki* has a strong, long-lasting fragrance apparent before burning, which improves with time.

West of Salalah, the arguments about quality classification become even more complex. Some local traders claim that the best resin comes from Wadi Qahshan high in the mountains beyond Mughsayl, others that 'Aydam, near the Yemeni border is the ultimate source. Three superior varieties emerge: *hujari*, *nejdi* and *hasiki*. Less well thought of is *shazari* from the south-facing Shazari Mountains between the Nejd and the monsoon belt. Everyone seems to agree that the incense produced on the coastal plain, known as *sha'abi*, is inferior to the rest, whether from valleys leading into the hills or from the coastal plain. As with wine-making, *le terroir* is all-important. At ports such as Aden, which today is the main export-collection centre for frankincense, experienced dealers, the inheritors of generations of traditional expertise, can detect the place of origin of a shipment, grading and pricing it accordingly.

The international aromatic trade has a grading system for frankincense depending on size, colour, degree of transparency, and of course fragrance, but it is generally acknowledged that *the* premium resin comes from *Boswellia sacra*. Colours change as quality deteriorates, from 'silver' (actually the palest cream), to a more reddish-gold. When the incense trade was at its height, demand was so

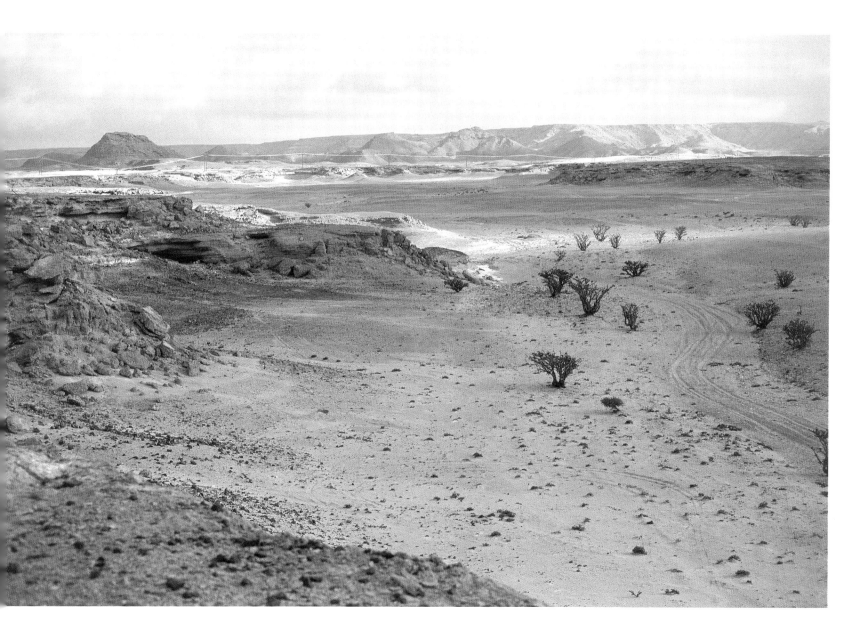

Above: Frankincense National Park at Wadi Dhowkah, a UNESCO World Heritage Site

intense that any sort of frankincense would do, even that of poor quality proving profitable, though it does seem clear that historically, Oman was always the major source. In modern times the number of trees in Dhofar has diminished, in part due to the increasing desiccation of the region. Other factors are the growing numbers of camels roaming wild, which eat the young leaves; and the once fierce restrictions imposed on the mountain people the Omani call 'Bedouin' having lapsed, they now use the trees as firewood and fodder for their goats and camels.

One of the four World Heritage Sites inscribed by UNESCO as The Land of Frankincense is Wadi Dhowkah. It is classified as a 'frankincense natural park', and was selected because of its comparative density of trees and the vicinity of the National Highway from Salalah to Muscat. About twenty-five kilometres north of Salalah, the flat wadi drains to the north behind north-facing cliffs, sheltered from the monsoon. This is ideal for the production of high-quality incense. The wadi and surrounding plains are now fenced off, to protect the trees from marauding camels, and from Bedouin.

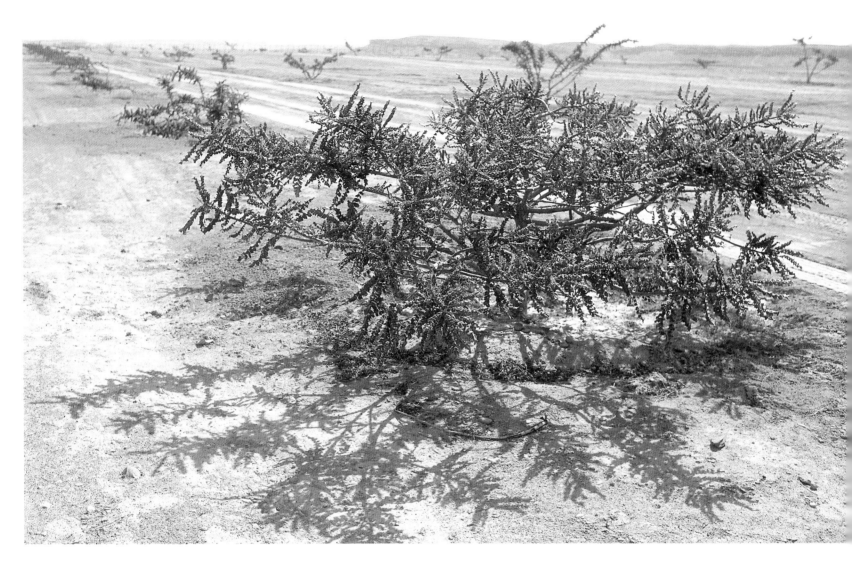

Above: Young frankincense tree at the Wadi Danoon 'nursery'

Right: Musallam Rehaba making his initial incision

Uniquely both Wadi Dhowkah and Wadi Danoon, another 'nursery' administered by the Salalah-based Frankincense Trade Centre, are being planted and irrigated. 'Traditionally, the trees are not watered', says the Coordinator of the Frankincense Land Sites, Ghanim al-Shanfari. 'But if they are, they grow fast, and can produce incense after five years or so. The five thousand new trees recently planted will be watered for two to three years, until they "catch" in the ground. We are planning to drill a well at Wadi Dhowkah to water the trees with a drip system. They will produce seeds of course, which will disperse and multiply gradually'.

Archaeologist al-Shanfari showed me a site at Wadi Dhowkah where there had been an ancient settlement for frankincense harvesters, with stone kitchens and storerooms. 'There were kitchens', he says, 'but it seems no permanent living quarters—they stayed in leather tents without their families. When the harvesting season came around, they met here, stored the incense, and then returned to Dhofar' (the original name for Salalah).

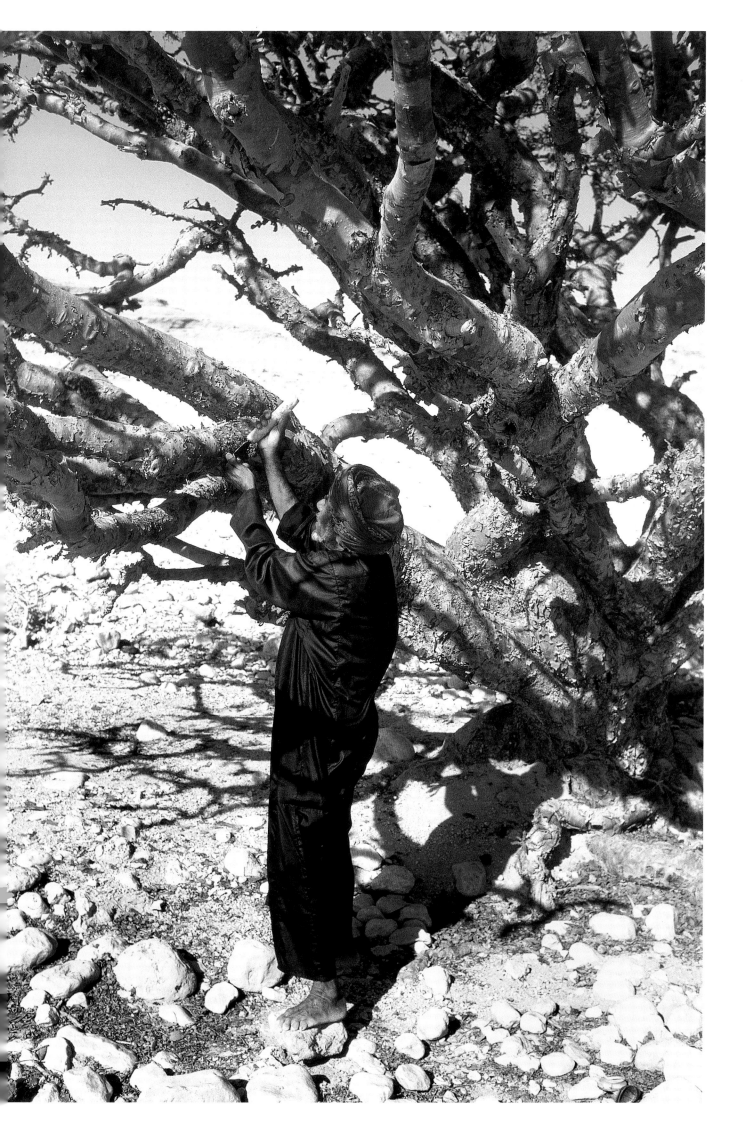

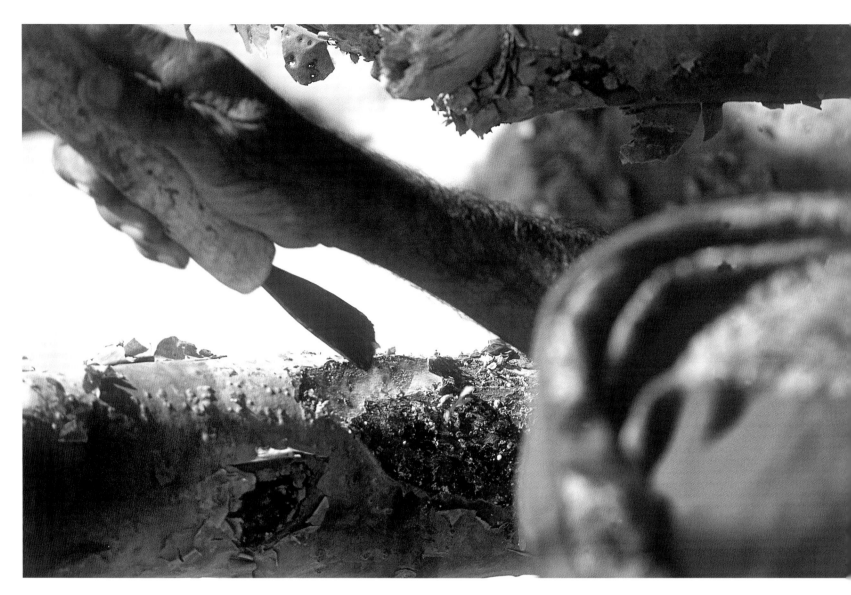

Dhofar is a great and noble and fine city. Much white incense is produced here and I will tell you how it grows.

Marco Polo, 1285

The trees themselves are a disappointment: low, twisted and peculiar, with no pretensions to beauty. Seldom growing higher than five metres (in Oman), more like a bush than a tree, they lack a central trunk. Fat prickly branches spread out from the ground, bearing small, crinkly leaves. But as soon as an area of papery, peeling, silver bark is pared away, drops of the precious white resin appear and begin to coagulate, already perfuming the dry air with their extraordinarily evocative fragrance.

The nineteenth-century travellers, Theodore and Mabel Bent, described the trees they found in Dhofar and Socotra: 'We passed through one of the districts where frankincense is still collected, in a narrow valley running down from the mountains into the plain of Dhofar. The valley was covered for miles with this shrub…. We did not see any very large trees, such as we did in Sokotra…. The shrub itself is a picturesque one, with a leaf not unlike an ash, only stiffer; it has a tiny green flower, not red like the Sokotra flowers, and a scaly bark.'[4]

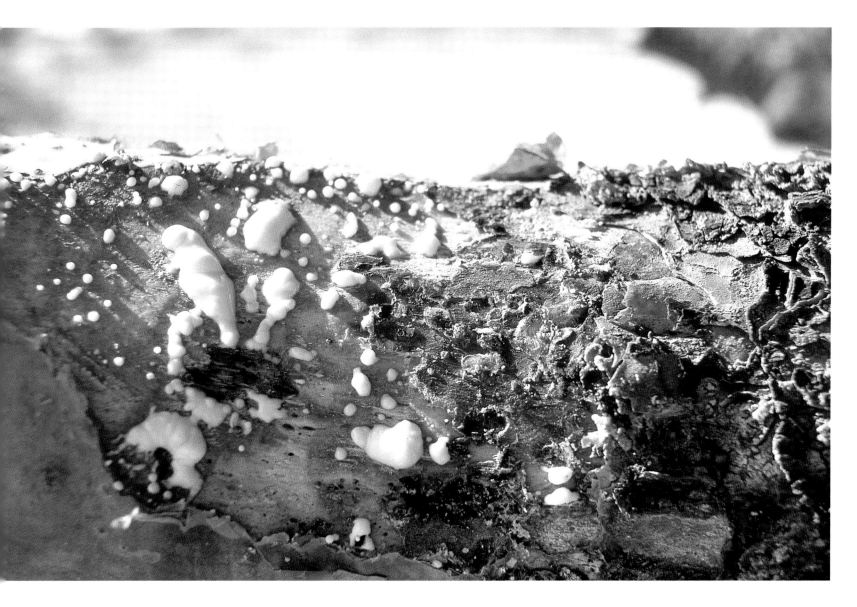

Left: A traditional harvester uses his *manqaf* tool to pare back the bark

Above: 'Pearls of the desert' ooze out within minutes of cutting, immediately releasing their fragrance

Frankincense is derived from around 15 species of the botanical classification *Boswellia*. This is part of the *Burseraceae* or balsam family, distributed over parts of Arabia, Africa and West Asia. Shahina Ghazanfar, an Arabian flora specialist at the Royal Botanic Gardens at Kew, specifies the 'drier regions from the Ivory Coast to Somalia and Arabia, south to north Tanzania and north Madagascar, Pakistan and India', (she omits Eritrea and Socotra). 'Only a few species produce frankincense, *Boswellia sacra*, which grows in Oman, Yemen and Somalia, and is reputed to produce the best frankincense. Other species, *B. papyrifera* in tropical north-east and West Africa, *B. serrata* in Somalia and India, also produce frankincense'.[5]

Arthur O. Tucker elaborates: '*B. carteri* and *B. frereana* are the main sources of frankincense today, native to Somalia, Iran and Iraq, while *B. papyrifera* was the principal source of antiquity and *B. sacra* was the principal species of classical times…. Inferior forms of frankincense come from *B. papyrifera*, found in Ethiopia, Sudan and East Africa…. In Somalia, frankincense is collected today from the

Mohr madow tree (*B. carteri* Birdwood), the so-called Bible incense or olibanum and the Yigaar tree (*B. frereana* Birdwood), the African *elemi* frankincense. Indian frankincense (Indian olibanum) is derived from *B. serrata*'.[6]

Frankincense is the crystallised sap from resin ducts under the bark of the *Boswellia* tree (whatever its species). Its main chemical constituents, according to Gabriel Mojay, are 'frankincense terpenes including pinene, cymene and limomene; alcohols including borneor'.[7] Locally frankincense trees are even classified according to gender. 'The female one is called the Golf or Magarah, and the male is called the Tays'.[8] Pliny adds: 'Frankincense that hangs suspended in a globular drop we call male frankincense…from its resemblance to the testes. The frankincense most esteemed, however, is the breast-shaped, formed when, while a previous drop is still hanging suspended, another one following unites with it'.[9]

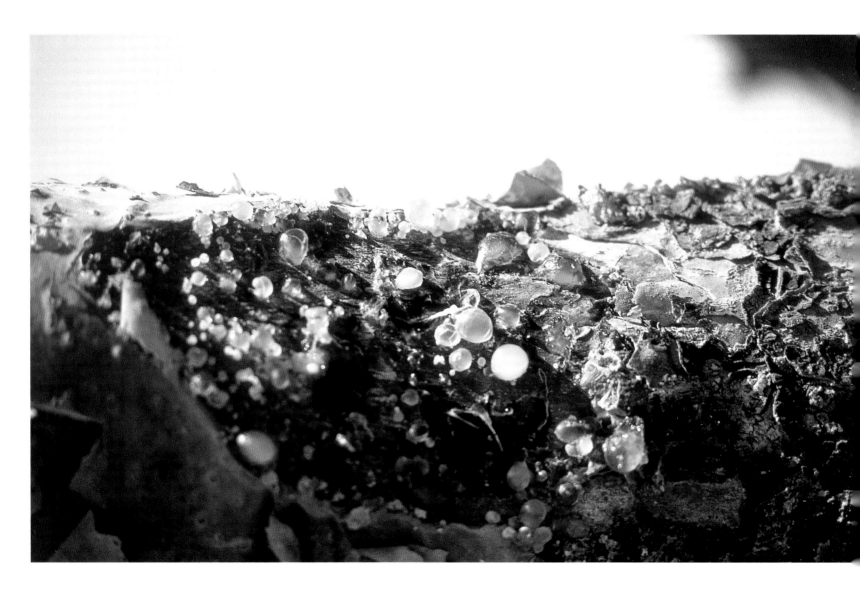

A fragrance fills the whole coastal region providing newcomers with a pleasure past seeing and telling.

Photius (Byzantine ecclesiast, ninth century BCE)

In the Jebel Mountains, the traditional guardians and harvesters of the frankincense groves are the Jebelis, who have for years depended just as much on their goats, cattle and camels for their livelihood. They are descendants of the 'Ad, whose cruel and dissipated lifestyle caused their city-state, to the north of the Jebels, to end in chaos, collapsing into a cavern overnight. The Jebelis are further divided into Mahra, Qara and Shahra groups of families, and in addition to Arabic, speak their own language, a relic of the ancient dialect of southern Arabia. The Jebeli language has a singsong, nasal, chirping quality, called 'the language of the birds' by early explorers. The larger Bait Kathir group, whose domain is more on the coastal plain, speak Arabic.

Left: Crystals hardening over a two to three-week period

Below: Collecting the third *tawq* or crop

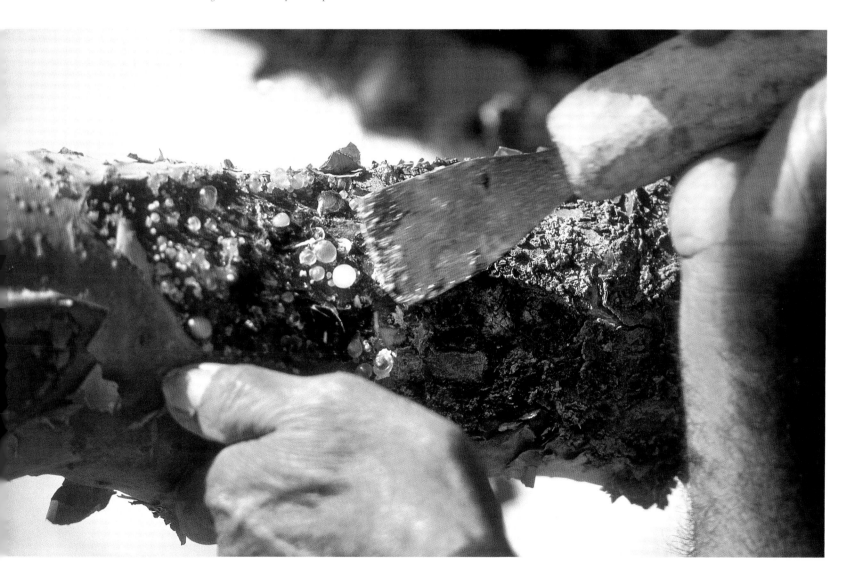

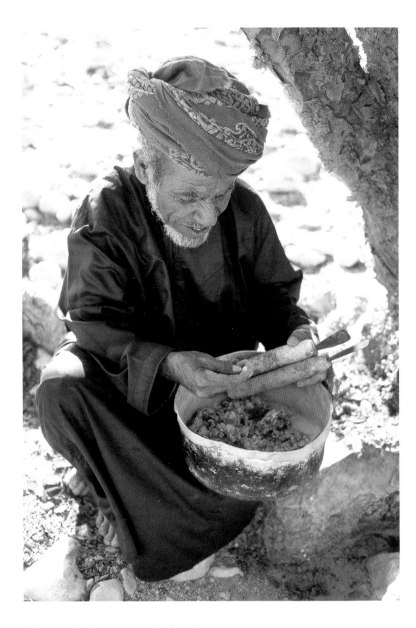

Some of the more isolated mountain people still live in large round thatched 'tents', whose walls and domed ceilings are made of fire-blackened, woven branches and tree trunks. During the monsoon they leave them to shelter in hillside caves. On the walls of some of these caves are pictographs depicting scenes which include an attack on an incense caravan, complete with red-painted bandits, defenders and an upturned, loaded camel in distress. There are also written panels in ESA, the Epigraphic South Arabian alphabet, whose inscriptions I saw at Sumhuram, a Yemeni-built fortress and storehouse for frankincense on the Dhofari coast, and also at the Great Dam at Marib in Yemen itself. These caves also contain pictographic maps showing the location of groves of *B. sacra* in the mountains.

The Jebelis have their own sartorial style. The older men, of slight build, wear a length of indigo-dyed cotton wrapped around the waist like a sarong, with one end tossed across the shoulder. Most carry weapons, either the engraved silver *khanjar* (dagger), or a casually slung rifle. Their hair is long, sometimes finely braided and tinted blue, tied back with a leather thong. Jebelis used to be poor, with a limited diet, but now that they have regular access to the markets of Salalah, their children have grown taller and the men tend to wear the generic Omani robe. The scent of frankincense shimmers round both men and women.

Above: Rehaba examines his hoard

Right: Once collected, the crystals are stored in a cave near the groves of trees, until after the monsoon

Older Jebeli women wear long black dresses and gold rings in their noses; the younger ones have brightly coloured clothes. Neither age group covers their head or wears a veil. Women do not own or inherit the frankincense groves of their families, a convention to secure ownership of the trees in perpetuity for one particular family, since a woman may marry outside her group. Their role in the traditional culture of frankincense is limited to classifying grades, sorting good-quality resin from poor, and then packing it for the men to take to market.

The groves are divided into small growing areas called *manzilahs*; rocks mark boundaries of each *manzilah* to avoid disputes over tree ownership. In the *manzilah* chain of command, the owner of the land is at the apex, followed by the tenant, supported by workers, guards and storekeepers.

At the height of the trade during the Roman Empire, Pliny reported that three thousand families were involved through hereditary succession. Nowadays the Coordinator of the Frankincense Land Sites assesses that there are about a thousand families who own trees, although hardly any young men participate in the work. There is actually a law whereby local tribes are supposed to take care of the trees and harvest those around where they live', Ghanim al-Shanfari says. 'But they have other jobs and harvest only when they are free, irregularly. It's not their main resource now, and it's hard to convince people to return to this trade.'

Since the early nineteenth century, and possibly before that, Somalis have travelled to Dhofar, paid rent to the owners of the trees and culled frankincense. Since they did not own the trees, they exploited them, cutting far too often, and causing them to wither. 'The trees need a rest of two to three months after every harvest, to build up resin again, and they suffered as a result', says al-Shanfari. 'Local people care about the trees, because they know they have given them life. They respect them and treat them in a friendly way.' After a recent government ban, Somalis no longer collect the resin, although private sector companies dealing in natural products are not happy about this. With fewer and fewer local people prepared to undertake the laborious, time-consuming work, which pays little today, the price of the resin at market has increased, due to scarcity.

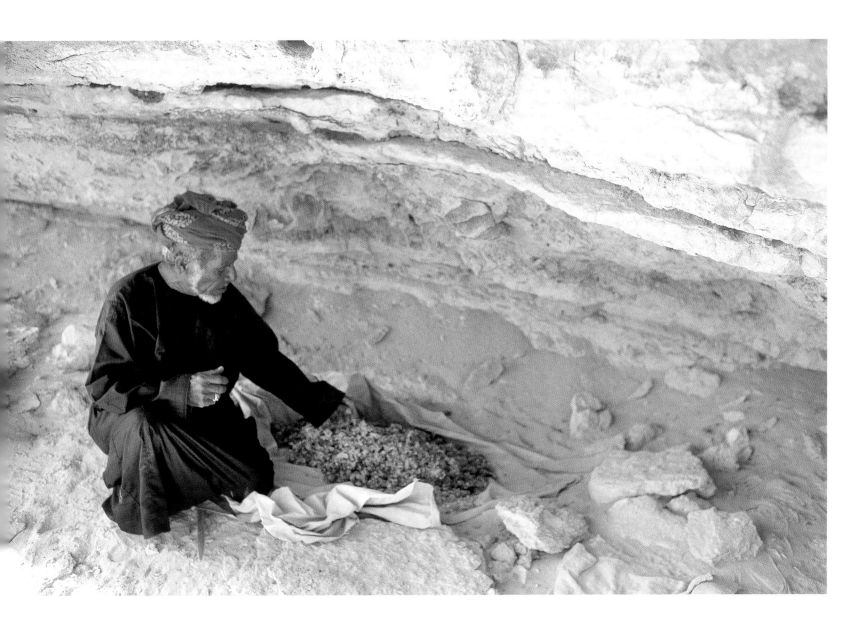

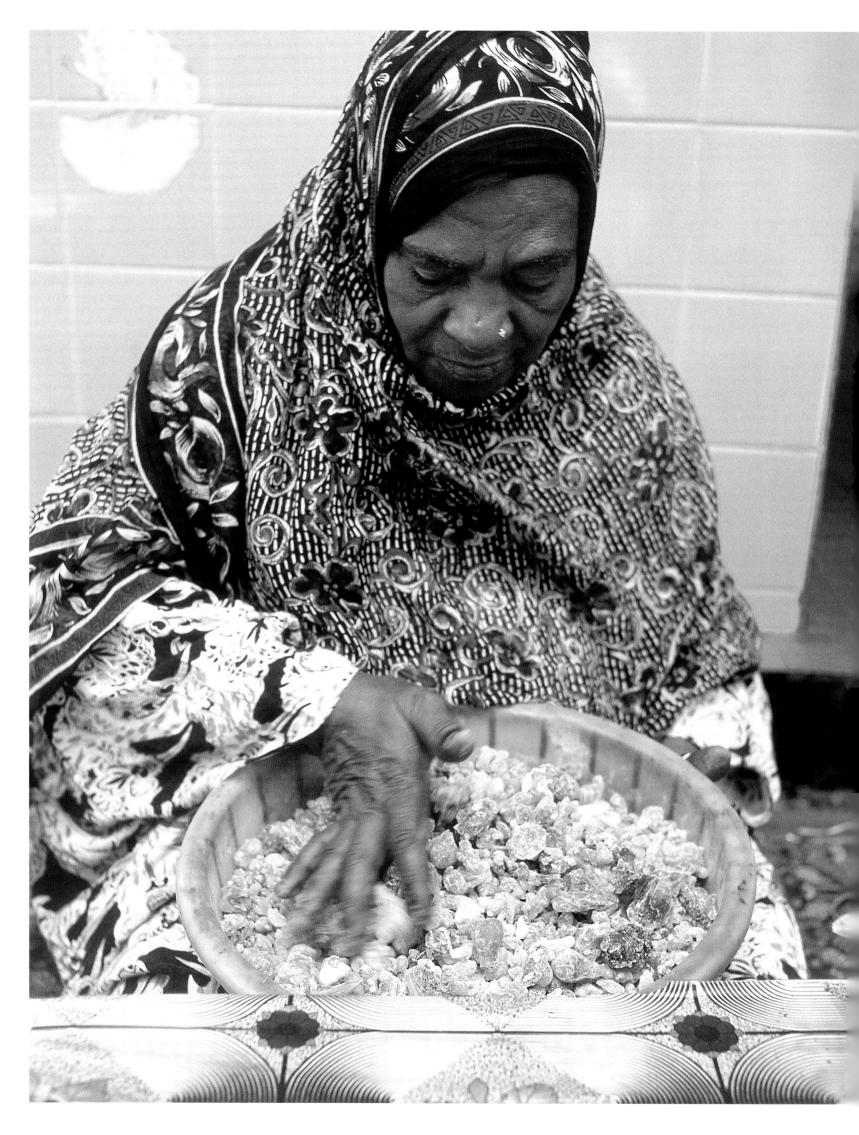

*Brilliant white and gathered at dawn in drops or tears
in the shape of pearls.*

Pliny the Elder (Roman historian, 23–79 CE)

The season for gathering the 'pearls of the desert' extends from late March or early April until the onset of the summer monsoon in July. Timing is important and in antiquity the harvest was augured by the appearance of the Dog Star. As Nigel Groom explains in *Frankincense and Myrrh*: 'The rising of the Dog Star was in Roman reckoning the beginning of July, when the "dog days", the six to eight hottest weeks of summer, commenced in Rome…. In south Arabia this fell a little earlier than in the Mediterranean, in May and June'.[10] When frankincense was in high demand, a second crop was harvested during November and December. Conditions were different during this colder season, as the resin took much longer to ooze out and to harden.

The seasonal pattern of cropping may have changed, but the method of extraction has remained the same for thousands of years, still surrounded by ritual. If timing of the harvest is important, more vital still is the care of the trees, and the way in which incisions are made so as not to harm them. We went to collect Musallam Rehaba from his substantial villa in Thamarit, high up in the Nejd. Then we drove to his family's remote frankincense grove, where I photographed him moving from tree to tree, chanting as he made incisions. His ancient harvest song was guttural, almost harsh, delivered with a driving rhythm, and punctuated by noisy exhalations of breath. Even early in the morning, the sun was fierce, as I followed Rehaba, stumbling over rocks in the ravines.

With practiced downward movements in time with his song, he used a special chisel-like knife called a *manqaf*, to carefully scrape away the silvery, outer bark in several places, in incisions about four to eight centimetres long, on the branches of specific trees. This cutting operation, called the *tawqi'* (in classical Arabic, the word *tawqi'* translates as 'to gall a camel's back'), has to be performed with great delicacy, since if the cut is too deep, the tree will become barren. Treatment of each tree differs according to age and size. With further precise strokes he pared away the first green layer he had exposed, revealing a red wound. Immediately, about a dozen or so beads of opaque milky whiteness appeared and, on contact with the dry air, began to harden before my eyes, so that within minutes they had changed to a spongy consistency and had become semi-translucent. This first *tawqi'* is not used: its function is to open the pores of the trees. Subsequent *tawqi's*, made in the same places at intervals of ten days or more, allow the gum to exude. The second cutting yields low-quality incense, but the third *tawqi'* produces the most, 'like a cow milking better the more calves she has', says Rehaba.

The crystals are left to harden under the summer sun between ten days and three weeks, becoming increasingly translucent. Rehaba went to collect them from trees he had previously cut. The air was laden with the piny, resinous, inimitable scent of frankincense. In the past, a two-handled basket of woven palm leaves would have been the conventional receptacle for collection, but Rehaba had only a battered tin bowl. No longer a young man, it had taken him several hours to fill his bowl, and so he paused to sit in the shade of one of his trees, examining his haul of once-precious resin. He is one of the last harvesters of a no-longer-profitable business—in Oman, at any rate. While we rested and

Left: Incense dealer and creator, Juma bint Saeed Thowaini, sorts silver frankincense

drank water, a small clay censer, shaped like a traditional Omani fort, was produced. Heaped with glowing charcoal, it was sprinkled with freshly harvested frankincense, and passed around. Following the custom, our water was 'purified' by having incense smoke wafted over it, and we fanned the smoke into our clothes, the men also perfuming their beards. Out in these fabled groves, the fragrant smoke coiled its way heavenwards, releasing a stream of ancient memories.

Later, just as his ancestors had always done, Rehaba carried a sack full of resin to a cave in the mountains, where it would dry out in storage until September, when it would be sent to market, or formerly, to the ports and starting-points of overland camel caravans. Before that time, the monsoon ensures that the mountain groves are inaccessible. It causes gales and stirs up the Arabian Sea, so that in the past small boats and even ocean-going dhows, could not set out. A portion of the local harvest is also kept back for domestic use.

Frankincense trees start to bear resin from their fifth year, but it depends upon the skill of the harvester to gauge whether a tree is strong enough to withstand tapping. If well tended, which includes being allowed to 'rest', they continue to exude crystals until they reach about forty years old. During the collecting season, the trees go on yielding from the same incisions, deepened as necessary, at intervals of approximately two weeks. Then they must be left to recover until the next year, or longer, according to their condition. Average production is about ten kilogrammes in a season, though some trees yield up to twenty.

Below: Frankincense oil and traditional censers at Al-Hosn frankincense souk, Salalah

Right: Oil and pomade processed from crystals at Salalah's main souk

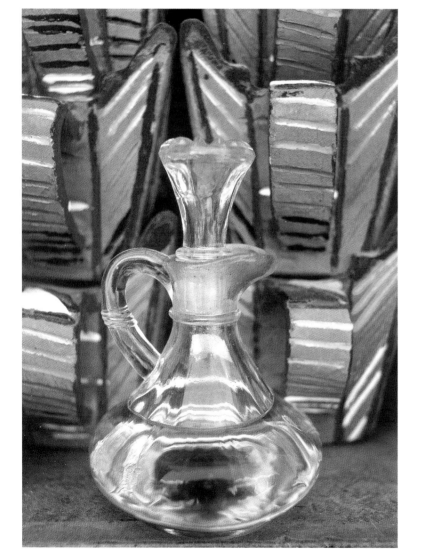

Before the monsoon, just after the first *tawqi'*, the Jebeli owners of the *manzilahs* descend on Salalah to meet the merchants dealing in frankincense, and arrange deals, primarily by barter. Analysis of this first *tawqi'* ensures that subsequent ones will yield sufficient high-quality incense, and then the merchants sign witnessed agreements.

By September, when the rain has stopped, and the ground is firm enough for camel caravans or jeeps to navigate, preparations are made to bring the incense down to Salalah. Emissaries are sent ahead to ensure that the merchants prepare a rousing welcome, and that their storerooms are ready to receive the resin. The September frankincense markets used to be the occasion for great celebrations. The Jebelis came into town brandishing their rifles, singing and performing the Habout, a traditional epic dance. This was a time when marriages could be arranged, but the main lure was shopping. Jebelis still travel to market to buy grain, dates, clothes, glass bangles and various kinds of oil, including sesame for their hair.

In former times, the sacks of resin were weighed on huge scales with stone weights of up to 32 kilogrammes. Until around 1940, merchants from Aden and ships' captains from further afield would

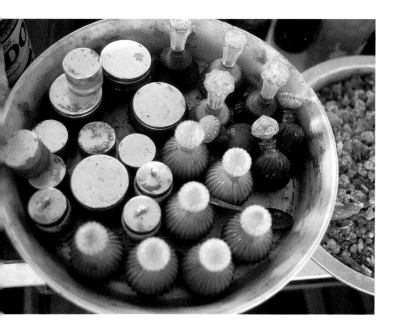

come to buy, some still using Maria Theresa thalers. In 1945 Wilfred Thesiger reported: 'As I entered the town of Salalah I passed a small caravan, two men with four camels tied head to tail, and when I questioned the guard who was with me he said that these camels were carrying frankincense. Today, however, the trade is small and of little value, hardly more important in the market at Salalah than the buying and selling of goats and firewood.'[11]

Today it is primarily tourists who stroll around the frankincense souk, which in itself has only been in existence since 1994. When I first visited Dhofar, there was an aromatic and spice section in Salalah's main souk, with piles of incense crystals in sacks and flasks of frankincense oil. In September buyers for the perfume industry (most from the very active modern Arabian sector) arrive to arrange for supplies, but a few connoisseurs from the global trade also travel to southern Oman, to source the best frankincense in the world.

During the era of Arabia Felix, southern Arabians ensured that their contribution to the frankincense trade was cloaked in mystery, and visitors were discouraged. Early travellers described the forbidding shoreline wreathed in monsoon mists, the high cliffs rearing up, deterring investigation. Deep within the remote ravines, the harvest was a particularly secretive season, the trees guarded against trespassers. The collection of frankincense was immersed in ritual and hedged about by daunting legends to protect the Jebelis from malign influences. Some were true, others probably not, but together they drove away intruders, and kept the price of incense high. Pliny recorded that the three thousand families involved 'are called sacred and (their men) are not allowed while pruning the trees or gathering the harvest to receive any pollution, either by intercourse with women, or coming into contact with the dead.'[12]

The most extravagant warning of the hazards of the frankincense groves is based on fact—the 'flying serpents', which are believed to guard the trees. The mountains of Dhofar are infested with small snakes, carpet vipers, that coil, seem to become airborne, and strike their victim sometimes as high as the thigh. Within twenty minutes the viper's poison is deadly, both hemotoxic and neurotoxic, with no known antidote. Several classical authors warned about the 'flying serpents', including the natural historian Diodorus of Sicily, who wrote: 'In the most fragrant forests is a multitude of snakes, the colour of which is dark red, their length a span, and their bites altogether incurable; they bite by leaping upon their victim.'[13]

Local legends about the vipers are more fanciful: 'The guards that help the families in protecting the trees are namely small serpents with wings of different bright colours. They fly from the trees with large numbers sending fire and sparks from their mouths.'[14] Tim Macintosh-Smith writes: 'The Dhofari scholar Sa'id al-Ma'shani has noted the existence of a rock drawing from the region which shows a man's leg and a snake. Possibly, he suggests, this is an ancient "No Trespassing" sign.'[15]

In the fifth century BCE Herodotus too had warned of vicious flying snakes that guarded the frankincense groves. However, he also reported that storax, an oleo-resin obtained from the inner bark of the Liquidambar tree, and also known as Jewish Frankincense, was burned by southern Arabs while they were collecting frankincense from the groves. The smoke was reputed to drive away the snakes.

THE GREAT ROAD SHOW

INCENSE ROUTES FROM DHOFAR

■ 1. Oldest land route. From Ain Humran travelling north (in the classical period via collection points of Hanoon and Andhur); then via Wubar, across the Empty Quarter to Jabrin, Gerrha, Dilmun and Mesopotamia.

■ 2. From Sumhuram west (inland) to Shabwa, north to Jabrin, connecting there with Route 1.

■ 3. From Sumhuram (and other Dhofari ports) west by sea to Qana, then inland to Shabwa, Marib and Nagran. The main route led northwest, but an alternative one from Nagran connected with Jabrin and then to northeast Arabia as in Routes 2 and 3.

The main route from Nagran northwest led to Yathrib, Dedan and Hijra. But at Dedan alternative routes connected east with Gerrha and west with coastal Leuce Come.

From Leuce Come Routes 3b across the Red Sea led either to Berenice or Myos Hormos. Both those routes were destined for Alexandria. Back at Dedan, the main road (Route 3) led to Hijra. From Hijra, routes went west to Caenopolis and Myos Hormos across the Red Sea (and onwards to Alexandria). Alternatively, a route from Hijra led to Aelana and on to Gaza. At Petra the road branched in five directions— the most significant being to Alexandria (Route 3A), or to Gaza, or Jerusalem or Jerash and on to Damascus. From Damascus a trail went to Palmyra. A fifth route brought goods westwards to Petra from Ur (but probably did not convey frankincense east, as Routes 1 and 2 from the south to Ur, were shorter).

■ 4. By sea (the latest route) from Sumhuram and other Dhofari ports to Qana, up the Red Sea, calling at Berenice and Coptos, then down the Nile via Luxor and Cairo to Alexandria. Alternatively, at Coptos a route led straight to Alexandria.

■ 5. East by sea from Dhofari ports, including Raysut, Al-Balid (latterly), Taqa, Mirbat, Sad'h and Hasik to India, China, Indonesia etc.

■ 6. The least known route of all, by sea east from Dhofari ports, up the Persian Gulf.

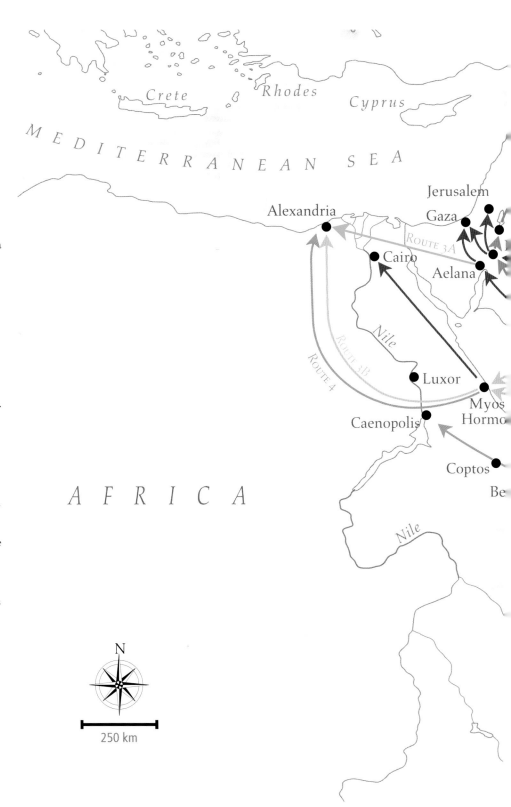

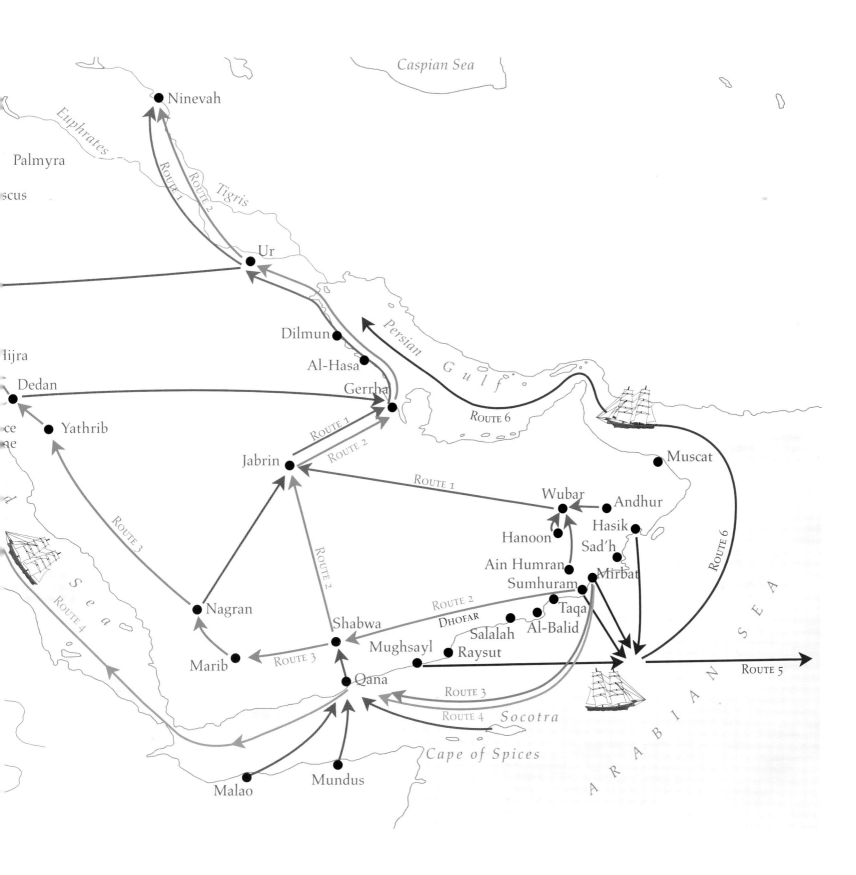

Caspian Sea

Ninevah

Palmyra

Euphrates

scus

Tigris

ROUTE 1

ROUTE 2

Ur

Hijra

Dilmun

Al-Hasa

Dedan

Gerrha

Persian

Gulf

ROUTE 1

ROUTE 6

ce

Yathrib

Jabrin

ROUTE 2

Muscat

ROUTE 1

ROUTE 3

Wubar

Andhur

Hasik

ROUTE 6

Hanoon

Sad'h

Ain Humran

Nagran

ROUTE 2

Sumhuram

Mirbat

ROUTE 4

Sea

Shabwa

ROUTE 2

Dhofar

Taqa

ROUTE 4

Marib

ROUTE 3

Mughsayl

Salalah

Al-Balid

ARABIAN

Qana

Raysut

ROUTE 5

ROUTE 3

Socotra

ROUTE 4

SEA

Cape of Spices

Malao

Mundus

81

Fragrance is our strongest link to the past, our closest fellow traveller to the future.

Tom Robbins, *The Jitterbug Perfume*

CHAPTER THREE

THE GREAT ROAD SHOW

THE ORIGINAL TRADE ROUTE

Of the three legendary ancient trade routes, rivers of commerce and ideas, the Silk Road was the longest stretching overland some twelve thousand kilometres from China to Syria, and eventually to Greece in the time of Alexander the Great. For over two thousand years the Spice Route connected South-East Asia and the Asian subcontinent to Arabia and Europe by a network of sea-lanes. The oldest was the Incense Trail, possibly the most intriguing, and certainly the least explored and documented. The three historic routes converged at Palmyra and Petra. Palmyra was an oasis junction of the Silk Road and Incense Trail, with caravanserais for travellers through Mesopotamia, Parthia and Central Asia. Strabo described some of the imports he saw at Petra—functional goods such as brass and iron, and also luxury items such as 'purple garb, styrax, crocus, costaria, embossed works, paintings, and moulded works (which) are not produced in their country'.[1] Petra was also the entrepôt for other luxury commodities such as silk from China and India, Chinese porcelain, pepper and spices.

Once harvested in southern Arabia the frankincense caravans trudged north on a four-month journey of four thousand miles to reach the Roman Empire over some of the most hostile terrain on earth. Efficient organisation and protection were required, such as road posts with soldiers and fresh beasts of burden. The merchants needed lodging and refreshment, and thus the famous caravanserais grew up along the Incense Routes. The prosperity of these hostelries grew. They became little towns, whose approaches and streets were paved with flat rocks; and eventually a succession of rich incense kingdoms flourished for nearly two thousand years. The wealth of now half-forgotten names like Sabaea, Ma'in and Nabatene enabled them to construct dams and sophisticated irrigation systems providing agricultural produce for growing populations, both indigenous and peripatetic. Before crumbling into the dust of history, they created alphabets and literature, religious and legal systems, great art and architectural triumphs, as well as engineering feats. The history of the world was shaped for thousands of years by the long-distance swathes cut by the silk, spice and incense routes, and their legacy lingers on. Along with luxury goods, they conveyed culture and technologies, spiritual concepts and conquering armies.

Political exigencies and geographical factors, such as a massive sand dune, would at times alter their course. Movement along the incense roads occurred in stages, not only with changes of animals, but of personnel as well. The kingdoms allowed only their own people to control the passages of the caravans

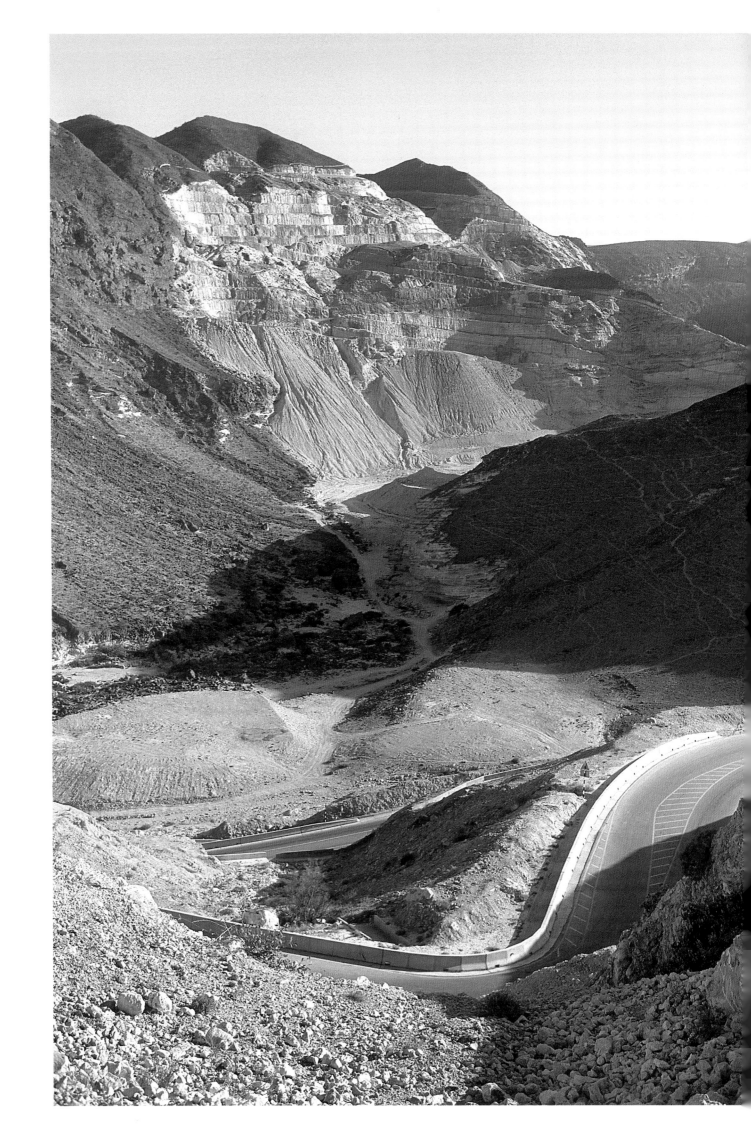

on their sectors, so that the entire operation was shrouded in secrecy, preserving monopolies as well as mystique. Just as it is highly unlikely that a merchant would have travelled from Ch'ang-an in China to the Syrian city of Palmyra on the Silk Road, so it is improbable that his incense counterpart would have undertaken the entire journey from Dhofar to Gaza, let alone Alexandria or Rome. Trans-shipping and deals characterised the conveyance of the precious resin, after which the merchants would hurry home.

There was a continuous coastal trade with India and further east for the exchange of frankincense for other goods. Arab dhows left Dhofari ports for India to take on board cotton, pearls, Golconda diamonds, emeralds and rubies and also, almost as precious, spices shipped from the East Indies. Pepper, cinnamon, nutmeg and cloves were as familiar in Roman kitchens as they are on supermarket shelves today. The *Periplus of the Erythraean Sea*, a narrative of a coastal voyage from Egypt to India, written by an unknown Greek sea captain or merchant between the first and early third century CE, lists other trade goods handled. At Qana in the Hadhramaut, an important port receiving frankincense from Dhofar, the *Periplus* reports: 'There are imported into this place from Egypt a little wheat and wine…clothing in the Arabian style…copper, tin, coral and storax…and for the King usually wrought gold and silver plate, also horses, images and thin clothing of fine quality'.

Much further along the journey at a Persian market town the *Periplus* records large vessels loaded with copper, sandalwood, teakwood and ebony. It notes that frankincense is brought there from Qana, so there must have been a sea route (see map route 6, p. 80) up the Persian Gulf. In addition, the *Periplus* lists 'many pearls, but inferior to those of India; purple clothing after the fashion of the place, wine, a great quantity of dates, gold and slaves'.

Written at a time when frankincense was the major export from South Arabia, the *Periplus* gives a fascinating insight into trading voyages from Egypt sailing south down the Red Sea. The ship calls at Berenice on the western coast, then 'eastward across the adjacent gulf, there is another harbour and fortified place, which is called White Village, (possibly Leuce Come) from which there is a way up to Petra to the court of King Malichas. It holds the position of a market town for the small vessels sent there from Arabia, and so a centurion is stationed there as a collector of *one-fourth* of the merchandise imported, with an armed force, as a garrison'. As we shall see, such tolls and other charges paid en route accounted for the extortionate cost of frankincense by the time it reached the Mediterranean.

The *Periplus* goes on to describe another port called Muza in present-day Yemen, crowded with Arab ship-owners and sailors: 'For they carry on a trade with the far-side coast…sending their own ships there'. The 'far-side coast' is that of north Africa, from which the south Arabians were obtaining supplementary supplies of incense at the height of the trade. Sources included Somalia on the opposing coast and the nearby island of Socotra.

Further east the *Periplus* describes Qana or 'Cana of the Kingdom of Eleazus, the Frankincense Country…(where) all the frankincense produced in the country is brought to that place to be stored, and to Cana on rafts held up by inflated skins…and in boats'. The *Periplus* must have sailed by the Dhofari coast during the monsoon, for it is described looming 'mountainous and forbidding, wrapped in thick clouds and fog, and yielding frankincense from the trees. These incense-bearing trees are not of great height or thickness; they bear the frankincense sticking in drops on the bark, just as the trees among us in Egypt weep their gum'.

Calling at Khor Rori harbour, surmounted by the fortress town of Sumhuram, the *Periplus* records that traders exchange cloth, wheat and sesame oil for frankincense, 'which lies in heaps all over the Sachalitic country, open and unguarded, as if the place were under the protection of the gods; for neither openly nor by stealth can it be loaded on board ship without the King's permission; if a single grain were loaded without this, the ship could not clear the harbour'.[2]

CAMELS AND CARAVANS, BANDITS AND TOLLS

If the *Periplus* gives us an intriguing insight into the part frankincense played in long distance trading voyages by sea, it is equally fascinating to conjecture what life was like along the overland roads stretching thousands of miles over gruelling terrain. Knowledge about conditions on map routes 1 and 2 towards Mesopotamia is more a matter of speculation and legend than fact, since far less research has been done—many maps and accounts do not include these routes. Much more is known about the other ones leading to the Mediterranean, with eyewitness reports and descriptions by classical authors such as Pliny the Elder. Pliny records that the whole journey was divided into 65 structured stages, with halts for rest and recuperation once every six days. Each sector was handled by local agents, hiring their own cameleers and mounts, with cargoes being transferred to new camels every three weeks or so. Hiring fresh camels necessitated transfer of loads, and therefore a longer halt, especially if repairs were needed.

The common factor for all overland routes was methods of transport. Over the millennia the survival of the people of Arabia depended on a sequence of animal domestication. Cattle and goats provided food and hides, and the Jebelis of Dhofar still tend theirs today. When donkeys and possibly mules became a part of Arabian life, long-distance travel became viable; but with the domestication of camels, trade routes were vastly extended. Donkeys need water and fodder more frequently than camels, which can live off the fat in their humps for a considerable time if deprived of water. The Arabian camel, the dromedary, has one hump; the Bactrian, its counterpart on the Silk Road, is slightly smaller and has two humps. In desert conditions, under a summer sun, a camel needs water every two to three days, depending on its load, breed and condition. In winter, provided it has sufficient green fodder, camels can last weeks without water. Furthermore, after camels superseded donkeys, the caravans could proceed like a plumb-line, no longer having to zig-zag about in search of wells or springs. An average day's journey would have been about ten hours, covering about forty kilometres.

Camel domestication was a lengthy business, but they were probably in use by the late third millennium BCE, possibly earlier, and the process was widespread by the second millennium. As Nigel Groom points out it was 'one of the most significant economic developments of the ancient Middle East. It enabled tribal groups to move into or pass through arid areas where life could not previously be sustained; it enabled raiding and warfare to be undertaken over previously impossible distances; it enabled heavy loads of goods to be carried considerable distances through waterless and previously impassable tracts'.[3]

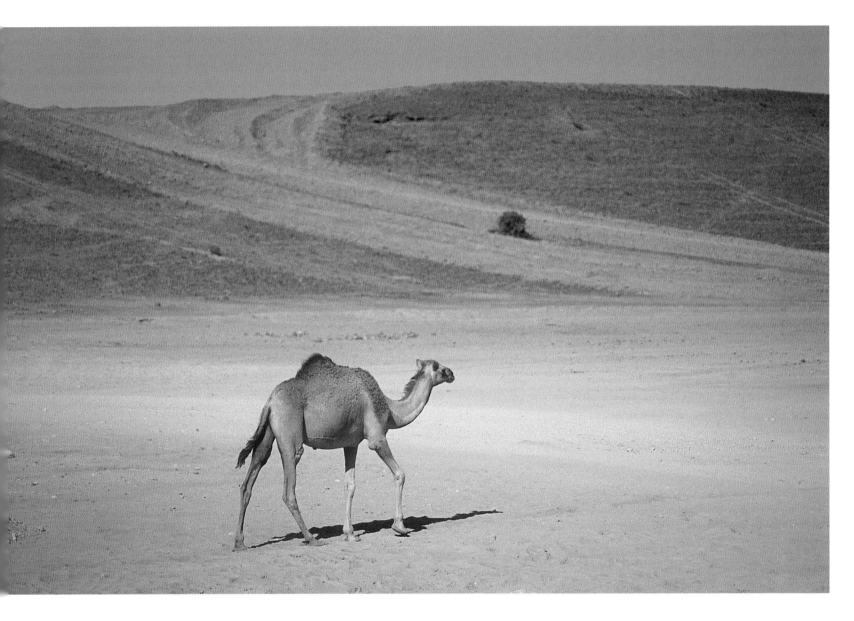

Above: The 'ship of the desert' traverses the sands of southern Arabia

Camels not only provided transport, but their milk, meat, hides and wool became an indispensable part of Arabian life. So greatly were they valued that they were called *ata Allah* (the gift of God) by the Bedouin, and the Qur'an instructs, 'on them, as well as in ships, ye ride'. In one of nature's most inhospitable environments the camel has become one of the most adapted creatures. It is equipped with long, sand-storm resistant eyelashes, and broad floppy feet that can slog through scorching dunes. Its endurance, on an unenviable diet of thorny desert scrub, (providing moisture as well as sustenance), is legendary.

At a time when the pace of the incense trade was quickening and camel caravans were increasing to two to three thousand, more than fifty 'houses' or breeds of camel were bred in south Arabia. Two different 'houses' were required for two separate functions, for which they had specific hoofs. In the

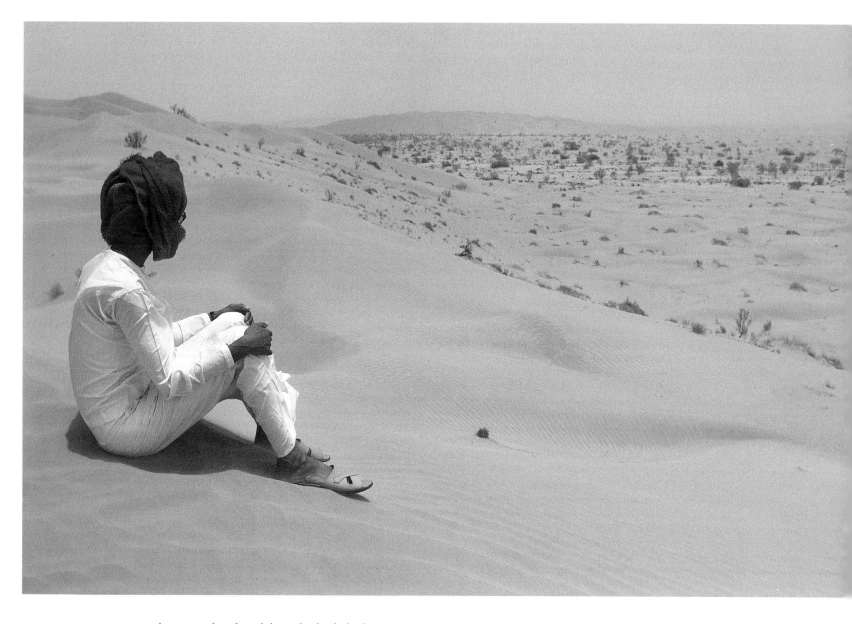

Above: On the edge of the Rub' al-Khali, the Empty Quarter, just north of Wubar

autumn, after the harvest and then the monsoon, the frankincense needed to be brought to collection points from the growing and storage areas. The incense was shuttled out of the mountains on camels with small, smooth hoofs. Then it was transferred onto large caravans ready for the journey across the sands on camels with bigger, calloused but soft-soled hoofs. Despite the camel's bad breath and bad temper, it often provided companionship—as well as a meal-ticket for its driver.

A specific form of architecture evolved in Arabia serving as lodging places for travellers and their animals. A purpose-built network of caravanserais evolved, some 25 miles apart along trade and later on pilgrimage routes, constructed to provide merchants, cameleers and animals with a secure place to rest, and spend the night or longer. Some were austerely practical with fortifications on a scale more befitting a castle than a motel, with curtain walls, bastions and towers. Others were ornately decorated, with stately arcades surrounding a courtyard. Almost all had just one entrance which could be closed and guarded. As Islam spread over Arabia, mosques were built on central raised structures in the courtyard of the caravanserai, while some had adjoining *madrasas* (institutions for the study of Islamic sciences, theology and law). Usually rectangular, caravanserais had at least two stories, the ground floor providing storerooms, loading docks and stables for animals, and perhaps a further open yard within the complex. The courtyard was also a hub of commerce, the arcaded porticos containing shops, kitchens and coffee rooms. Larger ones were equipped with bathrooms and workshops. The upper floors accommodated the travellers in dormitories, bedrooms and even lavish suites. Some caravanserais could house hundreds of people and animals, one courtyard leading into another, and the whole complex walled off.

Caravanserais evolved in response to travellers' needs, but their services had to be paid for. At the height of the incense trade it has been estimated that by the time the frankincense reached the Mediterranean, charges along the routes amounted to £400 million ($720 million/€584 million) a year or 688 *denarii* per loaded camel. Demand for frankincense always exceeded supply, and its high cost was due to the distance it travelled through different states, with their customs and service charges. To this would be added costs of local guides, entertainment such as dancing girls, bribes, and not least protection money for safe conduct to all the other charges. It is therefore not surprising that at the time of Christ frankincense was valued as highly as gold.

'All along the route they keep paying', wrote Pliny the Elder. He describes the scene at Shabwa, which he calls Sabota: 'Frankincense after being collected is conveyed to Sabota on camels, one of the gates of the city being opened for its admission: the kings have made it a capital offence for camels so laden to turn aside from the high road. At Sabota a tithe…is taken by the priests for the god they call Sabin…. It can only be exported by the Gebbanitae, and accordingly a tax is paid on it to the king of that people as well'. The Gebbanitae were probably the Minaeans who historically had controlled a considerable sector of the route north. Pliny continues: 'Fixed portions of the frankincense are also given to the priests and the King's secretaries, but beside these the guards and their attendants and the gate-keepers and servants also have their pickings; indeed all along the route they keep paying, at one place for water, at another for fodder, or the charges for lodging at the halts…and then again payment is made to the customs officers of our empire'. Shabwa, the Hadhramaut capital, always managed to hold onto its status as inland frankincense capital, despite later reliance on trade via the Red Sea. Except for special permission for ships coming from Sumhuram (established and controlled by the Hadhramis) and calling at Qana, successive kings of Hadhramaut insisted that all caravans must call at Shabwa, on pain of death for deviation, as Pliny commented. In this way they maintained complete control over the trade and its lucrative revenues.

At Wubar, the first major oasis after the caravans had left Dhofar, and the last before the Empty Quarter, there was not only a life-giving spring, but also a temple dedicated to their moon god. In settlements the routes passed through, the temples were also a means of acquiring wealth. The gods themselves needed to be fed and what better sustenance than frankincense, the very 'food of the gods'? So at Wubar a tenth of the cargo passing through would be demanded, and this was repeated at numerous other temples en route.

Bandit attacks on the straggling lines of thousands of camels loaded with the precious cargo were a constant hazard, and armed guards were hired to escort caravans through dangerous regions. In the early days of overland journeys, accessing sources of water was particularly risky. Brigands would swoop on congregations around wells, and fierce battles would break out, ending either in the caravan being robbed, or with the thieves getting injured or killed. Strabo mentions the Damascus region as being prone to attacks by brigands who 'have been robbing the merchants from Arabia Felix'. In narrow, rock-strewn mountain passes, through which weary merchants and their camels were plodding, roamed bands of nomads of shifting allegiance, who were not only perpetually falling out with each other, but were prone to pounce unexpectedly on the caravans.

The Himyarites, who had settled to the west of Qana, seemed to have been particularly pro-active, attacking travellers and at times threatening the strategic port of Qana. Their aggression forced the Hadhramaut regime to fortify mountain passes through which the caravans filtered to Shabwa. Eventually Himyar itself became a prosperous incense kingdom, and changed its tactics. Former bandits became adept at exacting tribute, otherwise known as taxation. 'Of these innumerable tribes', said Pliny, 'an equal part are engaged in trade or live by brigandage.'[4]

Travelling around southern Arabia in the years after World War II, Wilfred Thesiger saw that raiding for camels, cattle and goats was still a constant danger. He describes frequent murders, revenge killings and retaliatory attacks on women and children; as well as great courage, loyalty and hospitality.

Below: Fishing dhows at Sur
Right: Making pitch at a dhow building yard, Sur

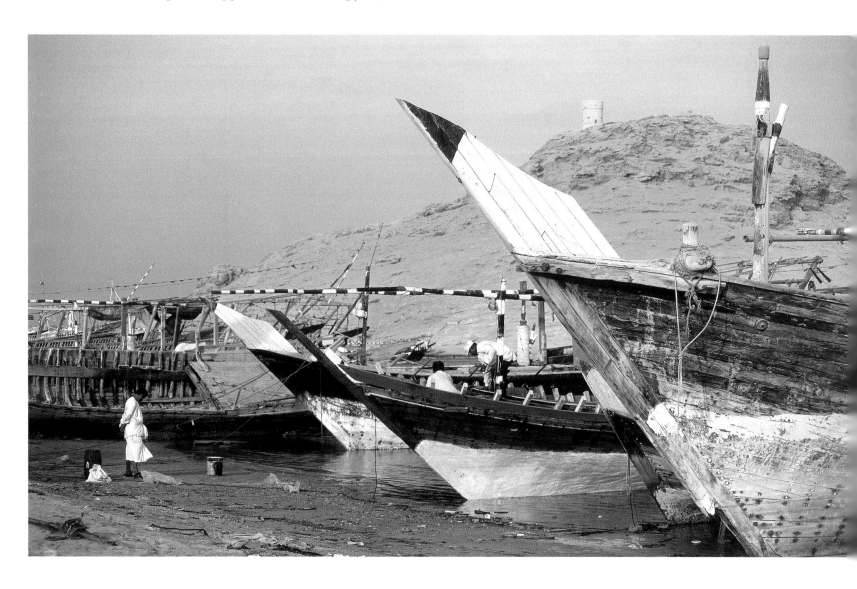

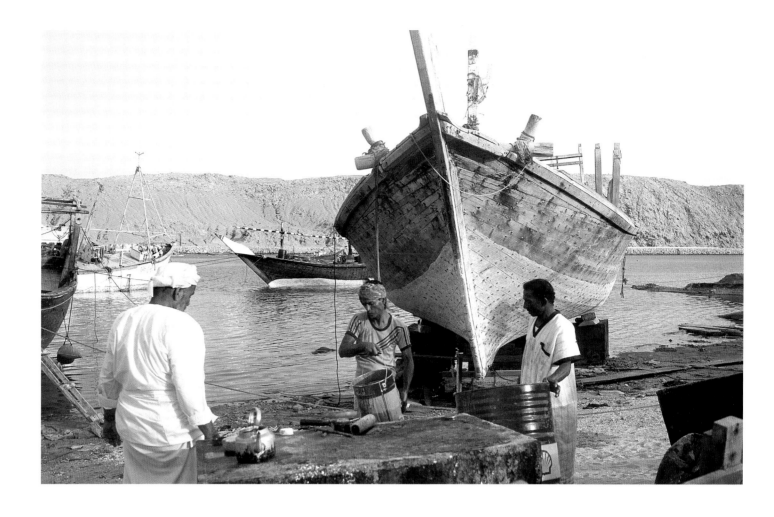

EASTERN ROUTES

What the eastern routes may have lacked in volume of trade, they make up for in the amount of time they have been in existence. Juris Zarins, one of the few to have excavated and researched sites in the region, estimates they were in use for eight thousand years. But the history of the eastern trade routes starts even earlier than this. Archaeological finds in the Nejd, and especially around the Shisr/Wubar area show that *homo sapiens* migrated out of East Africa across Arabia approximately one hundred thousand years ago. The region was wetter at that time, a climate which supported game, and at Wubar there were workshops for making hunting spears with large blades. Between *c.* 20,000 and 8000 BCE, the monsoon rains disappeared and so did human occupation. But the small scraggly frankincense tree prospered in these drought conditions, on harsh limestone soil which is intolerable for most other vegetation, but which it fended off using the toxic terpenes released from its roots.

Eventually the monsoon rains returned to Dhofar, and around 6000 BCE a fresh wave of immigrants arrived, who were Semitic pastoral nomads from northern Arabia (present-day Levant). Within the space of just two hundred years they repopulated the peninsula, reaching the Dhofar Mountains with their cattle. Zarins affirms: 'They are the people who established the ancient trade routes and distant-country links. Frankincense was first traded from Dhofar by them in response to Southern Mesopotamian demand'.[5]

Although frankincense trees had become established much earlier, it was not until the Neolithic era that the conditions necessary to create regular, long-distance trade emerged. The invention of writing by 3200 BCE enabled Mesopotamian and Sumerian *bullas*, clay tablets and other texts to provide proof of trade with eastern Arabia, notably Dilmun (now Bahrain and a section of the western coast of the

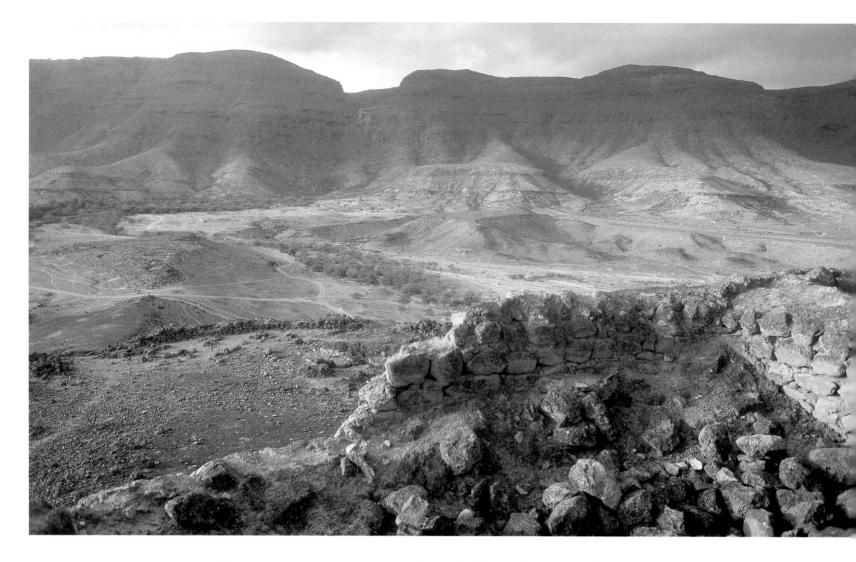

Persian Gulf). They mention 'aromatic material intended for use by priests/rulers'. Neolithic finds at Dhofar from the early sixth millennium BCE suggest links across the Empty Quarter with present-day Qatar, also in east Arabia. Large grinding basins and stones, flint cones, blades, marine shells and obsidian were unearthed at 16 sites in Shisr/Wubar. Shells and obsidian were traded along eastern routes, and seven obsidian beads originating in today's Yemen have been uncovered in fifth-millennium tombs in Qatar. Zarins concludes: 'Trade in aromatics was certainly in place in eastern Arabia (Dilmun) by the middle of the third millennium BC, and most likely by *c.* 5000 BC Since frankincense plant distribution was certainly restricted botanically to southern Arabia, the trade would necessarily have come northward either by land or sea.'[6]

Exports from Dhofar began to increase in volume and frequency linking the Gulf, the Red Sea and the Indian Ocean. By 3500 BCE Egyptians were in contact with Yemen on the east coast of the Red Sea, trading in obsidian, lapis lazuli, silver and Red Sea corals. At Nagada in Egypt several graves yielded incense resin around this time. Zarins also cites later archaeological evidence linking the Indus Valley to Oman (around 2500–2200 BCE). Mesopotamian texts mention construction and voyages of sea-faring boats from Magan not only to the Indus Valley, but also to Eastern Arabia and Sumer. It seems that trade links continued to flourish, since Magan was the ancient name for northern Oman, producing 48 to 60 tons of copper ore each year until medieval times. In the Sumerian language, 'Magan' denoted 'a sea-faring people', and its shipwrights were mentioned in Sumerian inscriptions of 2050 BCE. Dilmun seals at first show reed boats, then later wooden ones constructed of planks rubbed with fish oil, lashed together with coconut-fibre ropes. Magan also exported stone and wood, which along with copper and aromatics were reaching Indian and African shores. As this evidence shows, Oman's periods of prosperity have stemmed from intelligent exploitation of its geographical position, seamanship and trading acumen.

FROM AIN HUMRAN TO NINEVAH

Positioned dramatically on the top of a hill in the centre of a great plain, Ain Humran is the beginning of a speculative journey north tracing the earliest frankincense routes. After a considerable climb up through the ruins of a stone terraced village, I reached the gate of the hilltop fortress, passing through outer fortifications, then inner ones. At this altitude, late afternoon breezes gently buffeted me as I stood on the remnants of a tower overlooking what was once a fertile plain. To the north were the Al-Aswat Mountains, and it was easy to imagine incense-laden camels setting out on the first stage of their incredible journey. To the south, I could just see the Arabian Sea, and the safe harbour for dhows of Khor Janaif.

Left: Looking north from the promontory of Ain Humran, the first stage of the north-eastern routes

Below: Southern view towards the Arabian Sea from Ain Humran, with storage areas for frankincense in the foreground

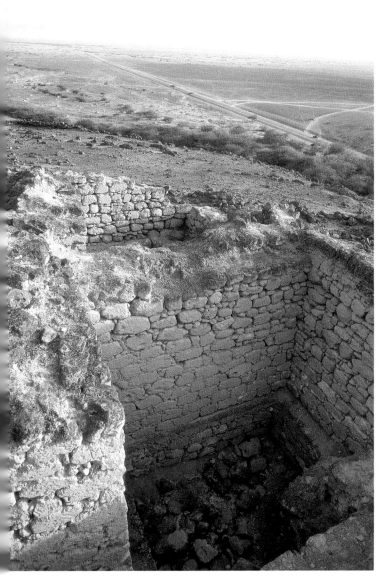

Ain Humran is little discussed and less researched than other major southern Arabian sites, nor was it selected by UNESCO as a World Heritage Site. Situated thirty kilometres east of Salalah, it has not been excavated since 1995, when after three successive summers of digs, Juris Zarins said that: 'The formal building complexes at Shisr and Ain Humran have contributed greatly to our understanding of the economic and political landscape of Dhofar.'[7]

Ain Humran is believed to have been Zaphar Metropolis, described by Ptolomy as 'the mother city', as it was much larger than Shisr/Wubar, with which it is contemporary. Both were established by 300 BCE and continued to be occupied into the Islamic period. They share pivotal positions in the incense trade and many architectural features. Walls and towers are similar in height and width, as well as having arrow slits and, most significantly as far as the big populations both cities served, both have access to a nearby permanent water source. Ain Humran means 'Red Springs', which supported a large agricultural community with dam systems which diverted water into fields from the main spring. As Nicholas Clapp points out: 'With a city on the coast and another inland, the people of 'Ad could have dispatched their frankincense to faraway markets by either land or sea'. Clapp continues: 'Each route had its hazards. Ships were prey to storms and pirates; caravans were subject to high tolls and the depredations of brigands. Each year the 'Ad could have chosen the most promising path or could have used both routes.'[8]

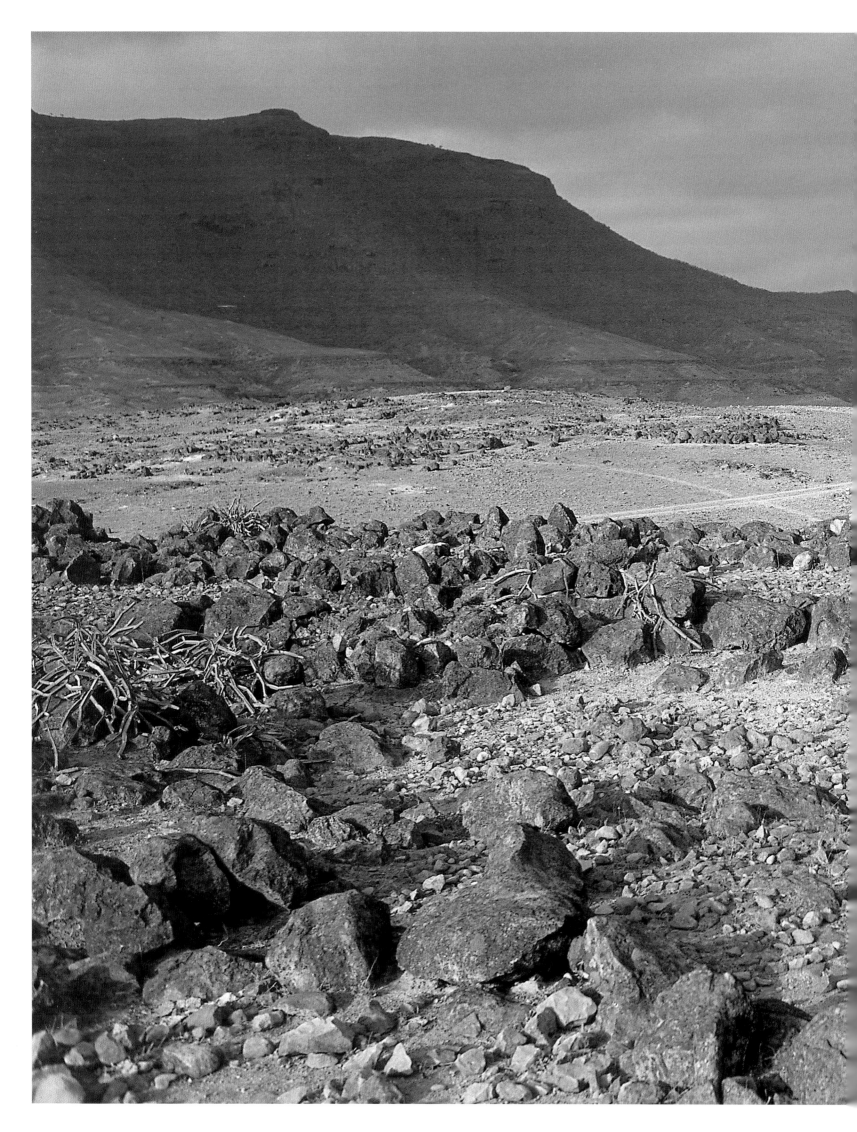

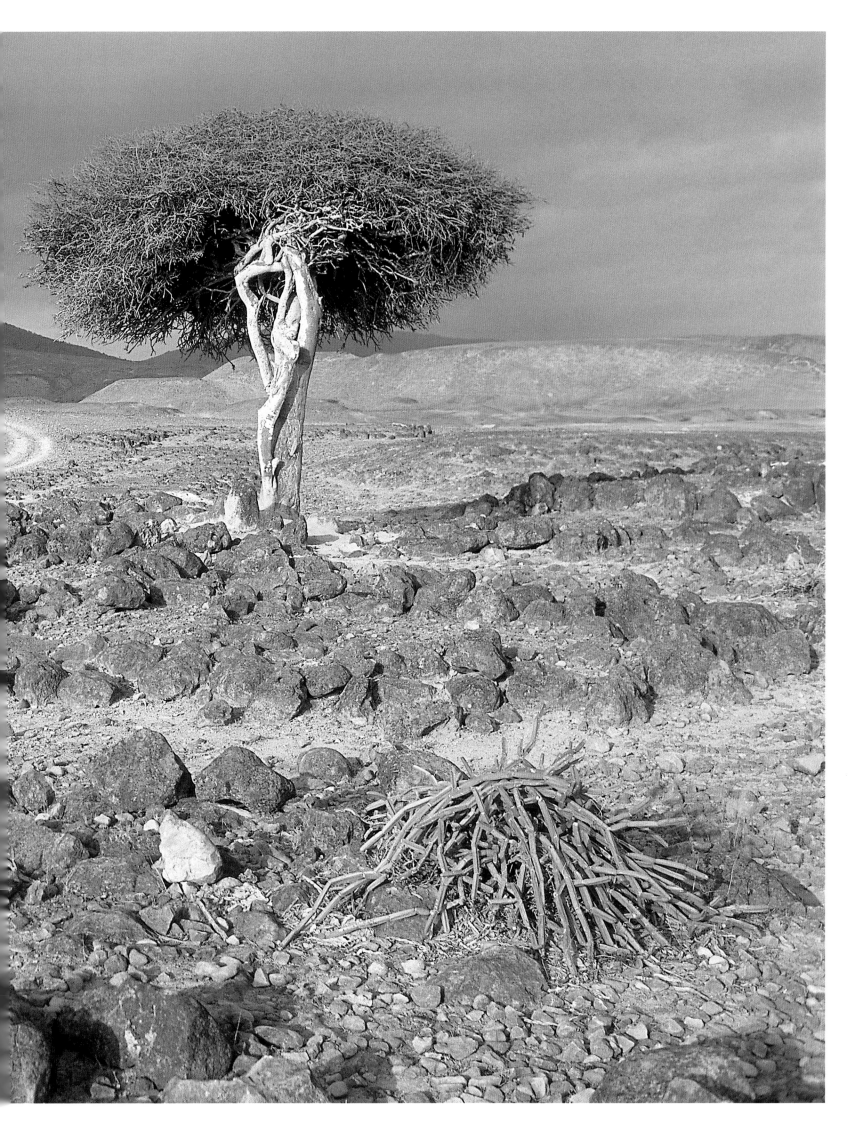

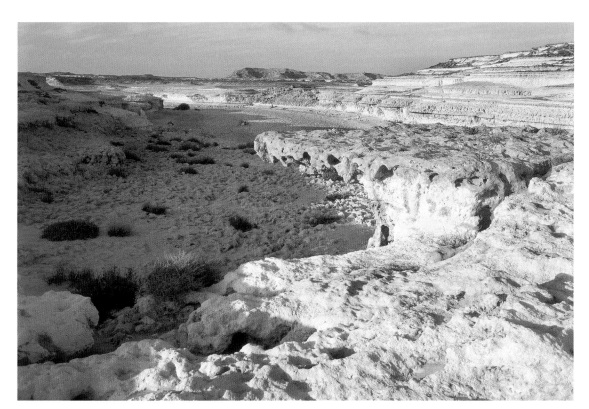
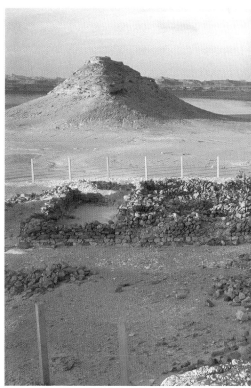

As a result of Zarin's excavations, the common heritage of Ain Humran and Shisr/Wubar has been confirmed, not just in their similar architectural layout, but also in their shared ceramic history. Most significant is the dot-and-circle decorated pottery, hallmark of the 'Ad people. Everywhere there were simple red burnished bowls and high-necked vessels, some with purple glaze dripped over the rim. One outstanding example was decorated with Christian cross motifs, others were of Ming Chinese origin, and down in the village, an endearing clay camel was unearthed.

WADIS HANOON AND ANDHUR

From Ain Humran, caravans travelling north would have stopped at Hanoon and Andhur, the most important seasonal collection stations during the peak era of the history of the frankincense trade. Unlike Ain Humran, they were never inhabited on a permanent basis, but were used to sort, store and guard the harvest. They had been established with military efficiency by the Hadhramis from Hadhramaut in present-day Yemen to further exercise their control over the incense business.

Travelling north over the Al-Awsat mountains, my journey to Wadi Hanoon was over bleak semi-desert, relieved every now and again by the appearance of an itinerant camel. Apparently bereft of herd or owner, these lone ships of the desert are in fact never wild; each always belonging to a farmer. Suddenly, the landscape was transformed. A stunning, immensely wide river valley opened out, painted with a sunset palette of spectacular colours. Wadi Hanoon has huge promontories sculpted by erosion; geological strata slice across miles of landscape. Near the empty riverbed were the ruins of a storage and temporary shelter site for frankincense also named Hanoon. It was once a frontier settlement at the northern edge of the Nejd, where the trees of nearby Wadi Dhowkah were producing top quality resin.

An inscription at Hanoon in the Old South Arabian script mentions the Hadhramaut-controlled fortress port of Sumhuram, to which it was sending incense, and the moon god Sin. It designates Hanoon as 'Sa'nan', a name still used by local people, referring to the region of Dhofar as Sa'Kal (or Sa'kalan),

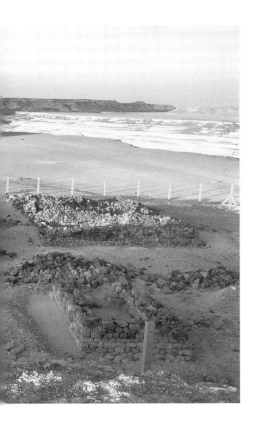
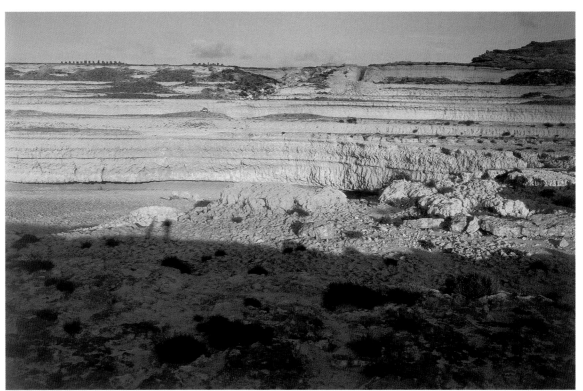

Previous double pages: Remnants of the walls of a village below the hilltop fortress of Ain Humran

Above left: The empty river valley of Wadi Hanoon
Centre: Former stores for frankincense at Wadi Hanoon
Right: Geological strata slice across Wadi Hanoon

also the country of the Sachalites, an incense kingdom in its own right. The inscription mentions Shabwa as the capital of the Hadhramaut incense kingdom, that city which for so long had an iron grip on all the incense that passed further west.

Some sixty kilometres north of Ain Humran, to the east of Hanoon, is Wadi Andhur, famous as a collection point for the best frankincense in Dhofar. Located in high quality growing territory, it received further supplies from the Hasik region, and also supplied Sumhuram. The impressive ruins of a walled fortress and temple are architecturally similar to those at Sumhuram and the masonry is identical. Wilfred Thesiger wrote: 'It was only at Andhur that I found the ruins of a well-constructed building… (which) seemed to have been a storehouse rather than a fort. The walls were built of cut stones set in mortar…. Along the top of the low outer wall were some mortar-lined stone troughs, about five feet in length and two feet in width and depth, similar to others which I had seen among the ruins near Salala.'[9]

Hanoon too was a colonial outpost of the Kingdom of Hadhramaut, though of a later date, *c*. 60 CE. From these two collection points for the caravans, Wubar was the next stop.

The Atlantis of the Sands'

T. E. Lawrence

An Arabian cross between Atlantis and Sodom and Gomorrah, Wubar has long haunted the imaginations of historians and explorers. The story of its discovery intermingles myth, legend, history and high-tech reality. Lawrence of Arabia had heard of the legendary city, which for so many centuries had been 'lost' in the sands, but died before he could find it. Several Arab historians were aware of Wubar, including Nashwan bin Said al-Himyari, who in the eleventh century wrote of it as, 'the name of the land which belonged to 'Ad…. There are to be found in it great buildings which the wind has smothered in sand'. *The Book of One Thousand and One Nights* refers to Wubar as 'surrounded by marble walls, set with precious stones and topped with golden roofs'.

Wubar was not just a specific town, but also a large oasis called Shisr, inhabited by the 'Ad people, known as the Wubarites, who were in competition with the Sabaeans. As the only source of water before the Empty Quarter, and the 'only permanent water in central Nejd' as William Thesiger discovered in 1948, incense-bearing caravans were obliged to stop there, and so it became wealthy. What is now a two-hour car journey from the Qara Mountains, took eight to ten days by camel: Wubar must have been an extraordinary sight on its rocky prominence, rearing up out of the desert, with its eight towers and a citadel, surrounded by defensive walls.

The story of Wubar's discovery has a *Raiders of the Lost Ark* flavour. A map drawn by Ptolemy had marked *Omanum Emporium*, the 'marketplace of Oman', in the land of the Wubarite people. 'Whenever he noticed a major trade centre, he'd mark it with a little castle with turrets', said Julius Zarins, chief archaeologist at what was eventually inscribed by UNESCO as a World Heritage Site. Nicholas Clapp, a film-maker

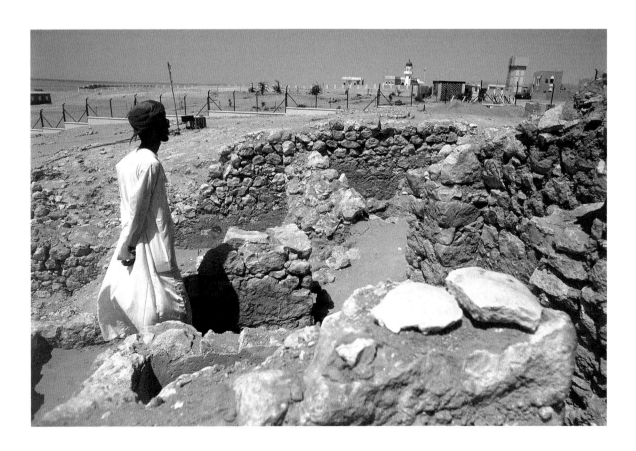

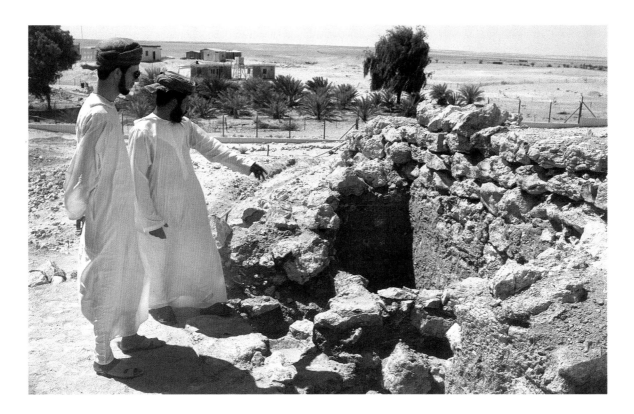

Left: Citadel of Wubar with modern Shisr village beyond

Above: Fireplace at Wubar

and author, had a hunch that this was indeed Wubar, but he needed more than a second-century map to pinpoint its location. He assembled an international team to locate Wubar, including Sir Ranulph Fiennes, who knew Oman, spoke Arabic, and had written of Wubar as 'the epicentre of the sands, where the lost city was to be found'.

After several frustrating forays into the sand dunes, Clapp contacted the US Jet Propulsion Lab, which had used LANDSAT images to reveal an ancient riverbed hidden beneath the Sahara. LANDSAT, together with the French SPOT satellite, revealed the faint lines of ancient caravan trails, using the near-infrared portion of the light spectrum. 'We were looking for the Incense Road going out into the Empty Quarter', said Zarins. Ancient donkey and camel tracks in parallel grooves over a hundred yards wide had been buried beneath towering sand dunes. These tracks were visible by satellite because they had been ground down by countless hoofs over the millennia and had reflective qualities which differed from the surrounding sand. They converged on the area Ptolemy had labelled *Omanum Emporium*, once the boomtown of the incense kingdom of Sa'kalan.

On my way to Wubar, I met Professor Zarins, who had just completed two full seasons of excavations. He had revealed the remains of an eight-sided fortress with walls over three metres high. At each corner there were once square or horse-shoe-shaped towers ten metres tall, of which two remain. For kilometres beyond the walls of the site of the main settlement, are the remains of hundreds of fire pits, left by caravaneers.

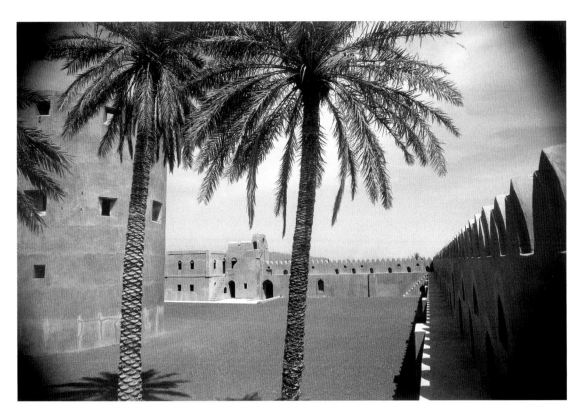
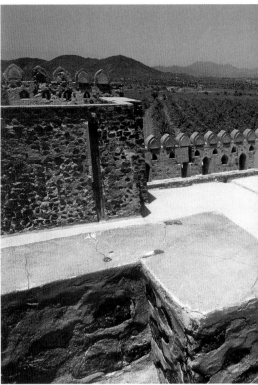

Zarins showed me some of the finds at Wubar, whose radio-carbon dating suggests that the region had been occupied almost continuously since 5000 BCE, making it the oldest caravanserai in southern Arabia, although the current city structure dates from around 1000 BCE. Along with uniquely decorated Iron Age pottery and Red Polished Indian ware, indicative of Mesopotamian/Persian influence, there was also Sung and Ming celadon porcelain confirming Wubar's position as a major trading centre. It seems also that the people of 'Ad invented the wheel for pottery, though not for transport. As Zarins said: 'They were illiterate people with a cosmopolitan culture, evidenced by blue and brown coiled and wired glass bracelets—a very sophisticated technique', which apparently entranced the Chinese. The 'Ad were prosperous enough to have leisure time to use gaming boards and play chess with soapstone pieces from north India, dating from around the seventh century CE. Other finds from Syria, Greece and Rome indicate that routes from Wubar could have led much further west.

According to legend, and Qur'anic comments about Iram (City of Towers), the 'Ad became decadent, arrogant, unjust and irreligious, so they were punished by the wrath of God. The city of Wubar was destroyed in one night between 300 and 500 CE, and although people continued to live among the ruins of their past glory until the fifteenth century trading in horses and spices, the rise of Christianity meant a fall in demand for frankincense. In reality Wubar's cataclysmic collapse was most likely triggered by an earthquake, causing most of the city to fall into a huge limestone cavern beneath it. As Nicholas Clapp writes: 'The legend of Ubar [Wubar] climaxed as the city sank into the sands…. Of all the sites in the ancient world, Wubar came to a unique and peculiar end, an end identical in legend and reality'.[10]

JABRIN TO GERRHA

Across one of the largest deserts in the world, the Rub' al-Khali or Empty Quarter, stretching over 100,000 square kilometres, lies Jabrin. No one crossing the desert bypassed it, since like Wubar, it was a permanent source of water. Although the castle we see today was constructed in 1671 CE, the

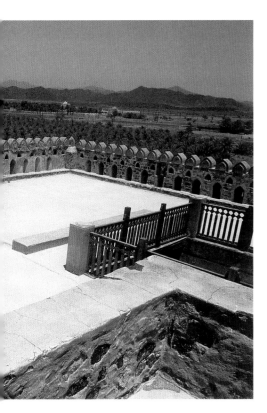

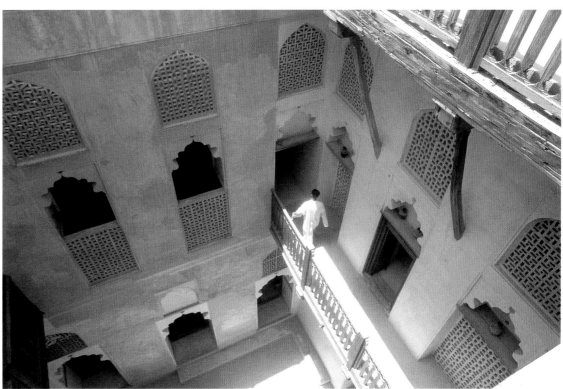

Left: Fortified palace of Jabrin, built in 1699 CE

Centre: View from Jabrin across its palm oasis

Right: Courtyard of Jabrin in the Persian–Mughal style

falaj (water channel) and two wells in the great central courtyard appear to have serviced the ancient frankincense route linking south to east Arabia from at least 5000 BCE. Zarins establishes its antiquity: 'Critical to our understanding (of the route) is the last major oasis on the north edge of the Rub' al-Khali, Jabrin. Known on Ptolemy's map as Labris…surveys at the site have yielded Hellenistic material…and other first millennium B.C. material…'[11]

Travelling to Oman today, if one visits only a single fort, it should be Jabrin. It is quite different from other Omani forts in several ways: it is more a palace than a fort, though it was adequately fortified. Jabrin never guarded a large settlement and looms now, huge and imposing over a small village, surrounded by an extensive palm oasis. Built by Iman Bilarub bin Sultan of the Ya'arubi dynasty as a residential palace, it hosted a civilised, learned lifestyle, and was designed as an elegant country home. Verandas and superb arched doorways in the Persian–Mughal style overlook the central courtyard, and the main staircase has poetry inscribed in its richly plastered, domed roof. Jabrin had a library, a small *madrasa* and a mosque with an exquisitely painted ceiling. What makes Jabrin so unique is the beauty of its murals with their flowing curves and delicate flower patterns in the Mughal tradition. Such embellishment was a feature of central Omani domestic architecture, but nowhere is it more subtle and sophisticated than at Jabrin, in the mosque and five well-proportioned rooms.

The next stop on the frankincense route from Jabrin was Gerrha, a port on the Persian Gulf, whose merchants had mastered the business of trans-shipping, taking over the cargoes of incense from the people of 'Ad at Jabrin, and conveying them to both Mesopotamia and the Mediterranean. The Wubarites must have resented the outrageous cut of incense that the Gerrhaeans demanded, but pragmatically appreciated that they were a buffer against the predatory armies further north. For all their empirical power, the forces of Alexander the Great and the Emperor Augustus never colonised the incense lands.

At present, there is no conclusive proof as to exactly where Gerrha was, but it would appear to have been near present-day Dhahran, a city in a formerly much larger Bahrain, then called Dilmun, now part of Saudi Arabia. Zarins associates Gerrha with the Salt Mine Site, noting finds there of Neo-Assyrian-Achaemenid period cylinder seals, as well as stamp-seals with South Arabian characters. This important community, who traded primarily in aromatics as far as Palestine to the west, became very wealthy. Strabo comments that 'from their trafficking both the Sabaeans and the Gerrhaeans have become richest of all'.

Below left: Painted wooden ceiling in the Sun Room at Jabrin

Below right: Detail of a gate at Jabrin

Facing page: Arched doorways and well in a central courtyard at Jabrin

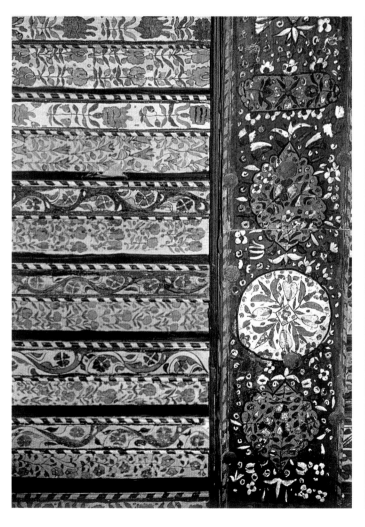
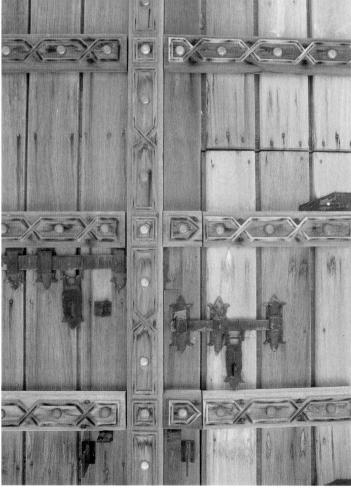

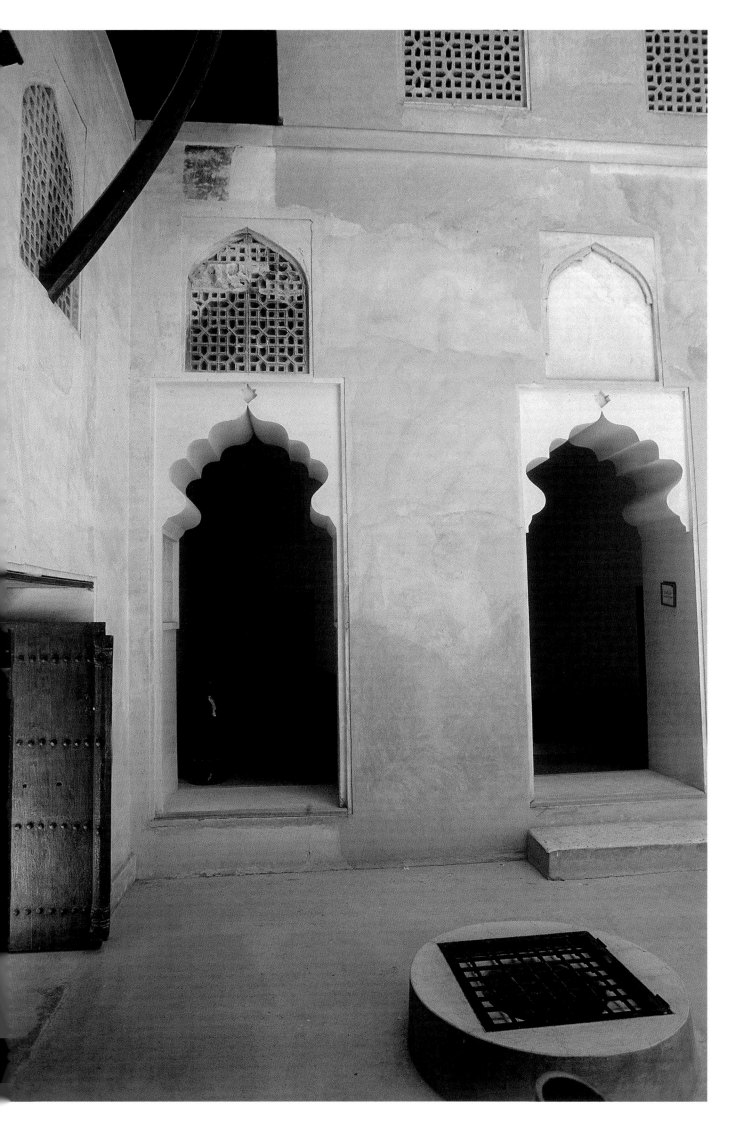

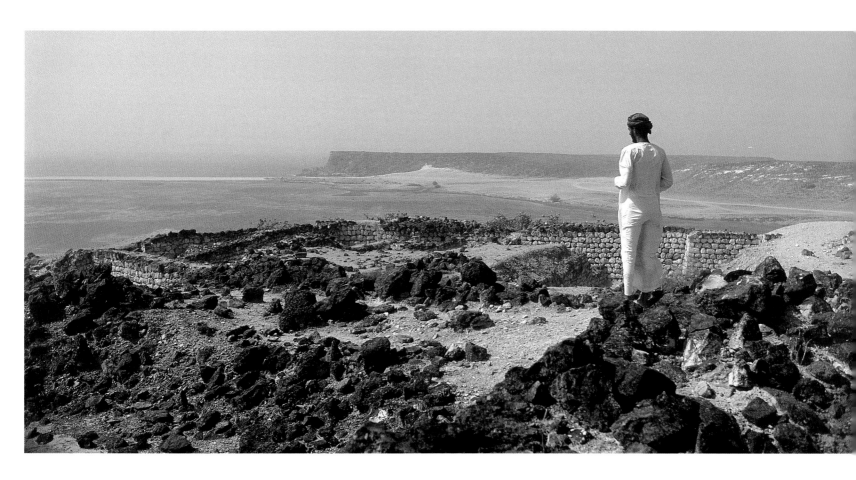

SUMHURAM / KHOR RORI

Control of the incense trade, sometimes turning brutal, was a much-coveted prize. Wubar had played its strategic role as the only caravanserai and provider of water for the overland incense route north-wards for thousands of years. Meanwhile comparatively late in the history of the frankincense trade, as the first century BCE was closing, ports on the Dhofar coast were being established to service the growing sea trade between the Red Sea, Persian Gulf and Indian Ocean. At the same time domination of the frankincense industry at its source was under threat. The incense kingdom of Hadhramaut was relentlessly expanding eastwards, and in order to control maritime routes, established the fortified port of Sumhuram.

At the eastern end of the Salalah plain, situated on a sheltered lagoon named Khor Rori, lie the ruins of Sumhuram, known to the Greeks as Moscha Limen. It was purpose-built by the Hadhramis to organise the shipment of frankincense. Even its name implies a military operation: Sumhuram translates as 'The Great Scheme', which it certainly was. It also had a second meaning: 'The Plan is Great'. 'Khor' means inlet and Y-shaped Khor Rori was the best natural harbour on the coast, the largest in Dhofar, as well as being very deep, and thus ideal for ocean-going ships anchored to take on board cargoes of frankincense.

Sumharam traded incense with ships calling there, as well as exporting it in Hadhramaut-owned dhows. However, at the time the *Periplus* was written, it was a port solely for the king's shippers, and the only foreigners allowed there were the Indians who over-wintered at Moscha. They brought cotton, corn and oil and probably stayed in a valley settlement outside the fortress, waiting for the monsoon winds to turn around to take them home. As Michael Jansen writes: 'The whole valley seems to have been a single large cultural unit in which Sumhuram was a residence of the elite'[12]—as well as the military presence.

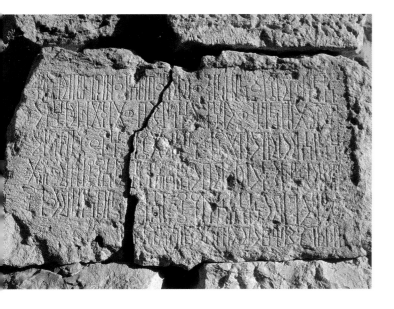

With the mountains coming right down to the sea, over which a great waterfall flows during the monsoon, it was an ideal location to build a fortress of substantial stone buildings. In what was Sa'kalan incense kingdom territory, the Hadhramis established a garrisoned colony under the rule of Shabwa, over six hundred kilometres to the west, which ruthlessly dominated frankincense export until the third or fourth centuries CE. The Khor had contained fresh water until eventually the sea broke through. A sand bar emerged right across the creek, preventing access, and mangrove swamps reclaimed the Khor. The site was abandoned, though the Sabaeans, whose own incense kingdom had in turn conquered Shabwa, may have forcibly removed the population.

At the entrance, the Hadhramis carved seven inscriptions, one of which commemorates its founding. It was built for Il'ad Yalut, king of Hadhramaut, named by classical authors as Eleazus, king of the Incense Country and Shabwa. As usual, confusion reigns over dates, and we have at least two alternative founding dates of first century BCE and first century CE. But these only relate to the present structure and the history of this settlement spans several eras. Archaeological excavation by the Italian University of Pisa has uncovered artefacts from the fourth century BCE. Carbon-dated finds of wood and charcoal indicate a previous settlement in *c*. 3000 BCE.

Left: Beyond Sumhuram is the deep-water lagoon of Khor Rori, once a thriving port

Above: Inscription at Sumhuram commemorating the founding of the city

Below: Massive stores for frankincense at Sumhuram

Butterflies dancing on long-abandoned stones were the only signs of life as I looked down into the tranquil emptiness of what had been such a thriving harbour. Where once the galleon-shaped dhows had moored, no doubt under close guard of Shabwan soldiers, a desultory camel bathed, the only action being the flight of some flamingos. Other birds such as egrets, gulls, sterns and waders feature in this undisturbed ecosystem. I had entered the town by a massive gateway with three successive gates a short distance from each other on the steep, narrow entry path. The ruins of a tower overshadow the access area, which changes direction several times, while ramparts flank the middle gate. 'The Plan is Great' was certainly an apt name.

Sumhuram had two temples, one a small structure by the gate; the other, found during excavations in 2003,

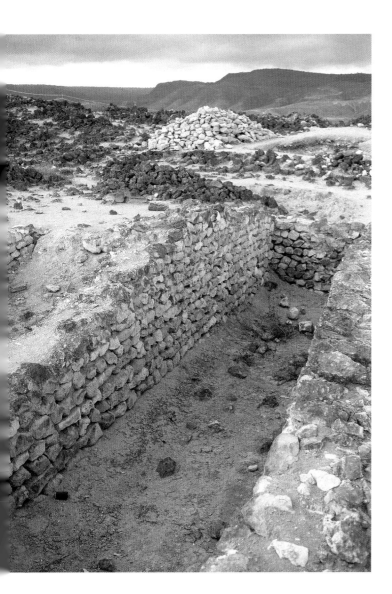

lies outside the walls. The first temple was dedicated to the South Arabian moon god, Sin. It contained an elaborate ablution system, two sacrificial altars and numerous bronze items. These included bells, an incense burner and ancient frankincense. One of the finds rings a personal note down the millennia—a bronze necklace with a camel-shaped pendant. An inscription reads 'Shafsay and his mother Nadrat dedicated to their lord Sin of (the temple of) Hum in Sumhuram for the protection of their persons and of their king'.

Sumhuram's buildings indicate a considerable degree of technical sophistication, with finely dressed stones, a deep well lined with smooth slabs, multi-storied dwellings, and of course many huge rectangular storage areas for frankincense. We get a hint of a cosmopolitan lifestyle from some of the archaeological material uncovered there. A bronze *yakshi* or Indian tree goddess, Salabhanjika, dating from the third century CE, bears out reports from the *Periplus* of the Indian merchants landing at Moscha Limen. A number of pottery finds, such as Nabatean painted shards from present-day Jordan, and wares from Iran, indicate provenance from thousands of kilometres north along the western incense route. A seminal bowl fragment combines Roman, Indian and local influences, the latter featuring the dot-circle motif seen on pottery found at Ain Humran and Wubar.

Below: Mosque at Al-Balid, the largest archaeological site in southern Arabia

Right: Excavating and restoring Al-Balid, a UNESCO World Heritage Site

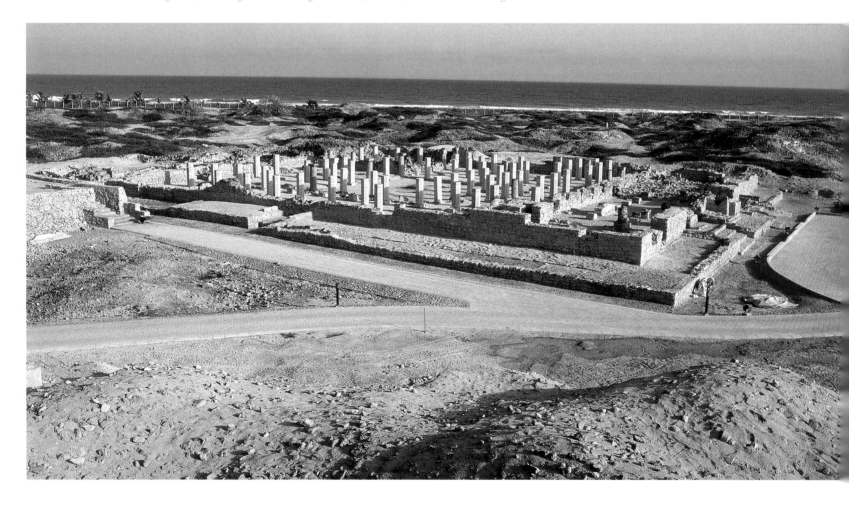

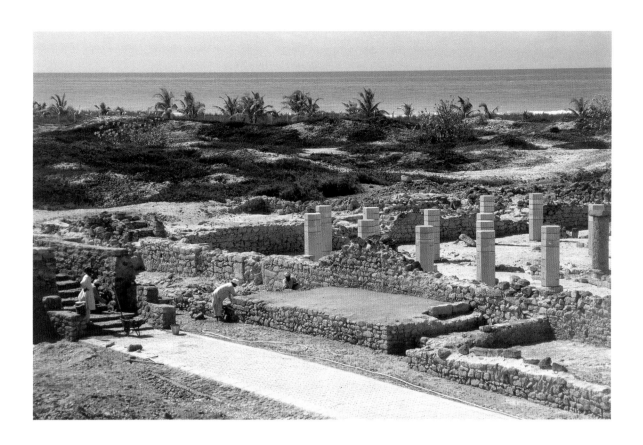

AL-BALID

A great and noble and fine city, it stands upon the sea and has a very good haven, so that there is a great traffic of shipping between this and India. Much white incense is produced here.

Marco Polo, 1285

Al-Balid is the largest archaeological site in South Arabia, and stunningly impressive. Much larger than Sumhuram, covering an area of 640,000 square metres, it was an extensive city rather than a fort. It took over from Sumhuram the main role in maritime trade into the Late Islamic period, or Middle Ages, and was one of the most important Islamic cities on the Arabian Sea. With links to ports in India, China, Indonesia, East Africa, Yemen, the Red Sea and Iraq, it played a significant role in world trade.

Immediately to the east of Salalah (which had no port of its own), Al-Balid was originally called Al-Mansura when Marco Polo visited it, then its name changed to Zufar, which became Dhofar, lending its name to the whole region, and indicating its importance as an urban centre and entrepôt, minting its own coins. Marco Polo also noted that, 'the city has under it many towns and villages'.

Although the splendid ruins of today date the site from the Islamic period, as with so much else about southern Arabia, the layers of history run deeper. Pottery and organic material discovered during extensive archaeological work show that it was inhabited from the end of the fifth millennium BCE. Other red shards with the now familiar dot-circle pattern give a later Iron Age date. Purple-decorated and black-polished ware resemble finds from Ain Humran. Excavations at the Tell or Citadel area reveal a substantial Iron Age city, dating from *c.* 325 BCE. As a city port it was re-established in the tenth century CE during the Manjawi era, but suffered numerous attacks, which necessitated constant re-building. Resurrected yet again in the thirteenth century CE during the Habudhi period, its architectural style echoes that of other major Islamic cities of the time, with massive walls intersected by towers and gates of monumental proportions.

Small wonder, then, that Al-Balid attracted invasions. It was built on an ideal, elevated site, with a natural harbour protected by a creek at each end, and a moat joining them. A *khor* running down from the mountains provided fresh water for the city and irrigated plantations of millet, barley and rice, alongside groves of banana, coconut and betel-nut trees. It must have been very cosmopolitan and grand, with a heavily fortified citadel or palace above a wide, open square called the Maydan. Some of the 144 columns of what was the largest mosque in Dhofar are decorated with a *fleur-de-lis* design, unique in this region. H. A. R. Gibb describes a typically impressive welcome at the port: 'It is their custom when a vessel arrives from India or elsewhere, the sultan's slaves go down to the shore, and come out to the ship in a *sumbuq*, carrying with them a complete set of robes for the owner of the vessel or his agents.'[13]

The visiting vessel may well have sailed from China, which traded extensively for *ju hsiang* (white milk), as documented in the southern Sung dynasty Zhu Fan Records of Foreign People, and evidenced by Chinese coins and Ming porcelain. If the ship had arrived from India, it may well have been taking on board horses as well as frankincense. Marco Polo commented: 'The merchants take hence great numbers of Arab horses to the market, making great profit thereby'. But by the late fifteenth century radical changes to trading patterns were imposed by European sea powers, notably the Portuguese. Al-Balid's position became dramatically less strategic with the discovery of an alternative sea route to India by Vasco da Gama. Its fate was sealed and it fell into decline.

Below: On some of the 144 columns of Al-Balid's mosque appear unusual designs

Right: *Fleur-de-lis* relief on a capital at Al-Balid

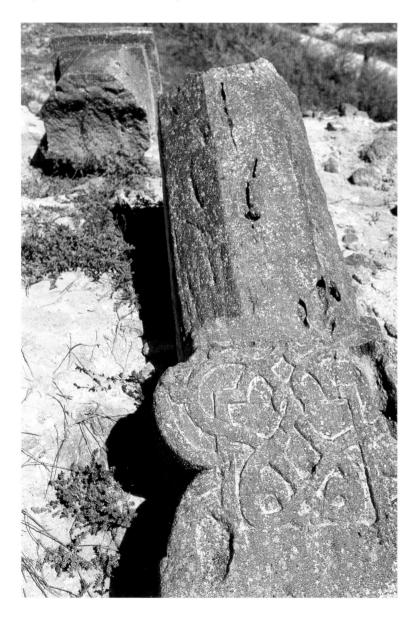

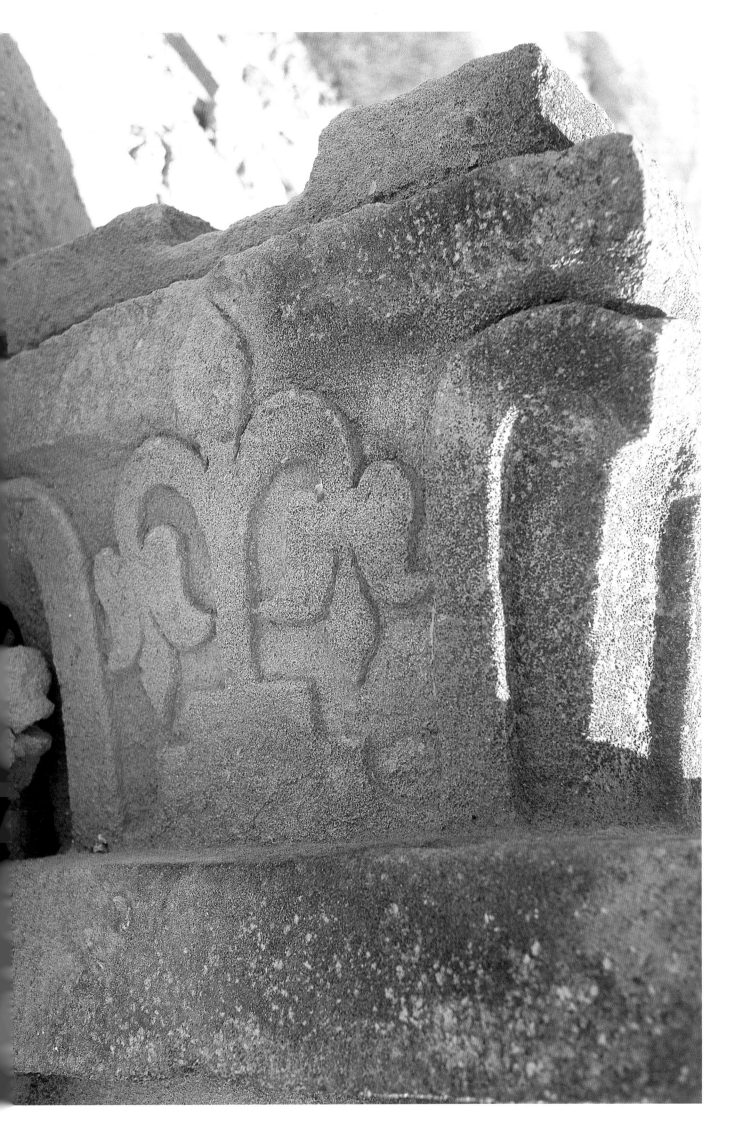

DHOFARI ANCHORAGES

One of the delights of visiting Oman's southern region today is exploring little fishing villages full of character. Behind idyllic beaches virtually empty except when the catch comes in, are picturesque streets of old merchants' houses many still luxuriating in faded splendour, with superb fretwork windows and carved doors. These villages feel somnolent, though they were once thriving entrepôts for ships sailing along the coast. They were not large ports with tight security such as Sumhuram and Al-Balid, but nevertheless they bustled with frankincense business, horse-trading and Eastern imports. It is possible that their success came at different times from the bigger ports, such as the period between the decline of Sumhuram in the third to fourth centuries CE, and the rise of Al-Balid in the tenth century.

A tarmac coastal road, recently named The Frankincense Highway, now links these appealing villages. It is a dramatically scenic route along the 56-kilometre-long Dhofari shoreline, plunging up and down hairpin bends in the mountains, along wind-swept cliff-tops overlooking glorious bays, little coves and lovely creeks, passing the ruins of ancient forts and cities. The Highway connects Hasik to the east of Salalah with Muqsayl to the west, through fishing villages steeped in the history of frankincense. Towards the Yemeni border to the west, Muqsayl is now the picnic place of choice for families from Salalah, with its

Below: Mirbat bay from the fort
Right: Now a tranquil fishing village, Mirbat formerly exported Arab horses and frankincense

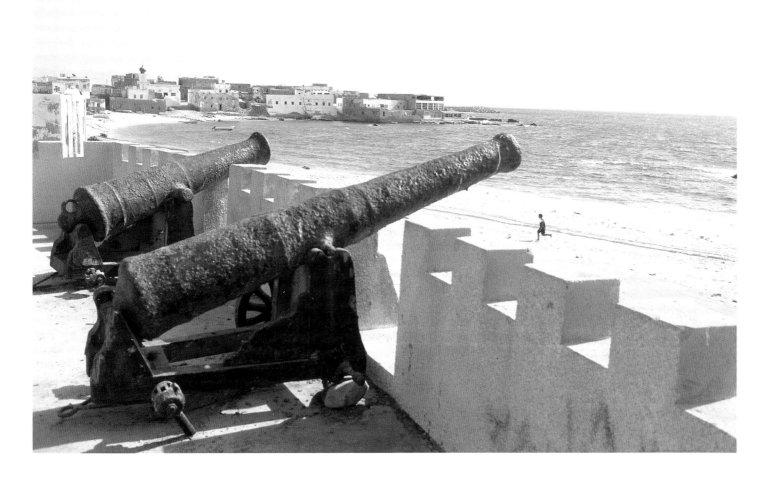

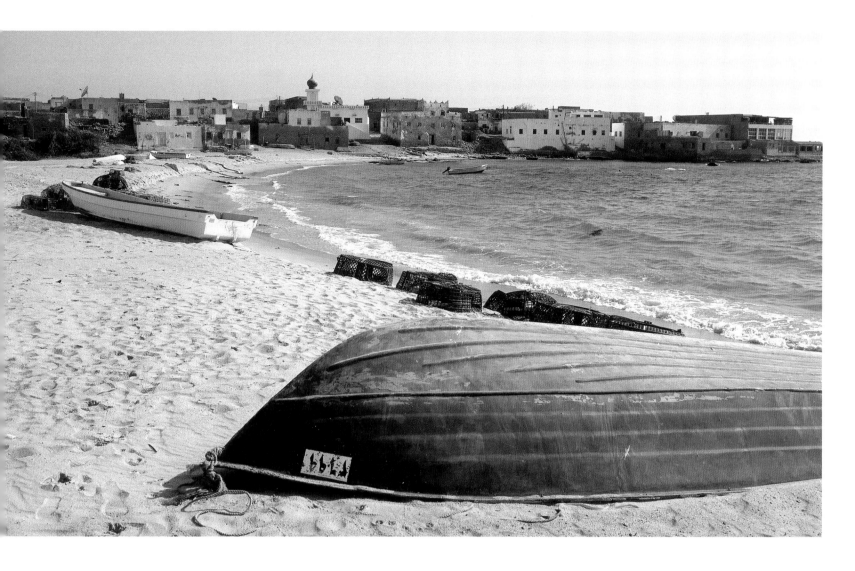

long beach of white sand and elegant sun shelters built in modern Islamic style. In the glory days of frankincense export from its shore, it had a dam and a small fort above a lagoon settlement.

Travelling east, the Highway curves around the sheltered bay of Raysut, another site of ancient history, now Port Salalah. The tradition of southern Omani trade has been revived at this ultra-modern, recently completed container port, which is massive enough to berth the largest container ships, trans-shipping six thousand containers at a time. Professor Zarins, who has excavated at Raysut, discovered there one of the most significant aspects of Iron Age settlements, the homestead. Along the entire *wadi* at Raysut, he located large-scale homesteads, with big circular houses, corrals for livestock and walls around fields, plus its own small fort on a promontory. Later, in 1221, Ibn al-Mujawir wrote about a road between Raysut and Baghdad, conveying Indian products from Raysut, as well as frankincense, and bringing back Iraqi fabrics.

The same author described a road that led to Kufa, also in Iraq, from Taqa, the next village on the journey east along The Frankincense Highway. Immediately beyond Salalah, its fishing fleet supplies the Dhofari capital's hotels and markets with crayfish, lobster, sardines, tuna and kingfish. Taqa has some fine old houses and the obligatory fort, this time not in ruins, but used until the 1980s as the office of the local *wali* or governor. The coastal road passes by farms and fruit plantations irrigated by the traditional and very effective *falaj* water channel system obtained from wells, springs or from the freshwater *khors* that run off the mountains to the sea. Here flamingos stalk elegantly and camels come to cool down.

The Highway descends down the mountainside from Sumhuram to a tranquil bay, around which curves the enchanting fishing village of Mirbat. Its large, dilapidated houses are built of mud brick, covered in stucco, and are usually several storeys high. Their arched windows are enhanced by carved wooden trelliswork screens serving as *mashrabiyas*, from which women could see out but not be seen. In recent years descendants of the old trading families have been restoring their heirlooms of Dhofari architecture, repairing the great teak doors, and renovating the fortress-like details at the corners of the roofs.

The grandeur of these houses indicates the former wealth of Mirbat. During the tenth century Persian merchants, the Minjawis, had established it as a principal trading port for frankincense and Arab horses ('Mirbat' means 'horse market'). Mirbat's only connection with frankincense today is the incense burners (*mejmars*) made here and at Taqa by women using tools made of shell and porcupine quills, and clay from the foot of the mountains. The shape of *mejmars* recalls the turrets of traditional Dhofari forts. These examples of folk art are painted in primary colours and sold to tourists, rather more than to local people, who prefer elaborately chased silver incense burners.

Until very recently the tarmacked road east ended at Mirbat, and even now The Frankincense Highway we travelled was 'in progress' in places. It passes through some of the most breathtaking scenery in Dhofar, huge metamorphic rocks of pink granite looming over passes, and soon the distinctive peak of Jebel Qinqau dominates the landscape. Our next destination was Sad'h, which has some particularly interesting houses. Beside a run-down little castle, still standing, was a merchant's home, its lime-plaster façade incised with two reliefs of sailing ships, one of which was a simplified version of a relief I had

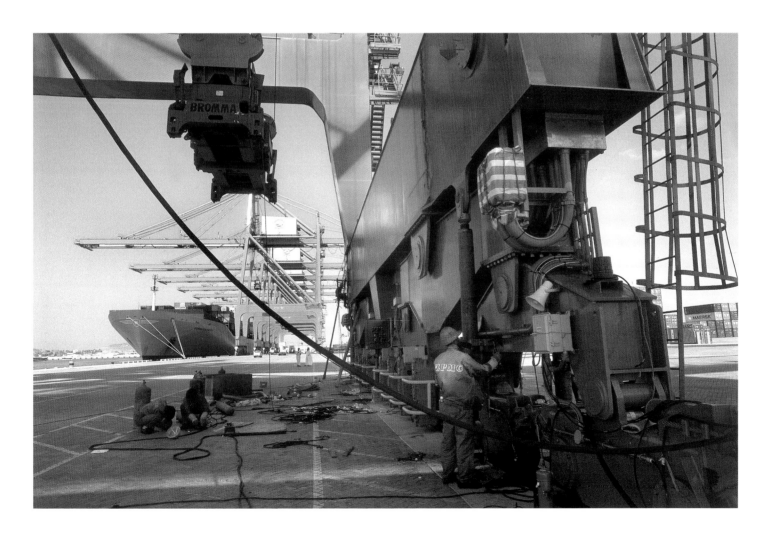

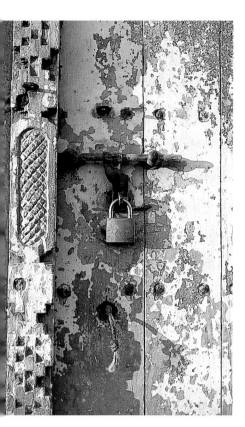
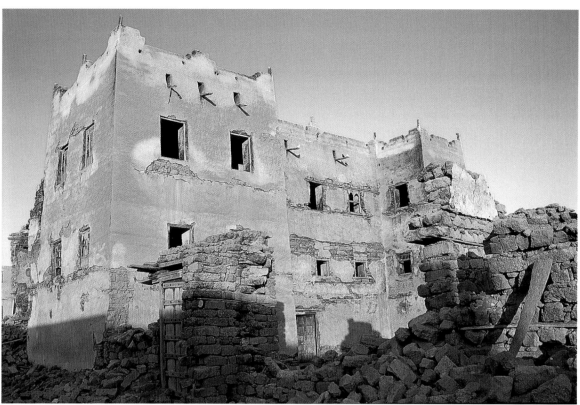

Left: Port Salalah free-trade zone, formerly Raysut port

Above left: Detail of a door at Mirbat

Above right: Eighteenth-century house at Mirbat. Most Omanis prefer to live in modern air-conditioned houses now

seen at Borobodur temple in Java. Another fine old house, with magnificent carved wooden windows was pointed out to me as having belonged to the chief trader in *luban*. Nearby were caves to store the resin. Sad'h's port, source of its former prosperity, which today is abalone, was filled with boats, mostly the small canoes known as *houry* and a few larger carved vessels, beached *boums* and *sambuqs*.

Until The Frankincense Highway was constructed, the only way to reach the most eastern of the Dhofari ports, Hasik, was by sea, unless you took your chances on a donkey through the passes in the mountains that surround it. Its harbour was once the first natural shelter during storms for boats traversing the shipping lanes from Mumbai or Basrah. The famous *hasiki* incense grows in the three wadis behind the town; and still further into the *jebels* beyond the watershed, is the source of the equally coveted *hujari* frankincense. The Mahri people, traditional guardians and harvesters of the crop in these mountains, speak a version of the ancient ESA South Arabian language, and Hasik itself has a remote, 'end of the line' feel. It certainly is the end of frankincense territory, for no more trees grow beyond this point.

WESTERN ROUTES

*And everywhere the air was heavy
with the scent of frankincense and myrrh.*

Qur'an, sura 34:16

Four hundred miles west down the coast from Sumhuram was Qana, the key port for the Hadhramaut incense kingdom, in present-day Yemen. To this day, the people of the modern port, Bir Ali, show their international trading origins—African, Malaysian, Indian and Arab. As we have seen, various incense kingdoms, including the Hadhramaut, had their own trees, but not in such quantity to satisfy international demand as those of Sa'kalan, nor of comparable quality. With its powerful cartel controlling the source of frankincense, South Arabia was the OPEC of its time, and Qana was the main 'pipeline' to the world beyond, identified as 'Canneh' in the Bible (Ezekiel 27:23). One can picture the little fleets setting out from the Dhofari fishing villages all along the coast, as soon as the turbulent seas and stormy winds of the monsoon had subsided in September. At Qana, the incense would be reloaded into larger ships that would carry it via Aden up the Red Sea. But this route was very hazardous, not only from storms and strong currents, but its shark-infested water concealed treacherous coral reefs. To add to the danger factors, pirates preyed on passing ships. It was not until Roman imperial rule effectively patrolled the waters that the Red Sea became a viable competitor to the overland camel route.

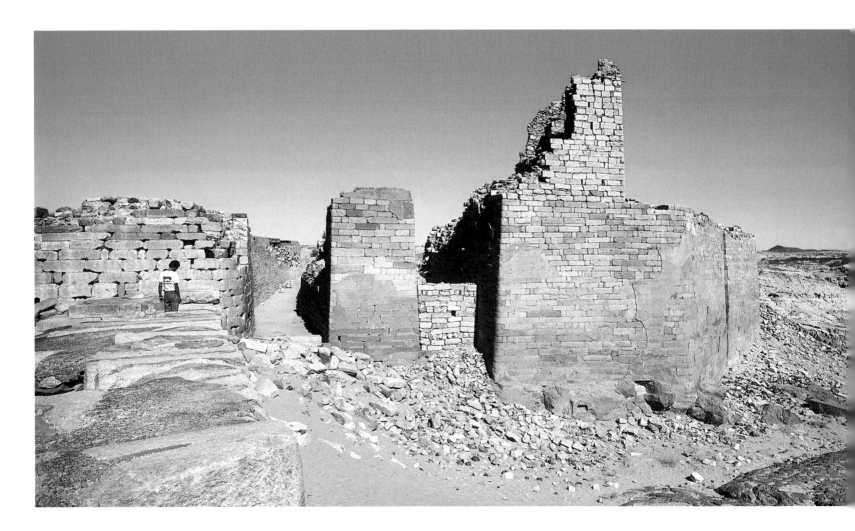

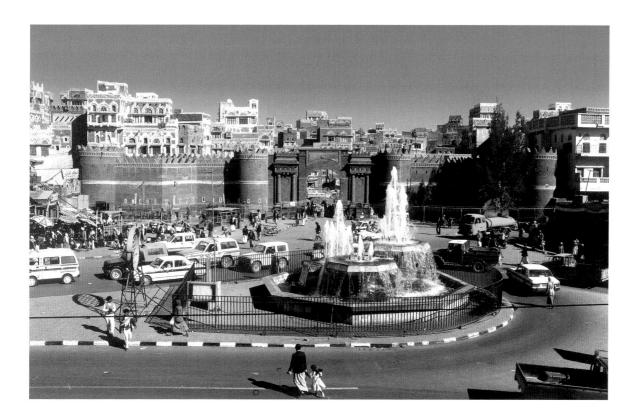

Left: North Lock of Old Dam at Marib, built by the Queen of Sheba

Above: Walls of San'a's Old Souk, once an important Yemeni caravanserai

From Qana the loaded camels were obliged to trudge to Shabwa, the Hadhrami capital, also known as Sabota, which maintained such a ruthless grip on the trade. Any caravaneers who avoided the city and its tolls were executed. Two routes led to Shabwa from Qana, both around 265 kilometres long. Although more gruelling, one of these routes through a narrow mountain pass could be controlled at that pass; while the other across a wide plain, was prone to raids and could be used to escape taxation at Shabwa by diverting straight to Tumna, the next stop after Shabwa. Both routes have long stretches of paved roadway, ruined towns, graffiti and inscriptions; but gradually the dominating position of Shabwa as Frankincense City was established, and it became one of the most powerful urban complexes in southern Arabia.

Beyond the city walls there were hundreds of fields, with a sophisticated irrigation system supporting around five thousand people who lived in suburbs covering 27 acres. Priests stood in lines by the main gate into the city, estimating the caravan loads for appropriate tolls for the temple, whose remains show two thousand years of continuous use. Besides the sacks of frankincense, the camels may have been carrying myrrh, silk, spices, ivory, gold and diamonds.

Having paid their taxes, the merchants set off in one of two directions. One route led to Jabrin and eventually north-eastern Arabia; the other, the route to the Mediterranean, stopped next at Tumna, the caravans now managed by the Minaeans. Tumna was the capital of the Qataban incense kingdom. An inscription from 200 BCE at its South Gate proclaims that dishonest merchants were fined fifty pieces of gold (while murder only merited banishment). City regulations established a monopoly for Tumna, ordered taxes (naturally), allocated market space, and installed overseers to control the caravans. Although the home of the Minaeans was north-west of Marib, the next destination and capital of the Sabaean incense kingdom, it seems that they maintained a position as controllers and carriers of the incense trade for many centuries from Shabwa at least as far as Dedan, much further north in present-day Saudi Arabia.

In each of the incense kingdoms there is evidence of extensive irrigation systems by dams and canals, supporting populations far greater than those of today. In addition, the paved roads that narrow in the mountain passes to funnel travellers for tolls, suggest well-organised central governance. Marib is surrounded by desert nowadays, though in the past it was rumoured that visitors could wander there for months and never once see the sky through the dense canopy of date palms.

Sabaea's wealth came from the incense trade, but its secret weapon was its giant dam. At 750 metres across at the northern end and fifty metres deep in the middle, it was one of the great engineering achievements of the ancient world. It watered a hundred kilometres of agricultural land, feeding fifty thousand people, and made Sabaea so fertile that it looked like an earthly paradise according to the Qur'an, with 'two gardens on the right hand and the left… A fair land and an indulgent Lord'.[14]

Once the largest city of the incense kingdoms, little remains of Marib, except for an oval temple for the moon god Ilumquh and some impressive columns, known locally as the Throne of Bilqis (see p. 27). Nowadays the town, built of stones taken from the site, is a rubbish-strewn truck stop between Oman and Saudi Arabia. The fabulous civilisation has long gone, except for the legend of the Queen of Sheba.

The vast ruined city of Baraqish is even bleaker, a deserted, desiccated arena of tumbled stone. This was once the capital of the last of the incense kingdoms, Ma'in. Just one of ten Minaean walled cities, it still has 57 bastions standing. A relief discovered on a temple magically brings to life what the merchants would have met at Baraqish: images of sacrificial ibex and gazelles, men carrying lyres, female dancers and amphorae of wine.

Next stop on the main Frankincense Route west is Nagran, from which an alternative road took off east to Jabrin and on to Gerrha. Nagran is situated in a rich oasis valley, whose northern frontier area also has inscriptions, thousands of them left in the sandstone beside a well at Bir Hima. Left by caravaneers presumably relaxing until the heat of the day passed, they date from 900 BCE to 500 CE. This time the dancing girls have long plaits, hunters wield spears, and there are depictions of date harvests and camel herds.

In addition to calligraphy in the Sabaean script, there are inscriptions in Thamudic, left by the Thamudite people from 715 BCE onwards. They prospered until the second century CE, occupying a large area at least as far as Hijra, and from the widespread legacy of their inscriptions would appear to have had far-reaching (literate) influence. Despite the fact that control and therefore safe passage of the incense caravans was so vital, the Thamudites do not seem to have tried to wrest that control from the Minaeans. A measure of law and order was somehow maintained over the long period of the overland routes by a working combination of bribes, ever-vigilant security measures, and dexterous manoeuvring between what must have been shifting balances of power among the various peoples of Arabia. In response to these fluctuations the route too must at times have been altered. But in general there was little deviation through a combination of factors. These included topography, restful oases with their nurturing caravanserais, availability of garrisons and, as always, customs stations. Later, this fixed incense route evolved into a path of pilgrimage, and also a road between great markets or fairs.

Appearing out of the desert heat haze, a giant caravan of a thousand or more camels, accompanied by merchants, cameleers and armed horsemen skirmishing around the stragglers, must have looked like a city on the move. Approaching Medina, formerly Yathrib, where the prophet Muhammad founded Islam, weary men would be anticipating traditional Arabian hospitality. The arrival of a great caravan would have been the excuse for extravagant celebration. These camel-sore traders may well have sought out some kinsmen, had saddles repaired, shopped for Syrian silk, and returned south to their families somewhat the richer.

THE NABATEANS

From Yathrib nine to eleven days would elapse until the caravans reached Dedan and then Hijra. The merchants, who had risked their lives as well as their profits, now left the protection of the Minaeans and entered that of the Nabateans, who in a brief but glorious civilisation of about five hundred years, flowering at the peak of the incense trade, grew rich by controlling the main route deep into present-day Israel, and much other territory besides. Their southernmost outpost, Madain Salih, was a frontier town with the Minaeans, a masterpiece of unique monumental architecture, in the same style as the more famous Nabatean capital, Petra.

The Nabateans were Semitic people from central Arabia, theirs being the last Arab kingdom on the frankincense route. Though their distinctive culture was built on the profits of commerce, they had been nomadic herders as well as traders until about 800 BCE. This is the time they seem to have settled down as farmers with evolved forms of irrigation, as their dams and clay water-pipe installations still testify. However, the grandeur of their cities derived from profits earned by acting as the middlemen of the Arabian incense trade, selling to the Greek and then Roman Empires.

Petra, in southern Jordan, is one of the most spectacular sites along the frankincense trail, strategically located on the crossroads of two of the great trade routes of antiquity—silk and incense—in a valley stronghold carved out of a fault in the mountains that surround it. Weary merchants would check into a caravanserai in the cosmopolitan city, where travellers from all over the ancient world would relax, burn frankincense at worship, exchange news and spend money.

They had entered, as I did, through a mile long, gigantic crack in the sandstone, known as El Siq. Rock walls one hundred metres high seem almost to meet overhead, with the result that the passage, no wider than the Roman carriages that eventually penetrated the mountain citadel, languishes in a gloomy half-light, echoing eerily with the sound of horses' hoofs that transport today's travellers—the tourists. A frightened bird darted by the antiquities that were beginning to appear, the first signs of Nabatean imposition on the dramatic landscape. Cut into the rock at intervals were initially small niches, then other, much larger, more elaborate alcoves, most carved with a lintel of the characteristic 'crow-step' design, hallmark of Nabatean architecture.

El Siq makes one more turn before, out of the gloom, the towering brightness of Petra's most famous monument, El Khasneh, the Treasury, is revealed. Turning right, what is now a ravine begins to widen dramatically, and after the second century CE the merchants would have passed a giant Roman theatre on the left. Suddenly the route opens into a valley plateau about three kilometres square, covered nowadays with ruins. Foundations of large, luxurious villas, elaborately carved, with towering gateways all clearly indicate the sophisticated capital of an organised state of possibly thirty thousand inhabitants.

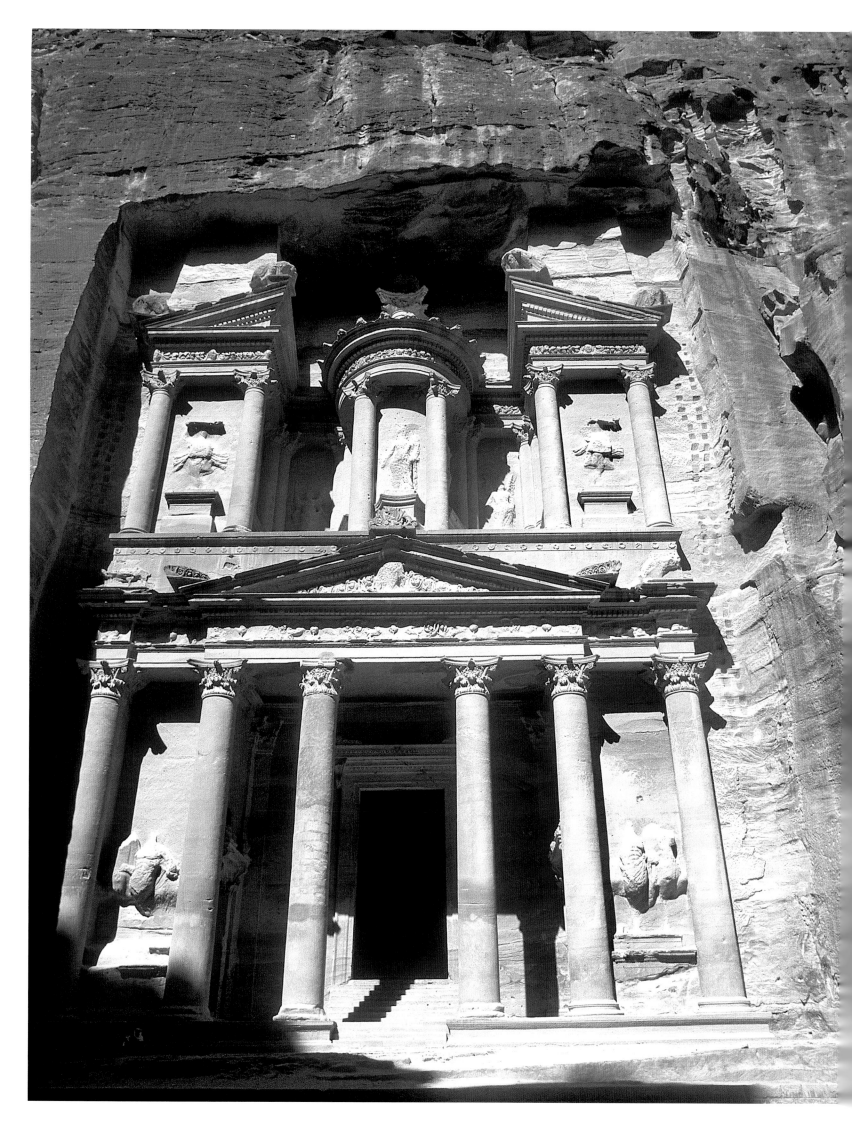

On either side of the valley the coral-coloured mountain walls are indented with ornate tomb facades. The effect is absolutely sensational. One can hardly separate man-made architecture from naturally sculpted geological strata, as the pink oleander bushes pushing through the paved streets bequeathed by the Romans perfume the air.

Originally an Arab people, the Nabateans were culturally familiar with frankincense. Many *unguentaria*, ceramic vessels to hold incense, unguents and aromatic oils have been excavated there. They worshipped the sun with offerings of frankincense, according to Strabo, and the magnificent Temple of the Lions has a grooved altar to contain fragrant materials. Strabo describes Nabatean society as essentially democratic, an interesting affinity with modern Bedouin peoples. Their kings were accountable to an assembly, and even took their turn in serving their subjects, since 'they have but few slaves'. Nevertheless as increasing numbers of Romans arrived, their lifestyle sounds increasingly hedonistic: 'The King holds many drinking bouts in magnificent style, but no-one drinks more than eleven cupfuls, each time using a different golden cup', writes Strabo, adding, 'they have two girls singers for each banquet'.[15]

Gradually Roman administration encroached to the extent that by 106 CE Petra had been incorporated into the empire, though with hardly any bloodshed. Nabatean culture thrived as long as there was frankincense trade, and some of their finest monumental architecture is dated from after this event. But its importance as the nexus of caravan routes was already declining as the development of Roman transport by sea began to threaten the viability of overland incense traffic. Petra's source of wealth vanished; its population became dispirited and depleted. A catastrophic earthquake in the fourth century decimated the city, reduced her splendour to ruins, and even her location was forgotten.

After Petra, frankincense routes branched in several directions. Gaza, to the north, was a critically important port for dispatching incense via the Mediterranean; but much of it travelled west to Alexandria for sorting and processing, and onwards to Europe.

DEATH IN DHOFAR

After the heyday of Arabia Felix, the frankincense trade crashed in the third century CE with the rise of Christianity. Already, by the first century CE the Romans had found a way to cut out the Arab middlemen using the monsoon winds to transport frankincense by sea. The dates of Al-Balid's flowering as a great city rich from its exports of incense, from the twelfth to the sixteenth centuries CE show that the earlier decline in use had not destroyed the trade. It was however, a mere shadow of its boom days.

From the sixth century CE, as Islam took hold, trading patterns changed. There were still huge caravans of two thousand or so camels travelling north, which did carry some frankincense, though increasingly there were more oriental and African luxury goods, and African slaves. Meanwhile, the Arabian perfumery industry was growing, requiring frankincense both as a fragrant ingredient, and as a fixative.

Increasing desiccation of southern Arabia, over-grazing and use of scented woods as fuel caused a sharp decline in the number of frankincense trees; and as prices fell, fewer trees were tapped, and many were allowed to wither away. The comparative decline of the trade continued until 1830, when Indian markets swelled appreciably with the re-export of incense in different forms from Mumbai. In 1895 the Bents reported that 450 tons of frankincense was exported annually from 'Zufar to Bombay'. New uses for the crystals were developed there: the volatile oil and powder were used in cosmetics, candle-making and mixed incense sticks, called *agarbati*. A Dhofari source recorded that in 1939 between six and seven thousand tons of frankincense were being exported per year, employing three thousand local people, and contributing 75 per cent of Oman's national income.[16]

At the outbreak of World War II, India closed its doors to foreign imports by levying punitive taxes, and the trade never really recovered. In 1947 the focus of the business moved to Aden, which had been receiving quantities of frankincense since the 1870s, and had imported some 105 tons in 1875. One third was sent to Mumbai, the rest to Egypt, Yemen and Saudi Arabia, as well as to the UK and Trieste in Italy, presumably for the perfumery industry.

But this was the beginning of the era of oil and with black gold supplanting white after the war, the fatal blow for the mass Omani export of frankincense was delivered by the development of a synthetic substitute. Scientists in Rome developed a brown rock-like conglomerate, using cheap chemicals. Yet frankincense production in Oman staggered on until barely thirty years ago. Now only old men gather the pearls of the desert. 'I am one of the last harvesters here', said seventy-year-old Musallam Rehaba, whom I had watched laboriously filling his battered bowl. 'It's barely a living for very hard work. Cheaper incense from Somalia and India spoils the market.'

At his wife's funeral in 65 CE, the allegedly heartbroken Roman emperor Nero burnt three thousand tons of frankincense—the equivalent of the entire annual production of Dhofar. Nowadays only approximately ten to twelve tons are exported annually from Dhofar, one of the last frankincense traders in Salalah told me, and almost all goes to the thriving modern Arab perfumery industry, though some is sent to Hong Kong, and a little to Europe and the US. 'Ten to twelve tons' is a stab in the dark according to Ghanim al-Shanfari, director of the recently founded Frankincense Trade Centre. 'Figures are hard to assess', he said. 'There is no central organisation for the marketing of frankincense and we don't have accurate records now'. The brief of his Centre, despite its name, is not to promote or even analyse frankincense trading, but rather to supervise archaeological digs, World Heritage Site matters, the newly planted nurseries of little frankincense trees and, in the future, the Museum of the Land of Frankincense now under construction.

Are we in at the death of a five-thousand-year-old culture? The offering that was once literally worth its weight in gold is now a gift pack retailing at about £3 ($5.40/€4.20) in the souk at Salalah. Search for frankincense on the Internet and a wonderland of shopping opportunities opens up. Although reasonably priced, this is incense imported from Somalia, Eritrea and India—not Oman, and the fragrance of these tiny brown crystals lacks the sublime epiphany of Dhofari silver *luban*. Why is this ancient heritage at risk of slipping ignominiously away? Apart from a small amount culled for use in Omani homes, commercial frankincense harvesting has virtually ceased. When I talked to one of the few exporters left in Salalah, he told me that when an order comes in, he cannot get enough *luban* from local suppliers, and has to dispatch Somalian incense. Said Yusef bin Harun is the grandson of a major trader in frankincense, but actually makes his living as a television cameraman. In the last two years he has exported only two containers of frankincense, to Egypt and Saudi Arabia. 'Before 1970 it was still an important business and there were 25 traders here at that time', he said. 'But now frank-incense has lost value and no one wants to harvest it. It's such hard labour and our young men would rather go into government service or oil'.

The young men have moved away from Dhofar, and those that are left, or who visit on holiday, prefer to dive for the highly lucrative abalone off the rocks between Sad'h and Hasik. In a two-month season, which is all that is permitted to preserve stocks, a diver can earn £25,000 ($45,000/€ 35,000), whereas Musallam Rehaba's annual harvest nets him about £80 ($144/€ 112). The shellfish sells for £100 ($180/€ 140) a kilo, while frankincense retails for about £1.50 ($2.70/€ 2.10).

There are, however a few hopeful signs. Aware of the situation, the government has set up an advisory committee, working in concert with UNESCO. One of the results has been the two tree nurseries at Wadi Dhowkah and Wadi Dhanoub. Showing me round Wadi Dhowkah, Ghanim al-Shanfari was optimistic: 'The private sector in Oman sees a big future in developing natural products such as frankincense'. When I asked him what he felt was the relevance of frankincense to the world today, he replied: 'Whether in temples, churches or mosques, we're using the same material to perfume and purify these places. I respect and adore this holy tree, because it creates a peaceful relationship between Omanis and the outside world. It brings Muslims and Christians, Muslims and Jews, together in worship, companionship and trade'.

Below: Mirbat harbour with working dhows in the distance

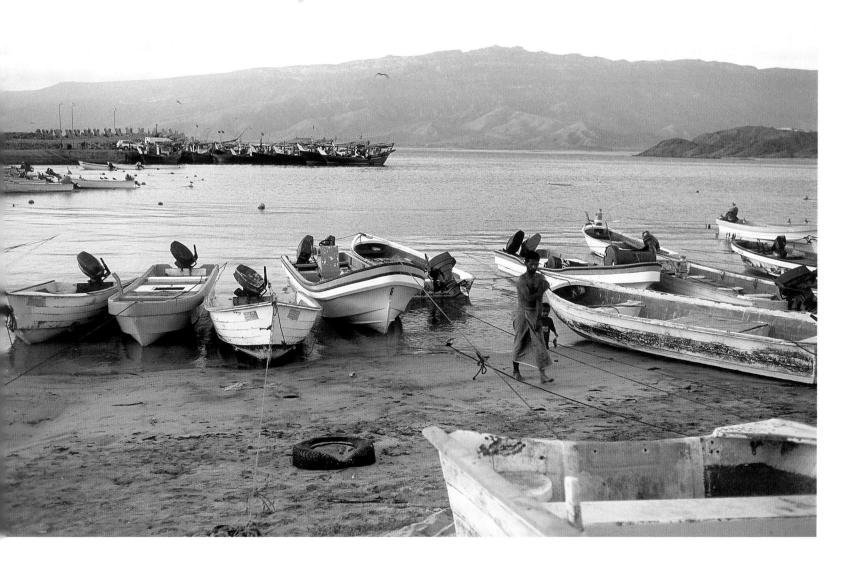

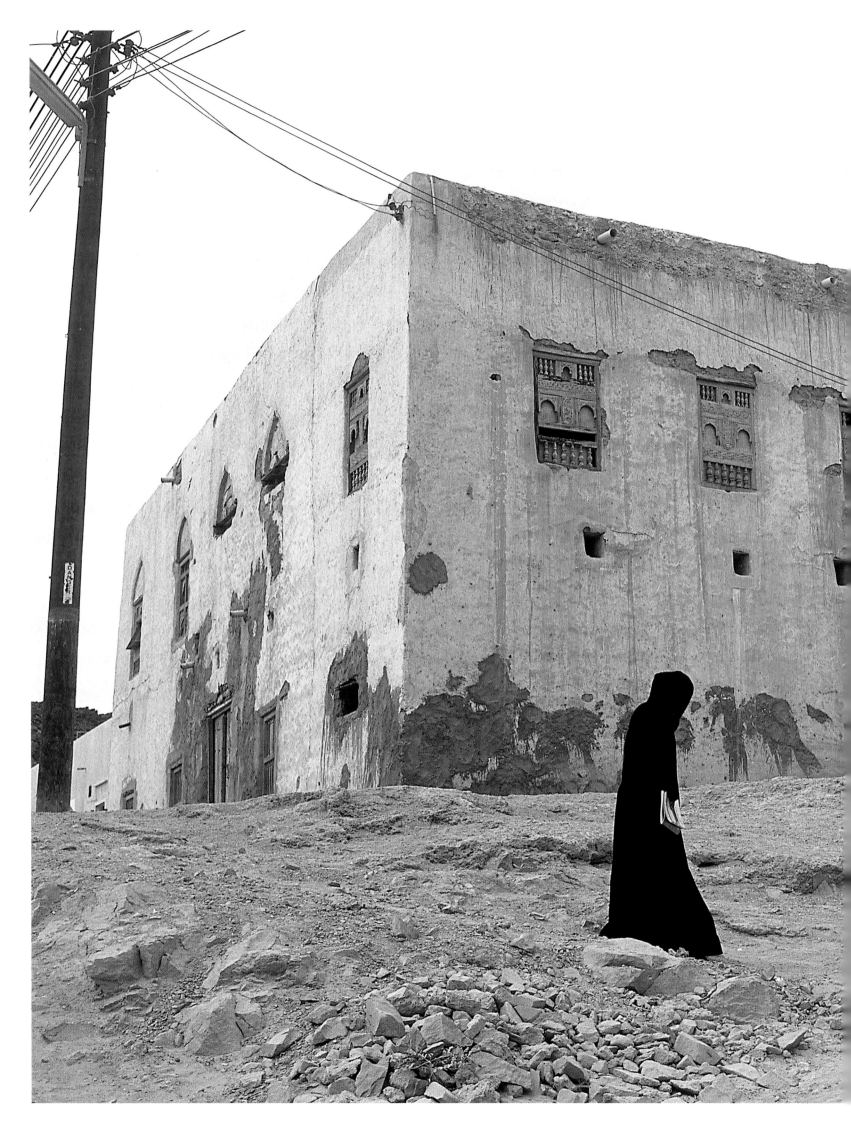

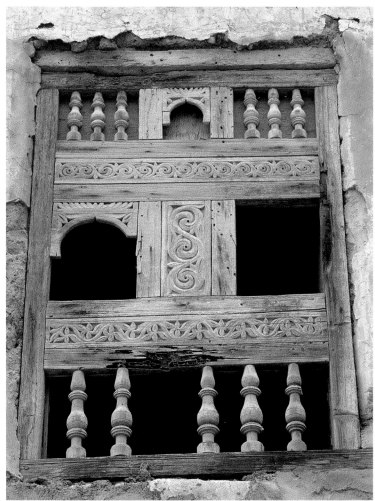

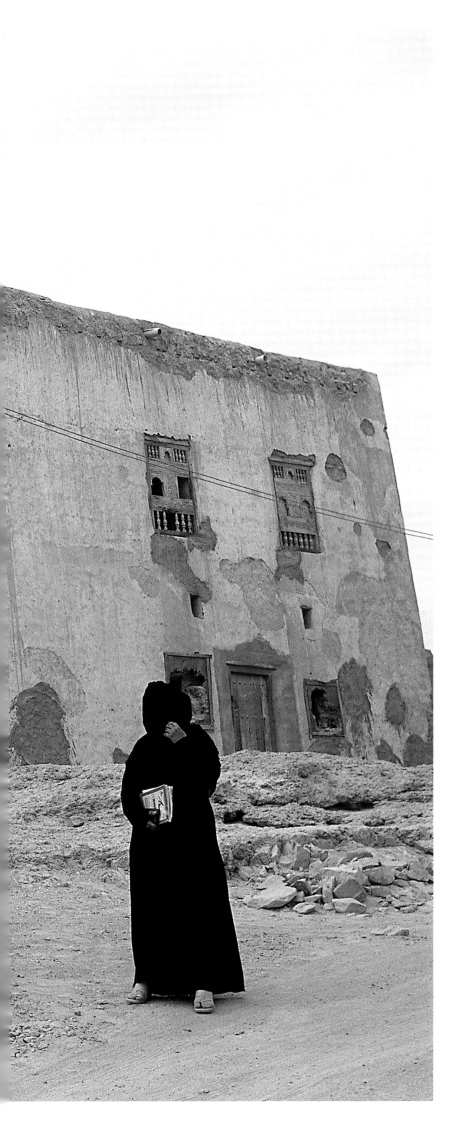

Left: The oldest house in Sad'h, once owned by the town's chief trader in frankincense

Above: Carved window of a trader's two-hundred-year-old house in Sad'h

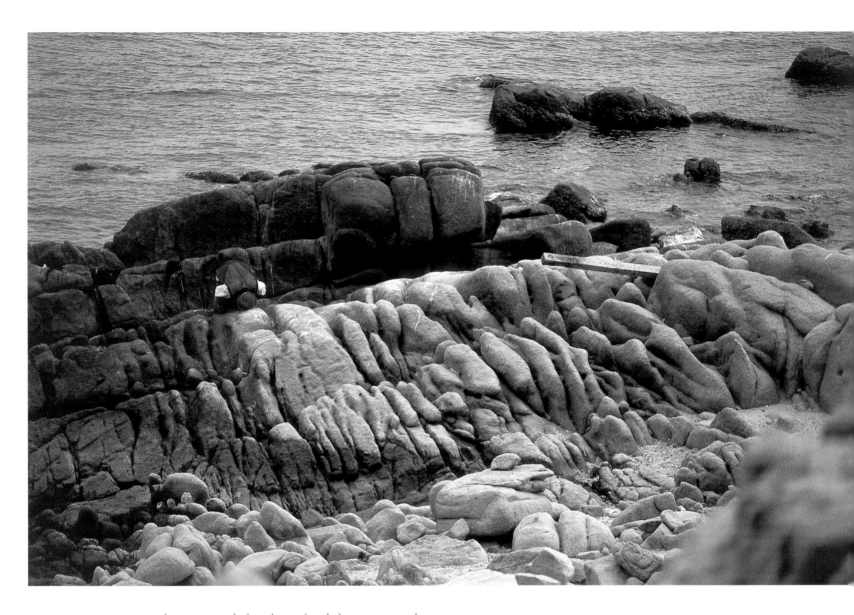

Above: Prayers before diving for abalone, near Hasik

Following double page: Weighing the abalone haul after diving beneath The Frankincense Highway

What an irony that just as exports of frankincense from Dhofar are now eclipsed by those from other sources, tourism into the region is being promoted, with great emphasis on the history of frankincense. Salalah already receives nearly forty thousand visitors a year, primarily during the *khareef* (the monsoon) and cruise ships call on a weekly basis during that three-month season. Although it may seem strange to inhabitants of more temperate regions, the lure of rain is a magnet for visitors from the parched lands of the UAE, Saudi Arabia, Kuwait and all over the Arab world, including Omani nationals. During the monsoon a green flowering carpet magically unfurls over Dhofar, and arid cliff-faces suddenly transform into poetic waterfalls.

And when it is not raining, visitors can explore the frankincense souk, whose sales soar astronomically at this time, before moving on to the atmospheric little fishing ports, and the archaeological sites. Oman has been receiving considerable media coverage in recent years, so increasingly international travellers swell the numbers of visitors who are determined to do more than just relax and eat fresh sea-food in Salalah's sumptuous hotels. An upmarket visitor industry is part of the Omani diversification away from oil and natural gas, and as the Adviser to His Majesty the Sultan for Cultural Affairs, His Excellency Abdul Aziz Mohamed Al-Rowas said: 'We want to find a way by which we can build up interest in our culture, without losing our identity, vital as far as tourism is concerned. We are conscious of the importance of frankincense to human culture'.

UNESCO IN DHOFAR

To celebrate frankincense and the history of the incense routes in 2000 UNESCO inscribed four new World Heritage Sites in Oman, collectively titled The Frankincense Trail, now renamed The Land of Frankincense. Under the criteria for nomination, the three archaeological sites of Khor Rori, Al-Balid and Shisr/Wubar, as well as the frankincense 'park' of Wadi Dhowkah were identified as a 'whole cultural landscape'. They 'represent the production and distribution of frankincense, one of the most important luxury items of trade in the Old World in antiquity'. As justification, these sites 'constitute outstanding testimony to the civilisation that from the Neolithic period to the late Islamic period flourished in southern Arabia and established economic, social and cultural links, reaching from the Mediterranean and Red Sea regions to Mesopotamia, India and China, through the development of the frankincense trade network'.[17]

Since 2000 the Frankincense Trade Centre, reporting to the Office of the Adviser to Sultan Qaboos on Cultural Affairs, has been working on a series of excavation, maintenance and conservation programmes in collaboration with various overseas universities. Part of the Centre's brief is to ensure that Omani archaeologists gain experience by participating at the sites. The Adviser himself, Abdul Aziz Mohamed Al-Rowas, told me: 'We are co-operating with UNESCO for guidance only'. Ghanim al-Shanfari expanded on UNESCO's role: 'Their experts have been giving us scientific advice and support on conservation and management, but not getting involved with the archaeological work. They have been very helpful and positive, offering workshops, meetings and lectures to build up our information and skills for protection and development, training us to develop techniques to UNESCO standards. For instance we get advice from them on placing visitors' centres at the sites, whether an on-site museum is advisable or not, and how to prevent disturbance of the original sites, like road-building or uncontrolled tourism'.

At present the Trade Centre also disseminates information about frankincense from sociological, spiritual and functional perspectives, as well as the historical background, a role that will be taken over by the Museum of the Land of Frankincense. This chimes well with UNESCO's emphasis on the *human* cultural story. 'UNESCO is promoting frankincense', added al-Shanfari, 'because they recognise that it has been a major gateway in human and religious history'.

A dedicated frankincense museum is being built at Salalah, close to Al-Balid. It will include a History Hall and a Maritime Hall. The first will present an overview of the history of Oman, with a special section on the sites of frankincense trade and the World Heritage Sites relating to incense. Although the official ribbon has not yet been cut, the History Hall has had a 'soft opening', and is available for visitors. The Maritime Hall will present the relationship of Omanis with the sea since antiquity, and their maritime prowess, including boat-building and navigation technologies. A small nursery of frankincense trees has already been planted and is flourishing next to the Museum site. The trees will gradually be transplanted into other production areas to counteract their depletion in recent years. It is hoped that the Museum's promotion of the role of frankincense throughout Oman's history will bring added visibility to the resin, and that through the phenomenon of 'patrimonisation', revitalisation of the trade will occur.

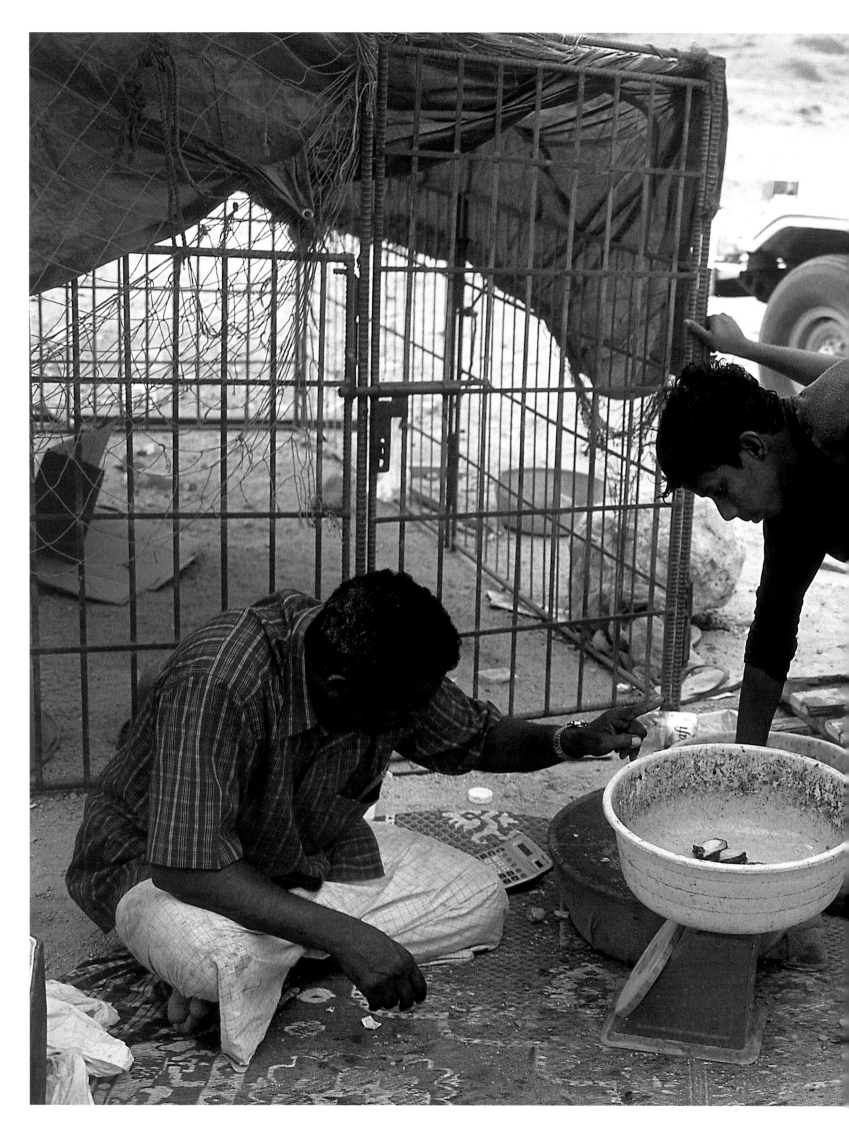

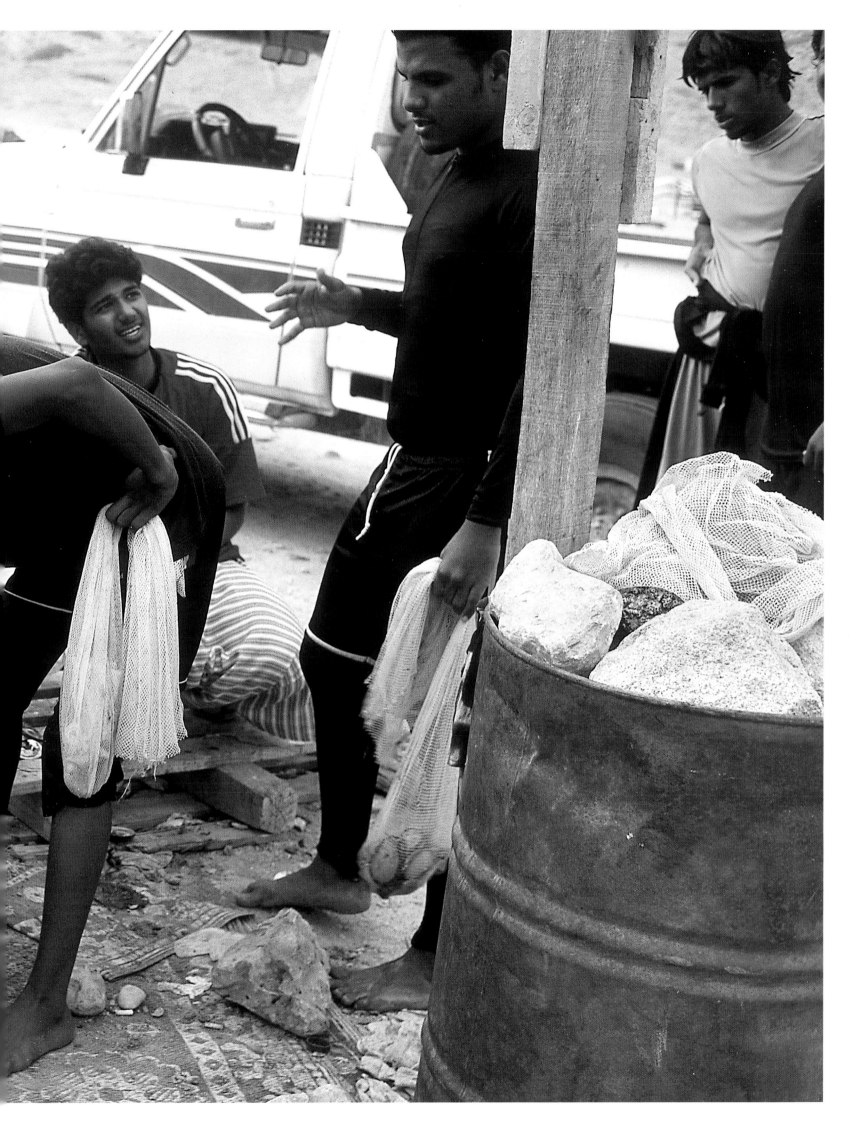

Ointment and perfume

rejoice the heart.

Proverbs 27:9

CHAPTER FOUR

THE DREAM FACTORY

Per fumum: the saga of scent, in which Arabia was the pioneer, evolved 'through smoke'. Incense is central to the development of that story, since aromatics were burnt not only in a sacred context, but frankincense remained one of the key ingredients in the subsequent evolution of perfume as an art of personal adornment.

The link between the fragrant smoke of frankincense all those thousands of years ago, and the international perfume industry of today lies in the development of Arabian perfumery. This, as we will see, gave birth to European scents. Of course frankincense was not the only aromatic precursor of this gradual development, but it was the most valued as a mood-altering substance, with its spiritual reference and soothing, evocative effect. As techniques evolved to produce scented ointments for the body, it was discovered how effective frankincense was, both as a base note to balance lighter floral essences, and as a fixative to make the perfume last. And frankincense is still used in these ways in thirteen per cent of premium international female fragrances and three per cent of male. This durability came about through the evolution of perfume in the Middle East.

Ancient Arabian 'noses' had the unique natural advantage that many of the finest materials grew almost exclusively in their region, enabling them to have a virtual monopoly on frankincense, myrrh, cinnamon and cassia. Through their mastery of maritime expertise and trading associations, they had the means to import a wealth of other ingredients. There is clear evidence of Arab and then Islamic trade or cultural and spiritual links with areas supplying perfume materials. Arab dhows and camels brought essential oils, spices and woods in great quantities from the Far East, Asia, Africa and the Levant.

Although expeditions on the spice routes are not as perilous today as they were for ancient mariners, sources for materials have not altered that much. The best vetiver still originates from Java, aloe-wood and camphor also from the Far East, sandalwood and spikenard from India. Except for a few imports of animal origin, notably ambergris, musk, civet and castoreum, which have now been replaced by synthetics, then as now, most materials are sourced from plants. These include floral essences such as Damask Rose (originally from Syria), now grown extensively in Turkey and Eastern Europe, and jasmine from Egypt and India.

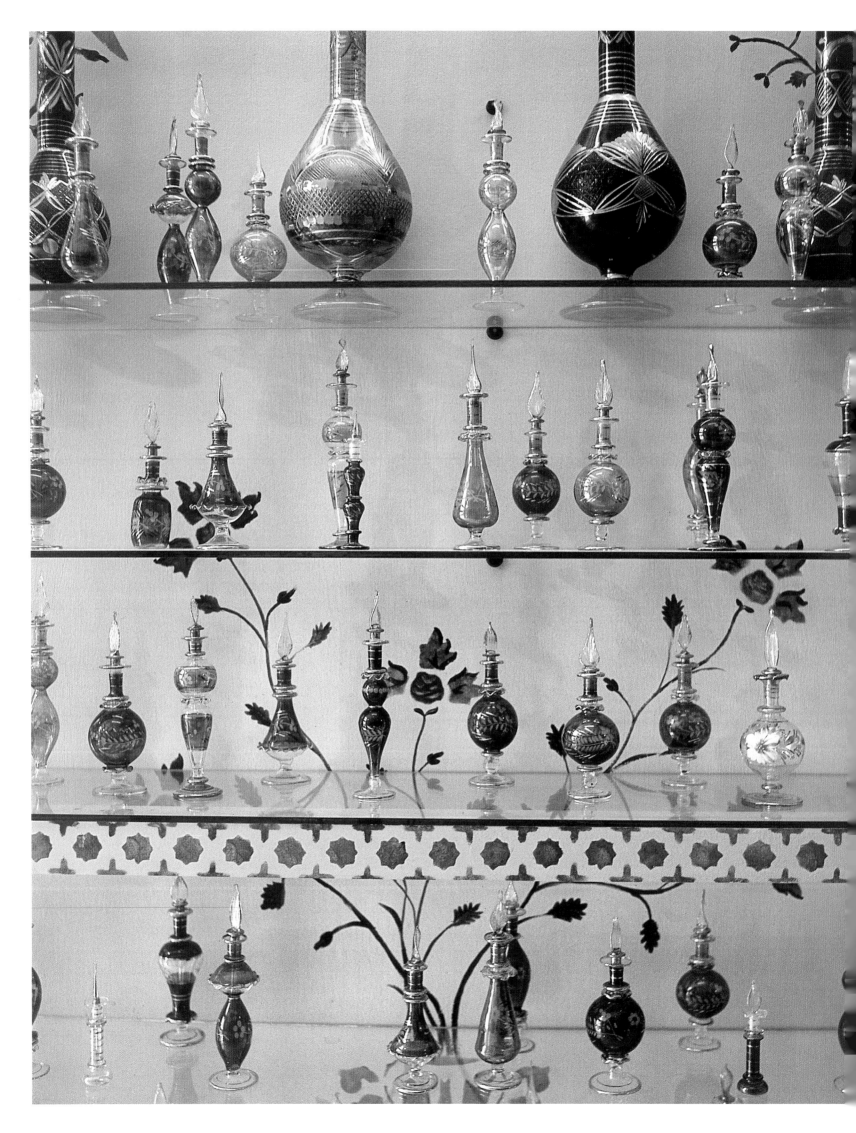

In the category of leaves, stems and roots, cloves are still sourced from Madagascar and Zanzibar, the latter colonised for several centuries by Oman to control the East African slave trade. Classical Arabian perfumery was unthinkable without resins, gums and balsams, that still feature today as base notes in the pyramid of perfume construction. These include Persian galbanum and benzoin from the Spice Islands of South-East Asia. Another indispensable category of the base or body note is that of mosses, woods and barks: cedarwood famously came from Lebanon; oakmoss from, among other sources, the Islamic worlds of Southern Spain and Morocco. The spices and aromatic herbs used by Arabs continue to play a key role in perfumery, including vanilla from East Africa and South-East Asia and coriander from the shores of the Mediterranean. The use of fruit has always struck a fresh top note in perfume creation, with bergamot and citrus such as orange and lemon from the Levant, and the warm tones of peach and apricot from Palestine and Iran.

Many of these substances are classified according to properties and function in the Arab *materia medica*, as perfume ingredients were often interchangeable with medical. The dating of the earliest recorded recipe from Syria, around 1750 BCE and ones from Egypt from 1600 BCE shows how early the Arab tradition of perfume making was developing. The region's perfumers were consistently the first to develop the fragrance technologies which eventually gave birth to the European industry, most of which are still used. The first fragrant products were ointments or unguents for the body; scented liquids came later, as skills evolved. Moisturising body perfumes came in the form of solid or liquid unguents, the latter fixed with a resin such as frankincense, as well as scented powders and oils.

The perfume creation process starts with the rigorous selection of base materials, which are weighed and mixed according to the specific formula created by the 'nose'. There are five methods of extracting the volatile essential oils. The most ancient process is maceration, also known as 'digestion', recorded in Mesopotamia *c*. 1800 BCE as well as in Ancient Egypt. This process is used primarily for animal ingredients, but also for vanilla, tonka beans, jasmine, iris and other flowers. The raw material is steeped in fat, oil, water or alcohol, and when its cells are ruptured, their aromas are absorbed, and then purified. When the process involves heat, it is known as 'infusion'. The cold method yields a 'tincture'.

Left: Perfume bottles at Sidi bou Said, Tunisia

Below: Antique bottles containing *aatr* at a Luxor perfumery, Egypt

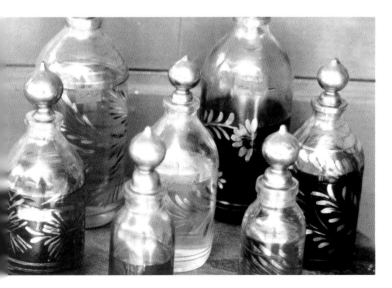

The technique of *enfleurage*, literally meaning 'to enflower', was developed in Ancient Egypt and is still in use, since it obtains a greater amount of essential oil than other methods, although it is labour intensive and therefore costly. The fragrant parts of the plant are again steeped in animal fats or oils, preserved in benzoin and sometimes a touch of rose absolute. This process can be lengthy, since some plants continue to release their essential oils over a period of time. From the seventeenth century, French perfumers have spread flowers between sheets of glass smeared with the selected grease for days at a time. The sandwiched flowers are changed again and again until the grease has absorbed as much odour as possible. It is then washed with a solvent which filters the essential oil into an 'absolute'.

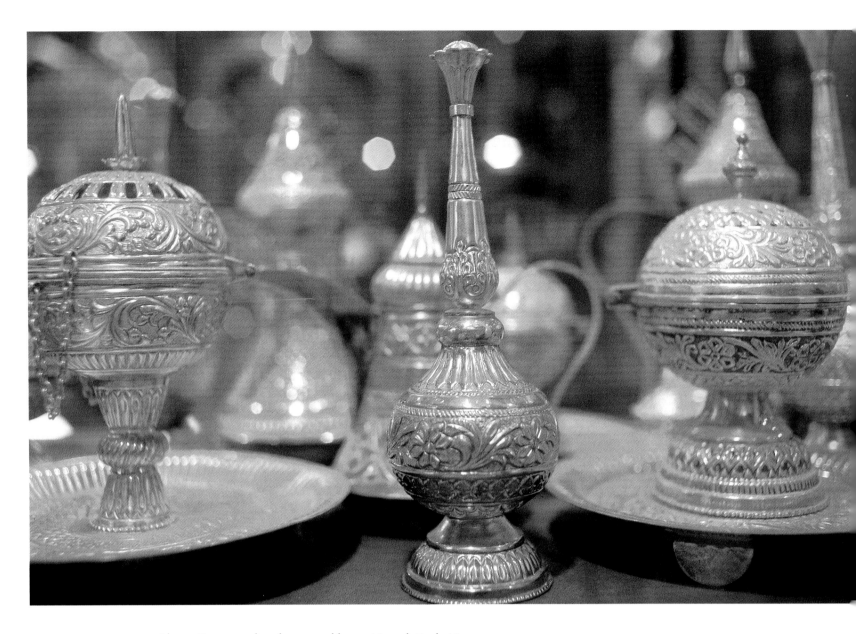

Above: Censers and perfume sprinklers at Muttrah Souk, Muscat

Right: 'Hostess trolley' for scent and incense at a Muscat perfumery

Far right: Elaborate incense burner and silver frankincense crystals at a Muscat shopping centre

Distillation is the third technique for extraction of essential oils. It is the main method used today, and comes with a lengthy pedigree. Stills have been discovered at Ninevah on the Tigris, in Mohenjo-daro and—again—in Ancient Egypt. Alchemists at Alexandria developed this method between 200 and 300 CE and then it was improved in the seventh and eighth centuries by the introduction of the alembic (from the Arabic *al-inbik*, meaning a 'still'). In the tenth century the Persian Avicenna further refined the method, enabling the pure essential oil to be extracted. The alembic is a cauldron in which plant material was originally suffused in boiling water, in later centuries only in steam. The heat breaks open the cells to release the essential oil. A pipe from the still directs the vapour into a collection vessel, after which the steam and oils condense back into liquid, collected beneath in another container. The oils rise to the top of the water, both of which are eventually used.

Expression, the fourth method, was originally used in Ancient Egypt, where flowers were twisted in a cloth bag until the oil was squeezed out. The method has been developed primarily to extract oils from the citrus family by means of pressing rinds between rollers to break down the cells, so that the resulting fragrant oil can be separated from the pulp. The fifth technique, extraction, conceived in the 1830s, is a comparative newborn in the history of perfume technology, using petro-chemical solvents by a method similar to distillation.

After any one, or all, of these processes comes the ultimate creative act—blending. With the chosen, processed essences to hand, a carrier is needed. Around the tenth century, when Avicenna was developing the still, great strides were being made by the Arabs in chemistry, alongside a battery of other sciences. Perfumers discovered how to make alcohol to be used as a carrier, enabling perfumes without a heavy, oily base to be created. Although the alcohol used is specially prepared and most certainly not for internal consumption, a branch of Islamic philosophy nowadays proscribes its use in perfume creation. Many modern perfumers in the Arab world, (echoed by some in the US), prefer an oil carrier to alcohol, since it 'fixes' more effectively so that the perfume lasts longer on the skin. This effect is known as the *sillage* or 'trail', and frankincense is highly esteemed in its creation.

Having established an oil or alcohol carrier and fixative, the fragrances are left to mature for several months until they acquire their final character. Today this stage is completed in stainless steel vats. Traditionally, in Arabia, this was done in stone or alabaster containers to keep the contents cool. The Arab progenitors of the contemporary industry exercised stringent quality control, and just as nowadays, each stage was rigorously checked.

Perfume artefacts preserved in Ancient Egypt from 3500 BCE testify to a sophisticated industry which exported luxury products the world craved. Alexandria was the end of the road for the frankincense route to Europe, where the crystals were processed into oil and other scented products. It was here on the Mediterranean coast that Egyptian perfumers led the field from the second century CE for several centuries. In tandem with alchemists, Alexandrian 'noses' made significant advances, attempting to

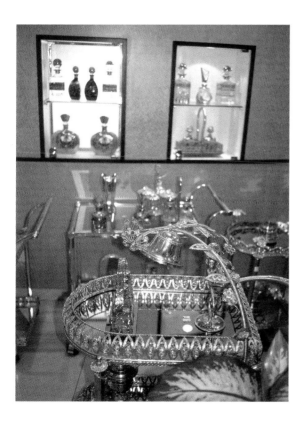
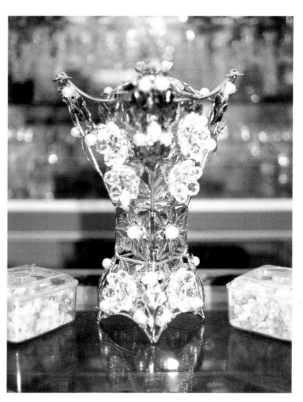

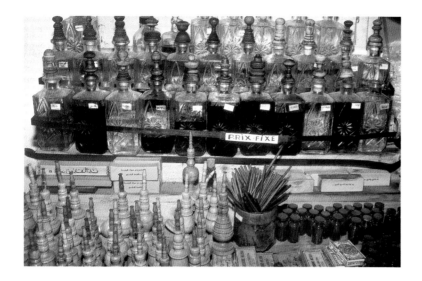

Above: Perfumes and make-up at the souk in Tunis

Right: Essential oils for perfumery at Nabeul, Tunisia

distil the 'spirit' of plants, and succeeding in distilling their essential oils. These early stills are credited to an alchemist known as Maria the Prophetess. A centre of perfume excellence also emerged in Aden, as Islamic influence began to expand, so much so that Indian merchants employed the masters in Aden to incorporate the use of fragrant ingredients from India.

As the Roman Empire finally disintegrated in the fifth century CE, the golden age of Islamic civilisation was about to begin. By the sixth century, musk, a key ingredient for its potent 'animal' aroma and efficacy as a fixative, was being imported from India, and its sensual aroma became incorporated into the very mortar of Arab palaces, and later into mosques. Both Arabian and Byzantine perfumers fell on it, as Constantinople acquired a leading reputation at the forefront of sixth-century perfumery. Local records show imports of frankincense and myrrh at this time, just as the rising tide of Christianity was so adversely affecting the rest of the incense trade.

With the advent of Islam in the seventh century, the Arabs became a world power. Classical Muslim culture reached its zenith in the ninth, tenth and eleventh centuries, its cultural and spiritual influence continuing to spread rapidly across the globe. From the seventh century onwards, the Arabs annexed and advanced centuries of learning recorded by the Persian, Greek and Roman Empires, many of whose texts were translated into Arabic. The study of chemistry flourished, enabling breakthroughs in perfume technology. Arab paper manufacture helped disseminate information from Cadiz to Canton, with bookstores springing up, opening windows of opportunity for the work of a host of writers such as Jabir ibn Hayyan (c. 721–815), who investigated perfume distillation, followed by Ar-Razi (c. 840–924), who pursued the same research in Baghdad.

From the eighth to the tenth centuries the Abbasid Caliphs of Baghdad colonised Persia, which was already renowned for its perfumery. Baghdad was the pre-eminent centre of the Arabian perfume industry at this time, and the epitome of a cultured city. Its artisans created exquisite glass flacons for lavish scented products, and its ships imported new ingredients from India, China and South-East Asia.

During the ninth century, at the height of the Abbasid Dynasty, a physician and philosopher named Yaqub al-Kindi, wrote some 250 works, including *A Book of Perfume Chemistry & Distillations*. His father, the governor of Kufa in present-day Iraq, came from South Arabia, and must have been familiar with frankincense. In the eleventh century CE another celebrated Arab physician, Avicenna or Ibn-Sina, took the by then highly developed art of Arab perfumery to Moorish Spain, probably its first introduction into Europe. Among the hundred books he wrote is the Canon of Medicine. His *materia medica* section includes essential oils such as clove, cinnamon and coriander, traditionally used in perfumery as well as medicine in the Arab world, but new to Europe. He also introduced Spain to steam distillation using the alembic or still.

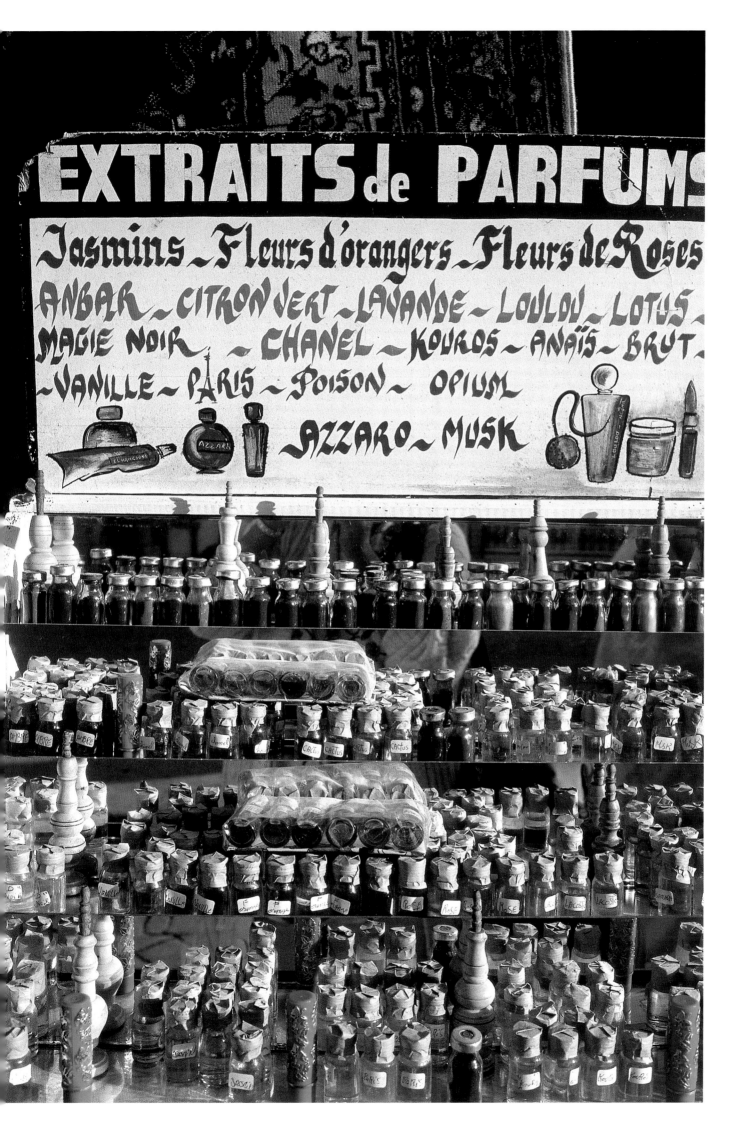

One of the particularly luxurious scents whose recipe was given by Al-Kindi is *Naddah*, mentioned in a fifteenth century book of Arab erotica called *The Perfumed Garden*. At the heart of Islamic culture is its reverence for gardens, flowers and perfume. It is said that a single drop of Muhammad's sweat, as he ascended to the heavens, created the rose. Two great Persian Sufi poets of the sixteenth century have immortalised flowers, Sa'di in his book *Bustan* or *Garden of Perfume*; and the impoverished Hafiz who passed by food-sellers in the souk, pausing only to buy a hyacinth, to 'feed his soul'.

Her thoughts are like the fume of frankincense
Which from a golden censer forth doth rise.

Edmund Spenser (1552–99)

A vibrant perfume culture still permeates Arabia based on both indigenous materials such as frankincense and imported ones. 'Perfume—my life would be a desert without it', my Omani guide said, spraying the tassel of his *dishdasha*, whose sole purpose on the garment, he told me, was to waft fragrance around. Aspects of this culture have survived almost intact down the millennia. In Oman, government buildings, offices, mosques and homes are censed with frankincense several times daily; and even in the corporate ambience of five-star hotels, an ornate censer on the counter beside the cashier billows forth that inimitable aroma.

There is a virtually unchanged cottage industry, with individual perfumers bottling their own creations, selling them in recondite little shops; and mothers handing down secrets to their daughters. But there is another twist to this tale of perfume, for so long the preferred luxury product of Arabia. The voracious clientele on whom new Western scents are often market-researched, have a highly developed modern fragrance industry of their own. Their factories test the efficacy of frankincense and a myriad other

Below: Frankincense burning in the Hilton hotel lobby at Salalah

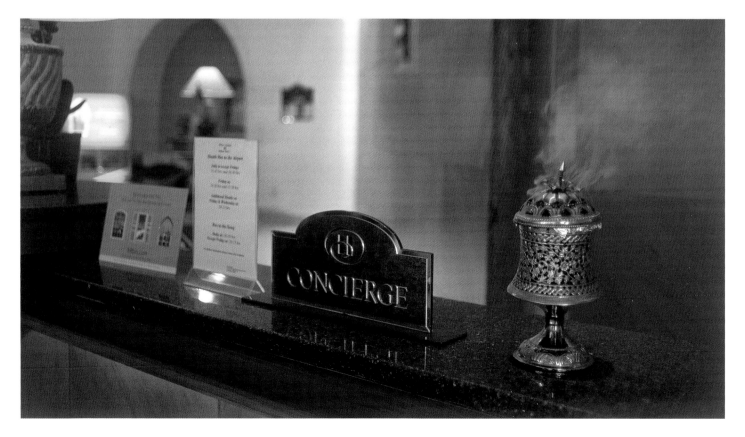

materials in household and culinary products, in addition to producing very costly scents in cut crystal containers as sumptuous as any Baccarat creation.

Stroll into the Perfume Hall at Harrods, or any of the glitzy shopping malls of the Middle East, and a sparkling array of crystal bottles containing *aatr*—Arabian perfumes—awaits you. (*Aatr* are commonly wrongly named *attar*. In fact the word *attar* in Arabic means a maker of perfumes, but *aatr* is derived from the Arabic *'itr*, literally meaning 'perfume', and also from the Persian *'atr jul*, which translates as 'fat of a flower', hence oil). Our grandmothers may recall Otto of Parma Violets, or Attar of Roses, both derivations from *aatr*. Some *aatr* are single note, such as amber, jasmine or frankincense; others are blended. Almost all *aatr* are aromatic oils extracted by distillation. They differ from Western scents in that they are strong and long-lasting, very different from the current marketing ploy of instantly forgettable and vanishing concoctions, which are not created to last. *Aatr* also do not contain synthetics or alcohol.

Some *aatr* are very expensive, literally hundreds of pounds for a modestly sized if beautiful bottle, particularly those containing *oudh*. This deeply evocative oil extracted from Burmese, Cambodian or Indian agarwood, is somewhat similar to frankincense in its resinous, austere yet sensual fragrance. After 130 days of mourning, a widow may scent her hair with *oudh*. It is by far the most costly ingredient in perfumery today. Already highly cherished by Arabs, so much so that the best is locked away in safes, it is now beginning to be explored by Western 'noses'.

'It is the tradition of the Arab people to use perfume', I was told by the branch manager of one of one of the multitude of Middle Eastern companies. They manufacture perfume for their own people, though the major ones have global distribution networks and advertising budgets to match. 'It is also a noticeable trend', he continued, 'that our people are returning to their roots, buying Arab perfumes rather than French. Eighty per cent of them buy products made here in the Middle East, because their oil base makes them long-lasting, and because they don't contain alcohol'. With factories in Ajman, Dubai and Sharjah, Al-Haramain's website claims that *oudh* is the source of its inspiration, that its *aatr* of Dehnal Oudh Maliki Ateeq took twenty years to produce and is 'one of the costliest perfumes on earth'. At one of their three shops in Oman, *aatr* of frankincense was part of a trio including *oudh* and rose, presented in Italian crystal bottles in a gilded casket for £2,000 ($3,600/€2,800).

Based in Abu Dhabi, *Yas: The Royal Name of Perfume* took that name from the Bedouin people of Bani Yas, whose descendants are now royal families such as the Al-Nahyans of Abu Dhabi and the Maktoums of Dubai. They adhere strictly to traditional ingredients such as *oudh* and frankincense, and traditional technology too. However, they market into Europe and the Far East. Kato Aromatic, founded in 1971 and with headquarters in Cairo, exports 'concretes' and 'absolutes' to international companies, as well as sixty essential oils, frankincense being a consistent seller. Kato has four sites for distillation and extraction, three for experimental plantations and one for aromatic chemicals, and are best known for their jasmine absolute.

Egyptian jasmine is world famous for its *indole* or 'animal' note. It produces its highest percentage of oil, along with its headiest aroma, at sunset; then it must be picked before the morning dew has dried off. The *aatr* of Arabia are called essential oils and have such powerful olfactory and medical properties because they are picked with due regard not just to the season, but to the hour of the day. Each oil is used as much as possible in its natural or terpenic state, and this includes frankincense, which is heavily endowed with terpenes.

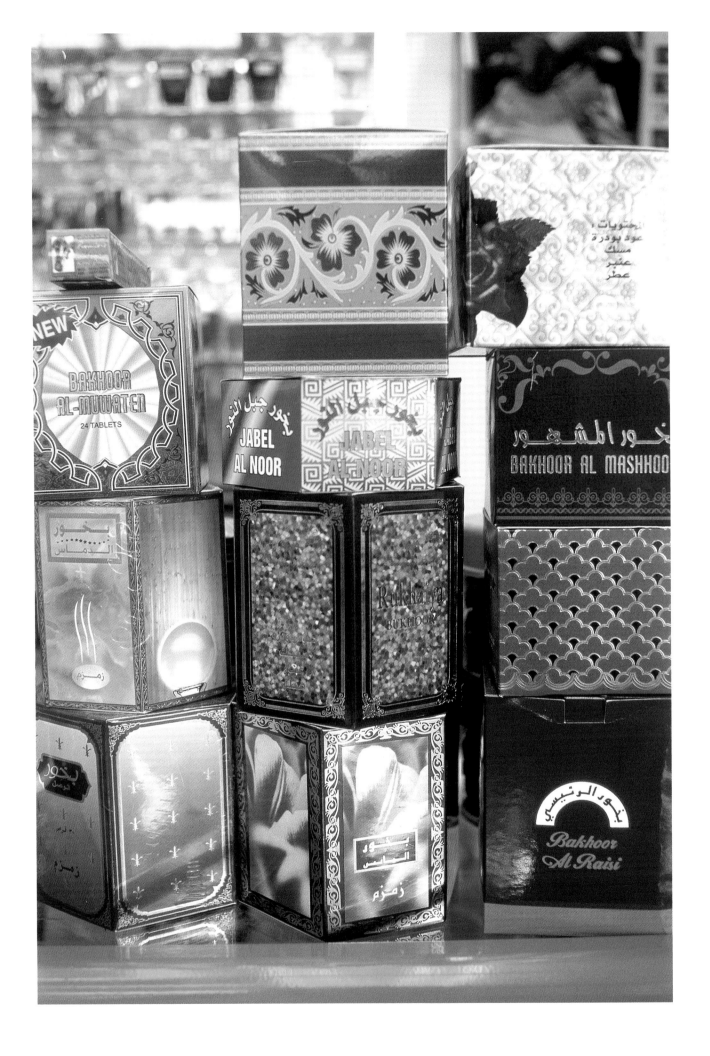

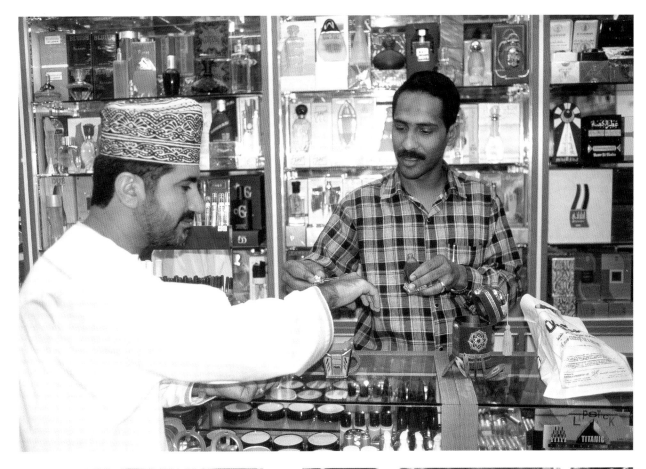

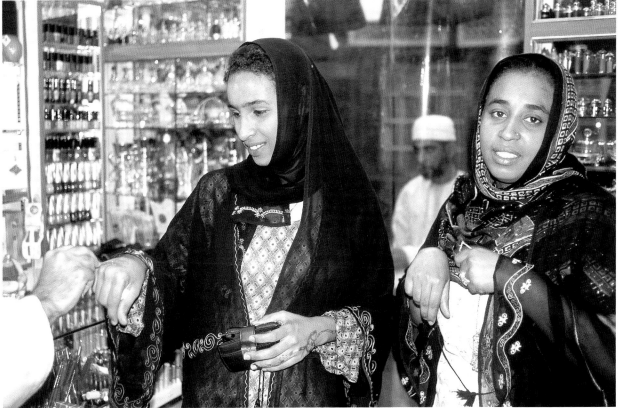

Left: Boxes of incense at the Old Souk, Abu Dhabi

Top and above: Testing fragrances at Muttrah Souk, Muscat

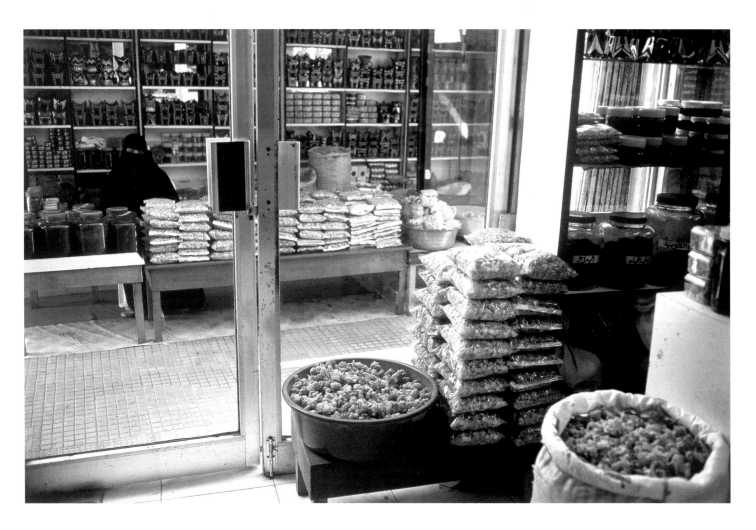

Above: Varying grades of incense at Al-Hosn frankincense souk, Salalah

Right, above: Blending essential oils, Cairo

Far right, above: Egyptian perfumer filling bottles

Right, below: Frankincense trader in Salalah's central souk

While in Egypt I visited a local perfumer on Sphinx Street, in the shadow of the Great Pyramid. He complained that French research chemists took his oils back to Grasse or Lyon, added chemicals and alcohol, gave the product a French name and charged a hefty price. His *Queen Cleopatra* scent, which contains frankincense, smells identical to the far more expensive *Bal à Versailles* by Jean Deprez, in which frankincense also features. 'The art of perfumery', he declared, 'lies in the blending'. He prepares his ingredients in precisely the same way Ancient Egyptians did, by crushing them in a wooden pressing machine to extract the oil. He gives the results wonderfully evocative names such as *Omar Khayyam*, *Harem Perfume* and *Arabian Nights*.

Another Egyptian perfumer at Luxor displays his fragrances in exquisite antique glass bottles, which he was not selling. He was, however, prepared to relate more about the art of blending *aatr*. As in Western perfumery, creating 'notes' of both dynamic and subtle characteristics is the goal of a memorable fragrance. The first is the fast-acting, quickly evaporating top or head note, to be followed by the moderately volatile main bouquet, the heart note. Finally, the base note, frequently containing frankincense, rounds off the *aatr*.

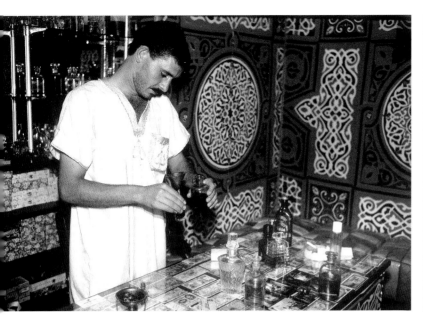
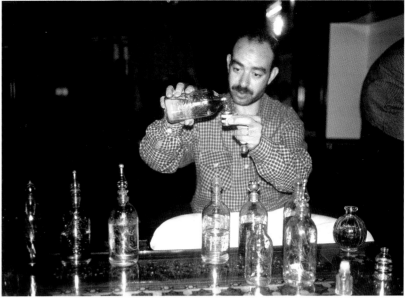

A tradition of generous, and at times courtly hospitality is woven into the very tissue of Arabian life, in which the use of incense and perfume is an indispensable part. At the entrance to many Arab homes, there is a room specifically for guests, the *majlis*, in which a censer burns, smouldering with incense. Arriving guests wrap their clothes expertly around the censer (so as not to catch fire), and in a minute or so become suffused in frankincense. At the end of a meal, guests will be given finger bowls to which a few drops of an *aatr* will have been added, or they may offer their hands to be sprayed with rosewater from an elegant silver flacon. While at a Western occasion, they might be offered chocolates, Arabian guests can choose to dab themselves from one of several small cut-glass flasks of different *aatr* on a crystal tray. Finally, when it is getting late, and the hostess would like to hint that it is time for the guests to go home, the censer will re-appear to be passed around. Once again, they will waft the timeless fragrant smoke of frankincense briefly through their clothes, breathe some in reverently, and make their scented farewells.

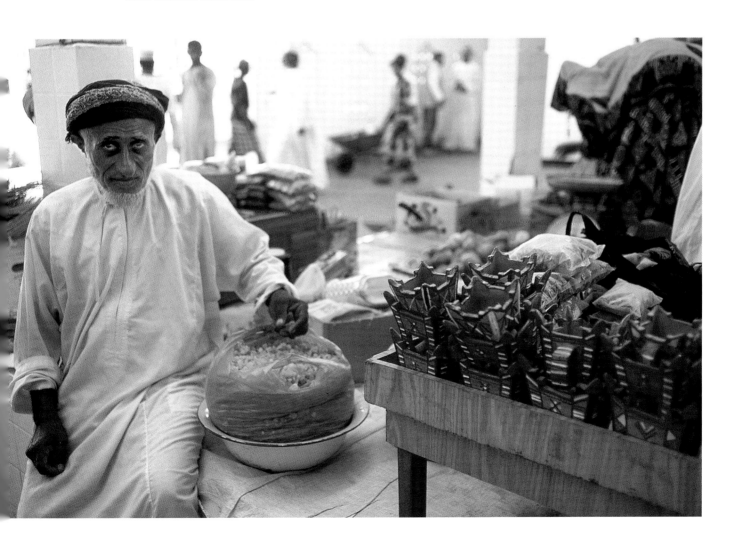

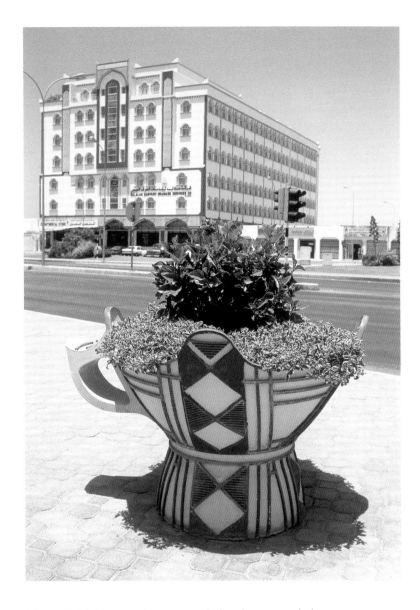

Above: Salalah's street furniture includes planters symbolising frankincense censers

Right: Giant perfume sprinklers dominate a city roundabout in Abu Dhabi

The pungent clouds of fragrance which envelop virtually every passer-by on an Arab street in the sweet aura of *aatr* of jasmine, or the spicier ambience created by *oudh*, sandalwood or frankincense, encapsulate the very spirit of their ancient culture. Giant sculptures of *mabkarahs* or censers in public places demonstrate the significance of incense in this society. As high as houses they dominate the landscape, like the elegant white one on a hill above Muttrah bay at Muscat, in which working dhows jostle with container ships. On either side of the entrance to Sultan Qaboos's palace, are monumental *mabkarahs*. They tower over roundabouts, often acting as fountains; and down in Salalah the censers feature frequently as street furniture. In primary colours they line the roads, doubling up as flower planters, their square, crenellated form recalling the coastal forts of Dhofar's trading history.

Steeped in perfume culture, many Arab households burn incense every day at sunrise and sunset. The purpose is not only to perfume the home and to ward off insects, but to protect those inside by purifying the atmosphere. The Advisor to HM the Sultan for Cultural Affairs, H. E. Abdul Al-Rowas, recalled that as a child in Salalah he asked, 'why do we do this?' and he was told, 'it drives away devilish spirits'. He continued: 'Frankincense starts your day beautifully, you see nature as it is. It helps you to become more transparent with nature, to have no barriers. Engaging with nature, we disengage from materialistic life'.

Frankincense is believed to offer spiritual protection. Ghanim al-Shanfari said that when he was a child, every morning and evening his mother burned it, 'wafting it around the childrens' heads and reading some holy words. At the Qur'anic school, when we had to recite long passages learnt by heart, my mother would give us water in which frankincense and some iron had been soaked overnight. It improved our memories and gave us heart before the test. Frankincense is the root of our culture, passed from generation to generation, and I pray that the new one will continue it'.

The transcendent yet sumptuous aura of aromatics saturates the air at Al-Hosn souk. Located at the heart of Salalah and hugely atmospheric, it was built in 1994 to replace former open stalls and now spreads over several streets. Most of the women, who control the trade, still prefer to sit outside on mats with their scales and bags of various grades of frankincense. Flamboyantly dressed in prints from East Africa or rhinestone-studded black velvet, they sport large expensive rings and jewelled studs in their noses. A formidable force, they are ready to haggle and entice customers into their shops to view the ranks of gaily painted traditional pottery censers, red and gold boxes of their own blend of *bokhur* incense and rows of *aatr*. Small silver kohl boxes called *makhal* contain eye make-up with medicinal

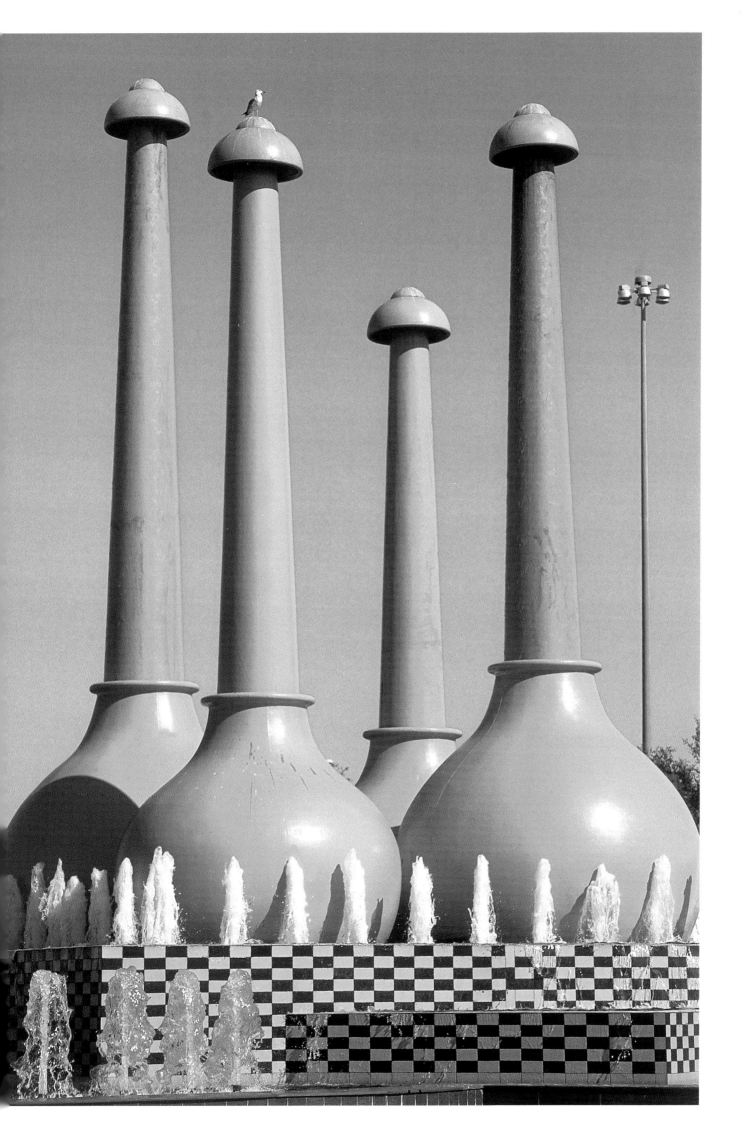

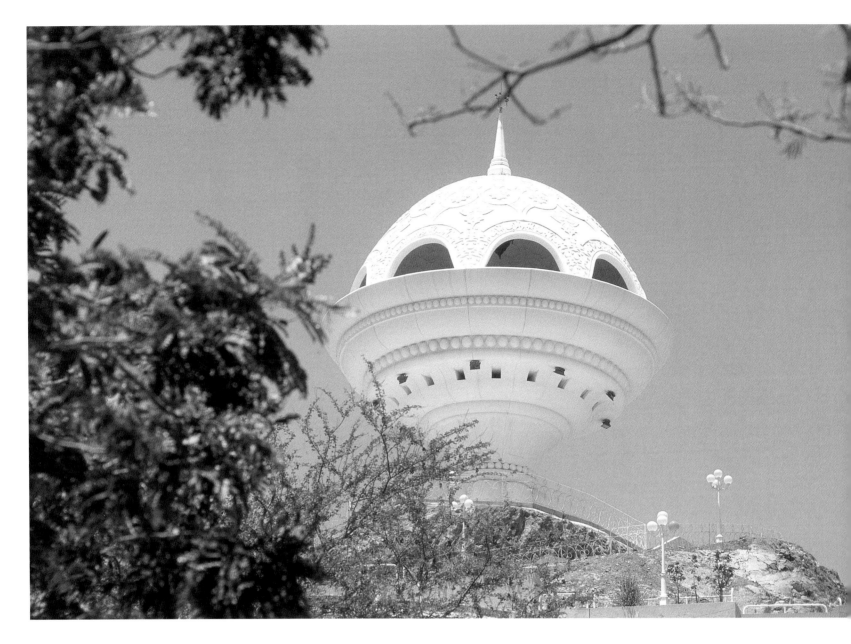

Above: Tower symbolising an incense burner above Muscat

Right: Massive censer icon at Abu Dhabi

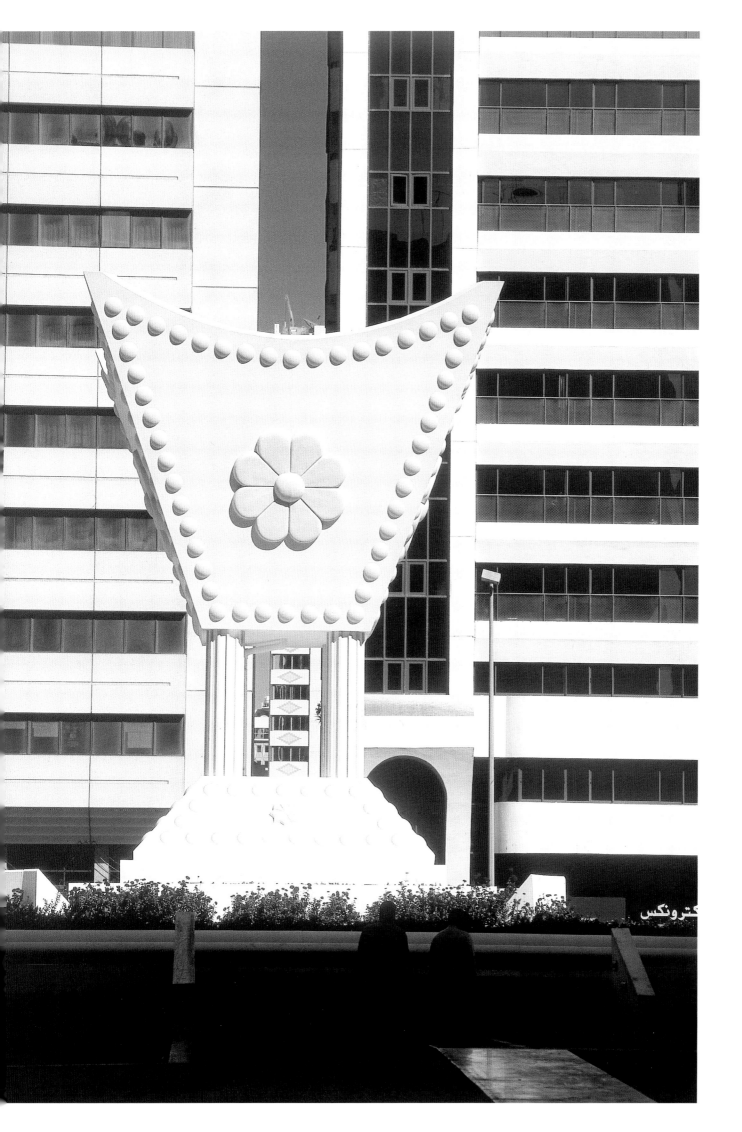

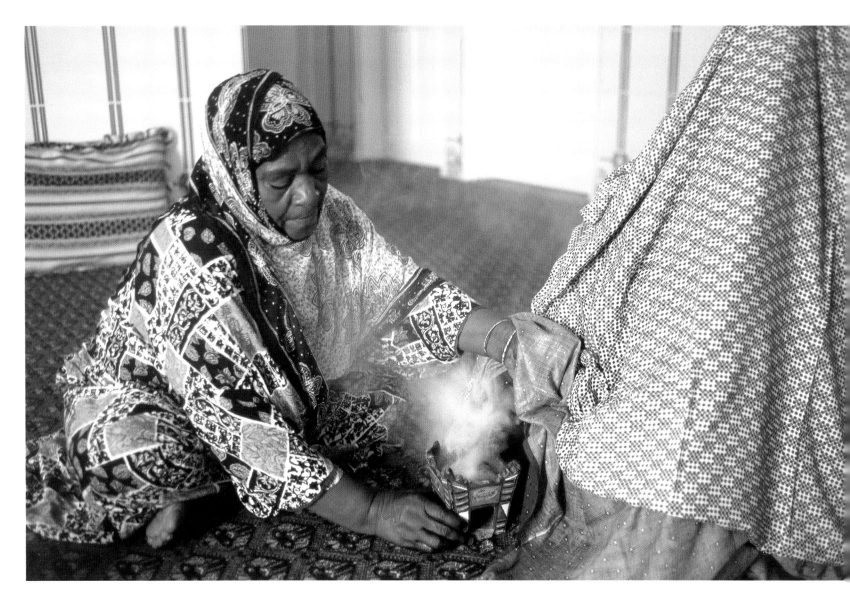

Above: Juma bint Saeed Thowaini places frankincense beneath her clothes frame
Right: Juma filling tins with her own *bokhur* incense

qualities. It is composed of frankincense sometimes mixed with antimony and the roots of *Aerva javanica*. Frankincense is also a constituent of perfumed pastes such as *mukhammara*, which is applied to the hair.

One of the most highly respected dealers and incense creators at the frankincense souk is Juma bint Saeed Thowaini, who learnt the trade from her mother. Such entrepreneurialism and secret skills have been passed down the generations. She took me to her mansion and first showed me how she censes clothes and bed linen. She draped them on a specially constructed wooden frame, which in the past would have been made of latticed palm stalks. After placing the frankincense in an hourglass censer called a *makbar* beneath the frame, she sat down to tell me the feminine side of the incense story. 'All Omani women know how to make their own perfume', she began, and traditionally, it contains frankincense. As a bride, she had been prepared for her wedding with a variety of scented body treatments. Rather like the Ancient Greeks, different fragrances are used for different parts of the body.

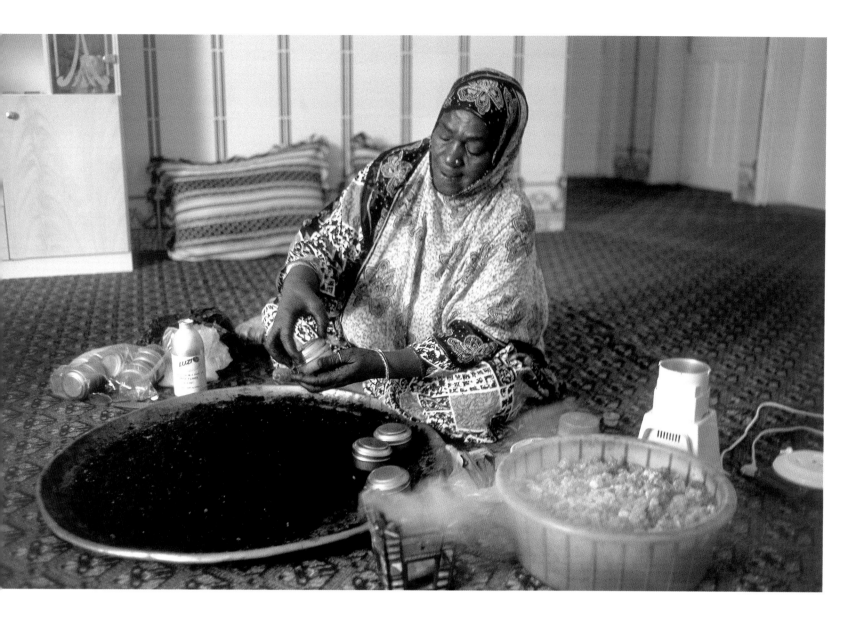

Just as the Ancient Egyptians applied frankincense unguent as an anti-ageing skin treatment, Dhofari brides have their faces smoothed with the oil or paste for its regenerative properties. At her wedding ceremony, Juma's female relatives started ululating and waving smoking censers high in the air. Meanwhile during a separate celebration, the relatives of her fiancé were dancing around censers. 'When the time came to go to my husband's house, I took with me my incense frame on which jewellery was hung. Dhofari women drink frankincense water to help deliver babies when they won't come out. After the birth of each of my children, both the baby and I were censed, to purify and protect us.' Juma also said that following ancient funeral rites, 'the dead are anointed with camphor, saffron and rose *aatr*, and for the sake of the angels, frankincense is burned'.

All the time Juma was talking to me, her hands were busy mixing *bokhur* incense according to the recipe passed on by her mother on her wedding day, and which she would not divulge. She did say that she blends expensive imported woods such as *oudh*, sandalwood and *jus* (perfume essence from Switzerland) but not frankincense. The prices she charges reflect these high costs, whereas local frankincense is available at around £1.50 ($2.77/€2.20) a kilo wholesale. Every woman blending *bokhur* has her own recipe, and some do indeed use frankincense. Juma grinds her ingredients in a coffee-grinder, and cooks it with sugar and rosewater. She exports her *bokhur* primarily to GCC (Gulf Cooperation Council) countries, but she keeps the best quality at home.

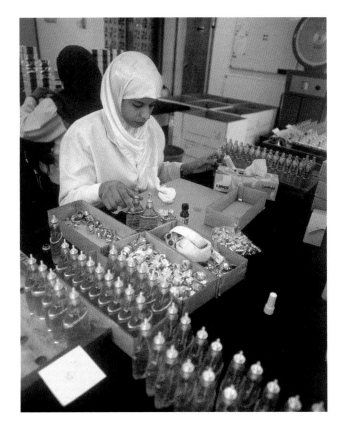

AMOUAGE – WAVES OF EMOTION

In 1983 a vision of reviving the great Arabian tradition of perfume creation became reality in Oman. It was originally a move designed to diversify Oman's trade away from reliance on the Sultanate's two present-day natural assets—oil and natural gas. Thanks to these revenues Oman had in just fifty years leapt from the Middle Ages into the twenty-first century, and today exudes an air of palpable high-tech prosperity. But supplies are finite, and one day a senior minister was discussing the problem with colleagues. He suggested that the traditional Omani skill of creating *aatr* from frankincense and myrrh could be re-established and transformed into a modern international industry.

Above: Gluing on bands and collar caps at the Amouage perfume factory, Muscat

Below: Distilling oil from resin crystals at Amouage

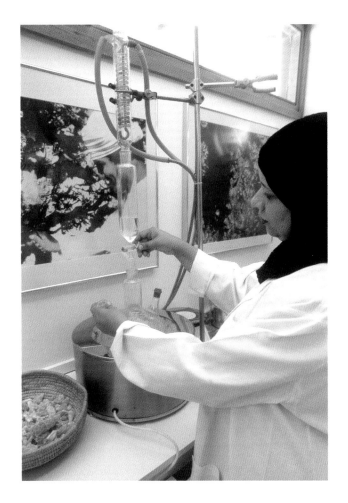

The minister was His Highness A'Sayyid Hamad bin Hamood bin Said, a member of the royal family, with a dynastic connection to the frankincense trade. In the Arab way, he consulted two of his sons, Sami and Badr, who were already running a flourishing international trading company named Sabco. Western-educated and leading lavish lifestyles, they decided that creating high-end perfumes would make commercial sense. The brothers formed a company, hired a British marketing consultancy and ordered a factory to be built on the airport side of the suburbs of Muscat. Within three months, working round the clock, shifts of Asian labourers constructed a *bijou* operation, complete with facilities for visitors, and offering guided tours of the factory, shopping opportunities and traditional Arab hospitality. An ornamental pool and landscaped garden containing—naturally—a frankincense tree, completed the dream.

Just as the three Magi took their precious gifts to Bethlehem, these two Omani entrepreneurs took frankincense to Paris. Their company, Amouage, made frankincense its signature in almost all their fragrances, which Badr called 'the best perfume in the world. It would be appreciated by women and men of both East and West, launched as a message to the world that frankincense still has value'.

For famous French nose, Guy Robert, who was asked to create a perfume 'for people who don't have to ask the price', and who had already created several classics such as *Madame Rochas, Calèche*

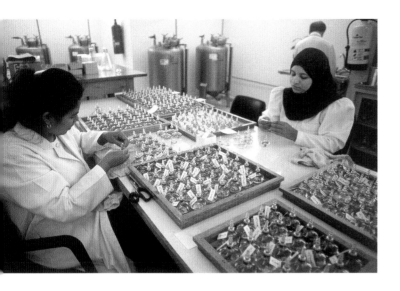

and *Gucci*, this was the opportunity of a lifetime. 'In my kind of work', he said, 'you always have a dream of creating *the* perfume, the one in which you are given free rein to use all the essences of your experience, your thought and imagination, no matter how expensive'. Having flown to Dhofar to imbibe the ancient culture of frankincense, back in his atelier, Robert set his nose to work mastering its olfactory nuances. With *carte blanche* to use the world's finest ingredients, he added them to silver frankincense and the delicate Omani rockrose.

At the press conference to launch Amouage as a company, as well the eponymous first fragrance, Badr bin Hamood said that for his family this was more than a business venture, it was an act of patriotism: 'Perfumes were produced thousands of years ago in the Middle East and Oman. And while we are delighted to re-establish this industry in its original birthplace, we also looked at our traditional silver craft, which was in a state of decline, and we felt that this too, should be part of the project'.

Accordingly, after *le jus* has been shipped from France, it is diluted, macerated and bottled in Oman. The finished product is presented in superb containers, revivals of the Omani tradition of silver working, centred on the fortress town of Nizwa. Centuries of craft expertise in chasing, engraving and granulating silver produced two designs for wonderfully ornate male and female perfume containers inspired by Arabian history. One is based on the handle of the now ceremonial dagger, the *khanjar*, an icon of Omani cultural pride which is incorporated into the Sultanate's crest. The other reflects the graceful curves of the *qubba* domes of mosques. These forms were developed by the London firm Asprey into hallmarked caskets of sterling silver gilded in 24-carat gold. Nearly 25 years later, they

Above: Placing hangtags on bottles of Amouage perfume

Below: Aatr, essential oils, at the Amouage shop in City Centre complex, Muscat

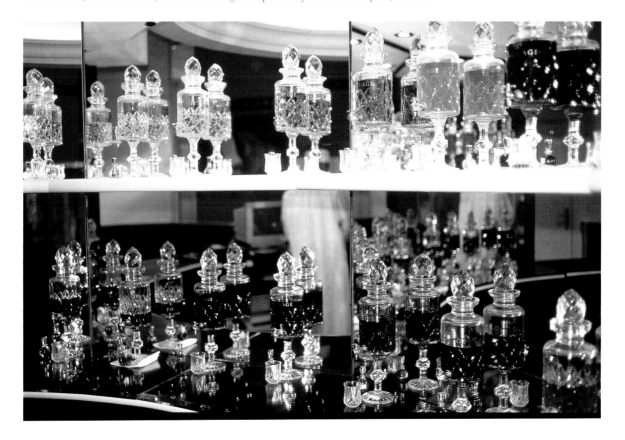

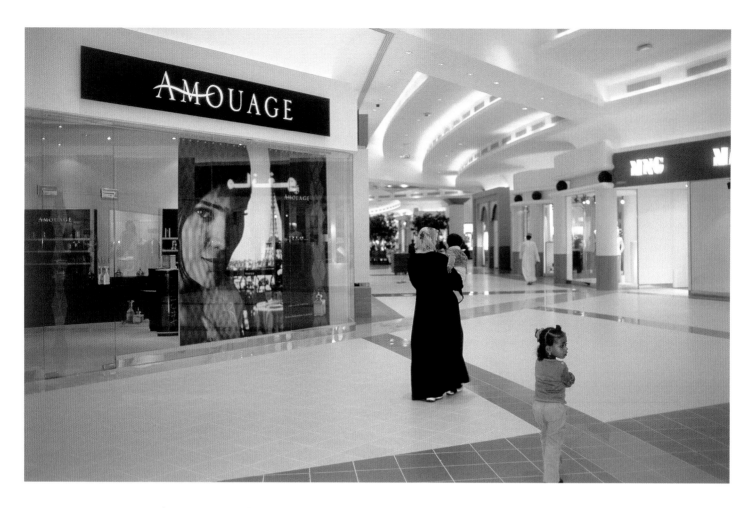

Above: Amouage shop in Muscat shopping centre

Right, above: *Dia* perfume in bottles embellished with pink gold
Right, below: The Amouage range

have become classics in Amouage's Heritage Collection, their Ultra Luxury range. For customers 'who don't have to ask the price', Amouage offers specially designed containers embedded with precious or semi-precious stones, or exquisite flasks of lapis lazuli, jasper or blue agate. Amouage is often presented to visiting dignitaries and has become the diplomatic gift of kings.

The name 'Amouage' is a French transliteration of the Arabic *amwaj*, meaning 'waves' (both marine and emotional). After a visit by the international media invited to Dhofar to learn about the new company and visit the frankincense groves, the perfume editor of British *Vogue* reported: 'There has never been a perfume created to be so special. Amouage captures history, culture, tradition and elegance'.

At first the international marketing campaign concentrated on evoking fantasies of exotic Arabia and the allure of the Eastern perfume heritage, as well as its unabashed extravagance: 'Amouage is the Rolls Royce of perfumes', Associated Press was told. In the lively perfume culture of the Gulf, the image of Amouage has been carefully burnished as offering 'the most valuable perfumes in the world', but they are certainly not the most expensive. Both there and in global outlets, the youth market is increasingly significant. Young women require 'freshness', not what they perceive as heavy, woody perfumes of the Oriental family; and they are not so responsive to pricey snob appeal. Amouage scents have subsequently

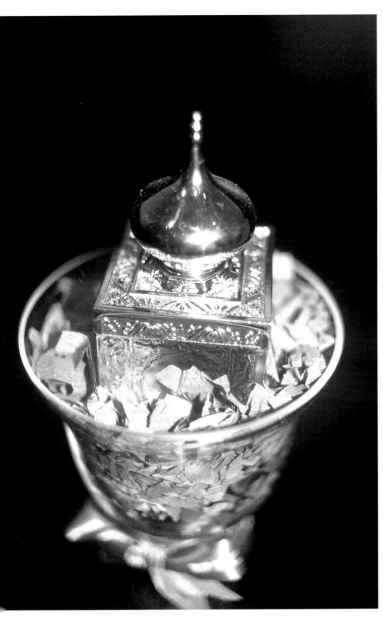

been developed in three ranges, from the Ultra Luxury of the Heritage Collection in its sumptuous flasks through Luxury and Premium to Youth. Using more modest materials to create containers that still make a bow to the Arabian connection, more recent perfumes evoke that contemporary idiom. Yet those same young women want value for their money and therefore longevity. Frankincense in the base notes gives them that tenacity and depth.

However, these modern yet timeless creations are certainly not for bargain hunters, nor are they available on every high street or Gulf shopping mall. Luxury will always lure its own market, just as frankincense did for so long. At the London launch of *Dia* (in the Luxury range), perfume editors sipped pink champagne to match the pink gold adorning scent bottles. As Sayyid Khalid bin Hamood, youngest brother of the family, and now Chair of Amouage, said: 'We are very proud of the way our products reflect the contemporary globalised world, combining the two-thousand-year-old heritage of Arabian perfumery with the best expertise European perfumery can offer'.

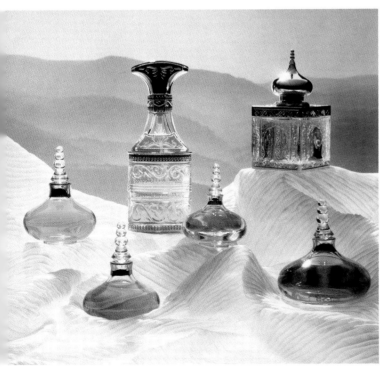

Here's the smell of blood still. All the perfumes of Arabia will not sweeten this little hand.

William Shakespeare, *Macbeth*, act V, scene 1

The modern European fragrance industry maintains the links that historically frankincense created with the Arab world. Writing about Al-Kindi's ninth-century *Perfume Recipes*, Nigel Groom pinpoints the link connecting frankincense—*per fumum*—through Arabian and finally European scents: 'I realised that in that work I had found key evidence to demonstrate how the medieval Arab perfume makers had been the bridge in perfume history between ancient and modern times. Perfumery could now be seen as an art with a continuous history of development since the dawn of civilisation.'[1]

Even when Europe was in the grip of the Dark Ages the sacred and medical functions performed by frankincense and other aromatics survived, and in privileged homes incense burners were popular to cover up unwelcome odours. But the use of perfume purely for aesthetic or hedonistic purposes was unthinkable. The early Christians had taken an ascetic stance: in the fourth century St Augustine forbade all pleasures of the flesh in reaction to Roman excesses, both in terms of quantity of frankincense burned for a multitude of gods, and profligacy in the use of perfume (the Romans used the very wings of doves to release trails of fragrance as they fluttered above the *vomitaria*). In France the Emperor Charlemagne attempted to imitate the perfumed fountains of the Roman Empire, but the scheme foundered on the philistine attitudes of the times.

Yet the yearning for scent could not be crushed. At medieval courts and great houses indigenous fragrant herbs such as rosemary were strewn on the floor and a flower essence (rosewater was a particular favourite) was on the table of every self-respecting northern baron for ablutions before and after meals. A thousand and one tales of the 'perfumes of Araby' began to seep into Europe, redolent with the promise of odalisque exotica. Crusaders returning from Arabia during the eleventh and thirteenth centuries brought home the real thing, and this had the effect of reviving ancient customs of personal hygiene. Arabian oils for bathing and skincare, and floral essences for hair-washing, became the rage for the fortunate fashionable few. Pomanders were the must-have accessories, after the Holy Roman Emperor Frederick I had been presented with one by King Baldwin of Constantinople in 1174. Pomanders were filled with solid perfume, hardened aromatic substances such as frankincense, and animal products including musk and ambergris.

Just as information about the source of Arabia's wealth—frankincense—had been closely guarded, so the skills of Arab perfumery were kept hidden from European eyes for a long time. But in the eleventh century the Arab physician and perfumer Avicenna went to live in southern Spain, then ruled by the Moors, taking with him his still, and thus Spain became one of the very first countries in Europe to manufacture perfume. After the Christians reclaimed Spain, the Arab perfumers, who were granted permission to remain, scrupulously guarded their secret formulae and technology. But little by little the Spaniards succeeded in penetrating their arts, and annexed all the accompanying trade.

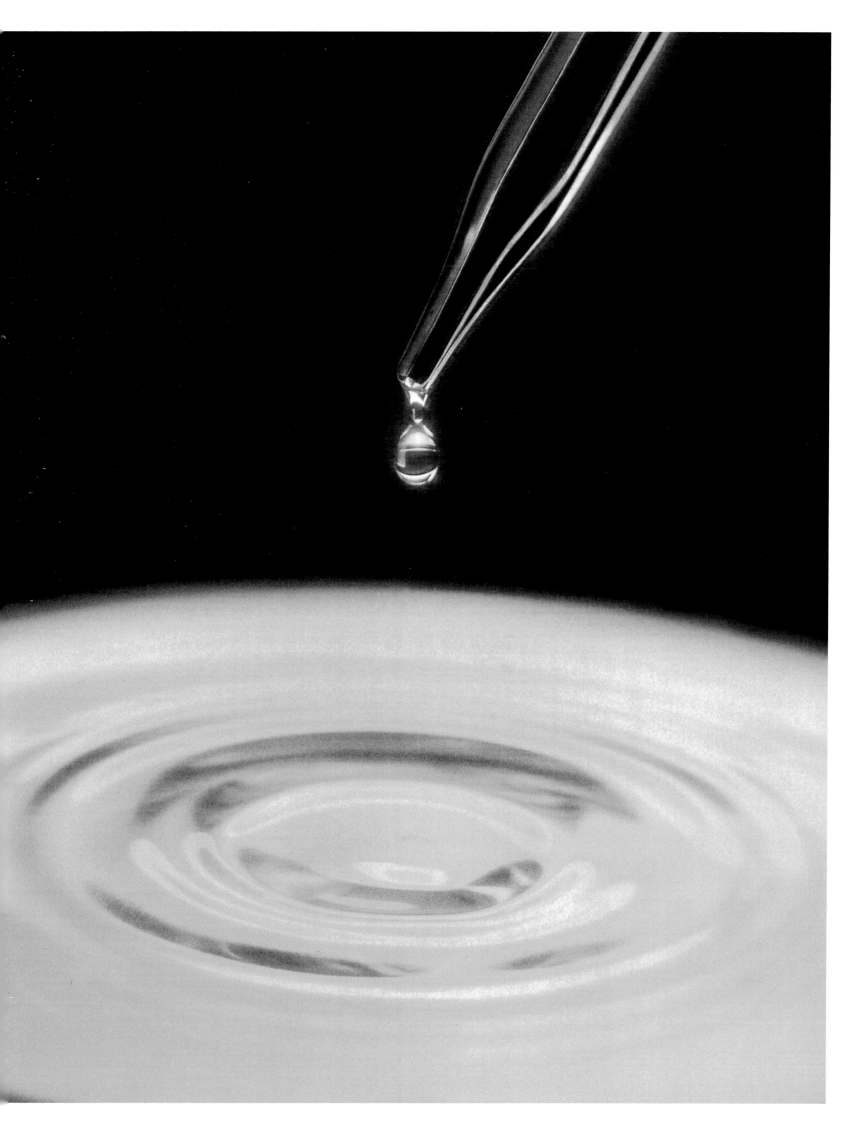

Although King Philippe Auguste of France had in 1190 officially recognised the creation of perfume as a professional skill, and granted the artisans a charter, France did not become the capital of the fragrance industry until the seventeenth century. As trade rapidly expanded with the East, it was Italy that spearheaded the Renaissance, leading Europe's creative and fashionable avant-garde for several centuries. Some Italian city-states were doing business with Arab and Persian merchants, but it was Venice which held a monopoly on aromatic, perfume and spice imports from the Middle East. The city offered access to perfume materials from Arabia, Egypt, India and China to the many innovative perfumers who worked there. As the Renaissance flowered, they catered for the European hunger for new and exotic symbols of luxury and style, experimenting with the woody, sensuous smell of frankincense, familiar in churches, but not for personal use.

Finally frankincense evolved, via the perfumes of Arabia, into those of France, which is still the undisputed heart of the modern fragrance industry. The year was 1533, and the catalyst an Italian princess, Catherine de' Medici. She came to France to marry the future King Henry II, accompanied by her perfumer, Renato Bianco, and all the sophistication of the Florentine court. She also brought Cosimo Ruggiero, her alchemist who, it was rumoured, was as adept at preparing poisons as operating his distillation equipment. He allegedly prepared the poisoned scented gloves which killed Henry's mistress and Catherine's rival, Diane de Poitiers.

As an Italian Catherine was fully conversant with the glories of Arab perfumery, and sponsored a laboratory to study perfume making, located in Grasse, an area of southern France ideally suited to the production of perfume plants. Already operating as a thriving centre of scented glove-making, the little town of Grasse became the foundation stone of the contemporary Western perfume industry.

Below: Jean-Paul Guerlain creating a perfume formula with paper wands

Right: Perfumer Maurice Maurin surrounded by his perfume 'organ'.

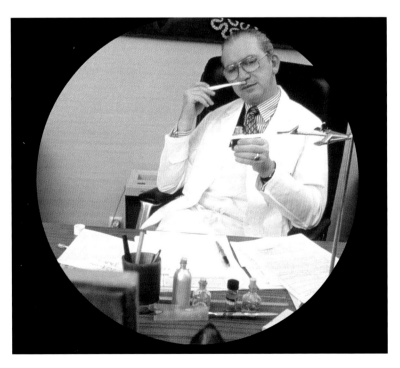

Long after one has forgotten what a woman wore, the memory of her fragrance lingers.

Christian Dior

How can one identify the elusive fragrance of frankincense as a keynote in a memorable scent? Is it possible to bottle such rich references? What role does frankincense play in the creation of the modern industry, with its £60-billion annual turnover? As Michael Edwards wrote: 'A great perfume is a work of art. It is silent poetry, invisible body language. It can lift our days, enrich our nights and create the milestones of our memories. Fragrance is liquid emotion.'[2]

Most perfumes containing frankincense belong to the Oriental group of fragrances, the incense usually a component of their base notes. Perfume is divided into four main groups, and further sub-divided into

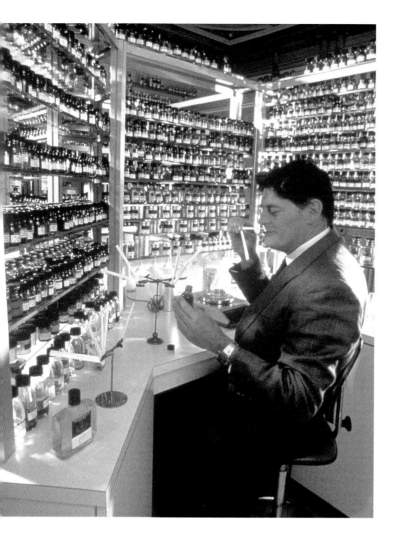

'families'. The groups are Oriental, Woody, Floral and Fresh. Within the Oriental group, the family names indicate how the divisions become blurred, as ingredients from other groups are blended with classically Oriental ones such as frankincense. At the heart of the Oriental group is 'Oriental' itself, whose notes include resins and musk. The French tend to call the whole Oriental group 'Amber' or 'Ambre', but for the rest of the world, there is a family named 'Amber Oriental', containing vanilla and synthetic ambergris (ambergris obtained from whales is no longer ecologically acceptable). 'Soft Oriental' perfumes contain other incenses, while 'Spicy Orientals' resonate with culinary spices such as cinnamon, nutmeg and cloves. 'Woody Oriental' is characterised by sandalwood, cedar, vetiver and patchouli; while 'Floral Orientals' bloom with orange flowers and sweet spices. Further permutations include 'Sweet Orientals', 'Fruity Orientals' and even 'Fruity Florientals'. The most recent sub-division of the Oriental group is the 'Sheer Oriental' family. As the name would suggest it is lighter and less dominating than the classic Oriental.

This Oriental group of perfumes tends to be strong, spicy and exotic, with a specific warm, heavy, sensuous sweetness, though frankincense injects a balancing freshness. They have a lasting quality derived from their base notes of frankincense, sandalwood and musk. The following fabulous fragrances all contain frankincense and yet are very different from each other: *L'Heure Bleue* by Guerlain, *Ysatis* by Givenchy, *Obsession* by Calvin Klein, *Chanel No. 22*, and *Frankincense & Myrrh* by Czech & Speake. Men could sample *L'Egoïste* by Chanel, *Dalí Pour Homme* by Salvador Dalí, *Jazz* by Yves Saint Laurent, and *Nino Cerruti Pour Homme* by Uniperf.

As well as contributing that opulent yet austere note to fragrance, the alcohol-soluble resinoid of frankincense is valued as a fixative in scents. The essential oil and absolute tend to be used as fixatives for creams, lotions, soaps and detergents, as well as in perfumes. The French, who are still the driving force in fragrance, speak of *la persistence*, the amount of time a scent lasts on the skin. The chemical function of a fixative such as frankincense is not only to prolong that olfactory tenacity, but also to ensure that the other materials of the composition last and bind together into a harmonious symphony. A fixative does this because it has a high molecular weight and less volatile constituents, giving it a slow rate of evaporation. This causes the rest of the ingredients to evaporate more gradually, progressing from one note into another as that ingredient fades away. Without an effective fixative to enable the fragrance to develop, it can be muddy or flat; a cacophony of impressions crashing into each other at once, producing a one-note tune.

Every great 'nose' is obsessed with ensuring that his or her creation leaves a memorable *sillage*—the olfactory trail bequeathed by its wearer. To create that subtle aura is a challenge, since with a substance such as frankincense, more than a judiciously tiny quantity can become over-powering. One has only to recall the impact of the launch of *Youth Dew* by Estée Lauder, which contains frankincense. It coined the phrase 'olfactory assault', and along with other knockout perfumes, was banned by some restaurateurs.

Another reason why perfumers are cautious about the amount of frankincense they use is that not only can it imbue a fragrance with dramatic effect, it also has a commanding aroma in its own right. In what has become a classic reference work for student perfumers, Steven Arctander describes the smell of frankincense, which he classifies as olibanum: 'It has a fresh balsamic, yet dry and resinous, slightly green odour with a typical, fruity-green top note…of unripe apples…. A certain pepperiness is mellowed with a rich, sweet-woody, balsamic undertone.'[3] Arctander goes on to describe the methods of extraction of the absolute, the oil and the concrete or resinoid of frankincense. 'Olibanum absolute is usually prepared by the large users themselves, since the preparation demands great knowledge of the raw material, and a strict control of the olibanum to be extracted'. (The Omanis would appear to have completely renounced the possibility of control of the processing of their raw material not only to Alexandria in ancient times, but to Europe and the US today.)

Arctander's book clarifies how contemporary perfumers use frankincense or olibanum as an absolute, obtained by alcohol extraction, the essential oil by steam distillation, and the resinoid by hydrocarbon or ethyl alcohol (ethanol) extraction. The classical use of frankincense, as we have seen, is as a key ingredient in many Oriental bases, Arctander noting that 'a truly "Oriental" note can be created by adding sandalwood, vetiver and cinnamon bark. It is also used in "powder" type perfumes, and gives delightful effects in citrus colognes where it modifies the sweetness of bergamot and orange oils'.

Recent research has revealed that the principle ingredient of gums such as frankincense and myrrh, resin alcohols, are very similar in chemical structure to the human steroid molecule, testosterone, the hormone which drives both male and female libido. Perfume has a piquant pedigree in aphrodisiac uses. In some languages, the word for kissing and smelling is the same, an intimate tribute of appreciation. To this day Sudanese women mix frankincense, cloves and cinnamon with part of a sea-snail, known as *Unguis odoratus*, apply it to their genitalia, and then strike the match.

To discover future trends in fragrance and how frankincense figures at the cutting-edge of this hugely lucrative industry, I visited the French Institut Supérieur International du Parfum, de la Cosmétique et de l'Aromatique Alimentaire (ISIPCA), which was founded in 1970 by Jean-Jacques Guerlain to train future professionals in the fragrance and cosmetic industries. The Institute is backed by the Versailles Chamber of Commerce as well as major commercial players in the business, and offers two-year university diplomas in partnership with the University of Versailles, as well as sandwich courses. Students on the European Fragrance & Cosmetic Master diploma course (EFCM) come from all over the world to spend one year at Versailles gaining expertise in the scientific, technical and historical aspects of perfumery. They spend their second year at either the University of Plymouth, England, or at Padua University, in Italy, acquiring marketing and business administration skills, with a four-month placement in the laboratories and marketing departments of host companies such as L'Oréal and Quest.

The Institute's International Manager, Annie Towhill, told me: 'We obtain frankincense crystals from Ethiopia and Somalia, which we use in preference to the synthetic. The crystals are processed into resinous oil by two methods: steam distillation or organic solvent. We find the first method gives a very powerful and aggressive top note; the second a resinous absolute, which is more a bottom note'. When pressed about trends, Towhill said that until recently the emphasis had been on floral fragrances, but the future looked distinctly Oriental. One of the senior lecturers and herself a perfume professional, Marina Jung-Allegret, agreed with this prediction, adding: 'Frankincense is one of those raw materials that we don't use much, but it would be interesting to re-discover, especially as the Oriental trend is coming back, even if it's lighter, more floral than in the past. I can imagine it being used again in trendy perfumes, perhaps marketed as an evening scent, or a 'private collection' perfume, something élitist and very special, as part of a niche concept. We have frankincense in our memory: because of its use in church there is a quality in perfume we call "on sent l'église" [smell of the church]. It's a very rich odour with many facets, warm, sensual and resinous, yet piney, almost sparkling and long-lasting'.

Master Degree students at ISIPCA create a project across the three disciplines they study—perfumery, cosmetics and food flavouring—to produce a scent, a beauty product and a culinary item. 'No one is creating a fragrance around frankincense,' said Jung-Allegret. But one of her students, Catherine Masson, added: 'I love frankincense: I think it's very sparkling compared to opoponax or myrrh. It's very under-estimated and under-used. It's certainly not explored here much, and it would be interesting to discover. Everybody says the future is for perfumes with stronger character, more daring—light, floral Orientals with lots of air and space. Personally, I hope that a combination of frankincense and musk will return'. But this student admitted: 'The difficulty for me in using frankincense is that it seems spicy and smoky, which I don't think are elements which appeal to young women, and in the last few years younger and younger markets have been targeted. An eighteen-year-old might say: "I don't want to smell old, like a thirty-year-old!" So I would be interested in making frankincense appeal to a younger audience, by playing on its duality, its freshness as well as its spice, maybe by using orange with it as a top note'.

I was surprised to discover that in the Cosmetics unit of the Academy, which includes skincare, the use of frankincense as an anti-ageing element, was unknown. However, another progressive student volunteered that she was aware that L'Oréal is pursuing research and development on this theme. It seems that even a giant multi-national company has heard of Cleopatra's secret....

CHAPTER FIVE

A GUIDE TO FRANKINCENSE TODAY

Oman is still permeated today with frankincense, and throughout the Middle East it is used in ways which combine ancient tradition and modern customs. A censer puffs away steadily in public-eating outlets from five star to fast food, as well as in the lavatories—not just for obvious reasons, but because this is where evil spirits or jinn are reputed to lurk. Animal byres are censed at sunset, again not just because of the disinfectant and fumigant attributes of frankincense, but to protect the animals from malign forces.

The Salalah incense trader, Juma bint Saeed Thowaini, related how she and each of her newborn babies were censed immediately after delivery, as both purification and celebration. On a strictly practical basis, frankincense would reduce the risk of post-natal infections and scarring, and aid the expelling of the placenta. The red section of bark revealed when a tree is cut is traditionally used to relieve morning sickness during pregnancy, and believed to increase the intelligence of the foetus. During childbirth mothers are censed to ease delivery, and afterwards, incense is burnt near the baby's cradle to honour and protect the new life. When the mother leaves her home for the first time after forty days, again she is censed.

Nowadays Western pharmaceutical practice in the Middle East interacts with what might be perceived as 'folk medicine'. Nevertheless, belief persists in the therapeutic value of an aromatic such as frankincense, which has proved so efficient over so many thousands of years. Limbs may no longer be splinted between pieces of frankincense bark made rigid and antiseptic by freshly smeared resin. It is rare, except perhaps in remote rural communities in the Nejd, that a 'sticking plaster' of the gum will bind together and help excrete any pus from an open wound. Modern dentists use filling material other than salt pounded with frankincense. But Dhofari people still add it to their drinking water to act as a diuretic and to cleanse the kidneys. I was given some too, to use as a chewing gum, intended to strengthen my teeth and gums, as well as act as a breath freshener. In many traditional societies, pounded frankincense, taken internally, was a cure-all for medical complaints of the stomach and liver, tumours and tuberculosis, shock, paralysis and fever. With its anti-inflammatory and analgesic benefits it was also used to treat inflammation of the urethra, vulva and genitals. As Karen Pereczes reports: 'The resin was often crushed, mixed with myrrh and dried aloe juice to make an antiseptic powder for wounds and was also used to stop internal and external bleeding… (It is) an inhalant treatment to relieve headaches, bronchitis, coughs and colds and asthma.'[1] This treatment is carried on today by Western aromatherapists. Pereczes continues: 'Ancient (Arab) books recommend it to treat joint pains and arthritis by suspending the aching limb over the smoke of equal parts of frankincense, mastic and lavender'. Current research in the West is investigating the anti-inflammatory properties of frankincense for the treatment of rheumatoid arthritis and rheumatism.

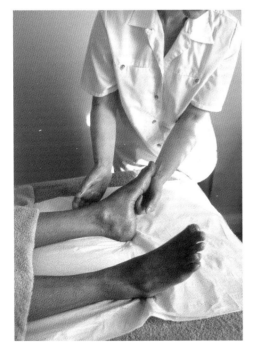 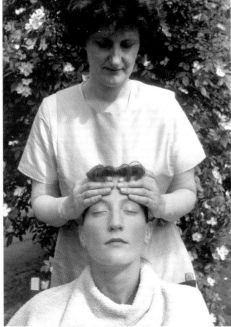 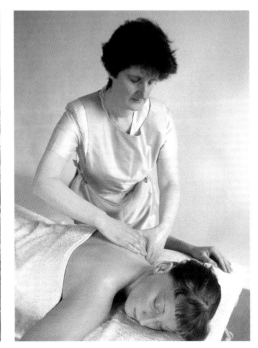

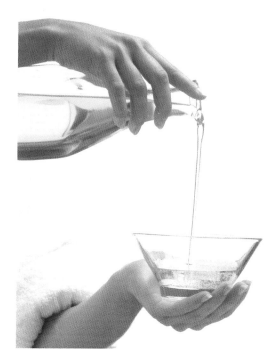

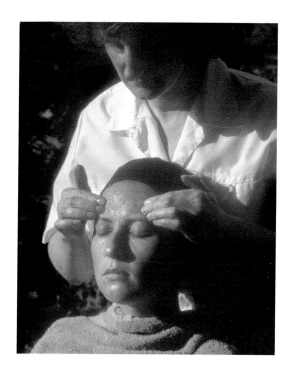

Far left: Foot massage using
essential oil

Left, centre: Temple treatment
with Meta Aromatherapy

Near left: Christine Westwood
applies shoulder massage

Right: Frankincense oil
for aromatherapy

Far right: Face massage

Martin Watt and Wanda Sellar write: 'Resin obtained from *Boswellia serrata* (local name *salai gugal*) has been used in traditional medicine in India for treating chronic inflammatory arthritis. Some of the resin's constituents called boswellia acids have been tested. In trials on isolated tissues these compounds were found to have an anti-inflammatory effect. Of particular interest was the report that boswellia acids seem to have a very low toxicity'.[2]

The Yemeni Al-Haymi comments that bathing with a blend of frankincense, honey and olive oil helps rheumatism. Interestingly, he adds that frankincense is 'an excellent stimulant of appetite in the 100-and-over age group'.

USING FRANKINCENSE

Every perfume is a medicine.

Ancient Chinese saying

At the Taxila Museum in Pakistan, I saw a terra-cotta object judged to be five thousand years old, from the Indus valley civilisation. It was a still used to extract essential oils from plants and discovered at Mohendojaro alongside a number of perfume and cosmetic containers. The science we call aromatherapy, which heals using the organic essences of aromatic plants, has always been inextricably linked with perfumery and ritual religious functions. In a plant the fragrance *is* its essential oil, and contained at the heart of this oil is its life force or soul.

Aromatic materials such as frankincense are central to contemporary complementary or holistic healing. Interest in this gentler, more personal form of therapy based on natural, traditional remedies has grown as it has become evident that conventional Western medicine, with its expense and often unwelcome side-effects, cannot answer all our problems.

Treatments such as aromatherapy are holistic in the sense that the practitioner will work with the patient to explore their mental, emotional and spiritual concerns, delving into the origins of the experience of *dis*ease or lack of ease. An essential oil such as frankincense affects the limbic system, that primitive region of consciousness, reaching deep into the psyche. On one level aromatherapy can be seen as a pleasurable anti-stress treatment, but there is increasing evidence that stress has a debilitating effect on the immune system. One of the main attributes with which frankincense is associated in modern aromatherapy is to support the immune system.

Aromatherapy works by introducing the life force—the energy contained at the heart of an essential oil—into the body and thereby releasing its therapeutic powers. With controlled delivery, usually by massage and via the olfactory system, the medicinal properties of the molecules or terpenes within the essential oil or blend of oils enter the bloodstream either through the pores of the skin or by inhalation, having a specific effect on target organs and acting as natural antibiotics. The synergistic effect of massage and pleasant smells affects the central nervous system, a fact corroborated by observation of pulse rate and blood pressure.

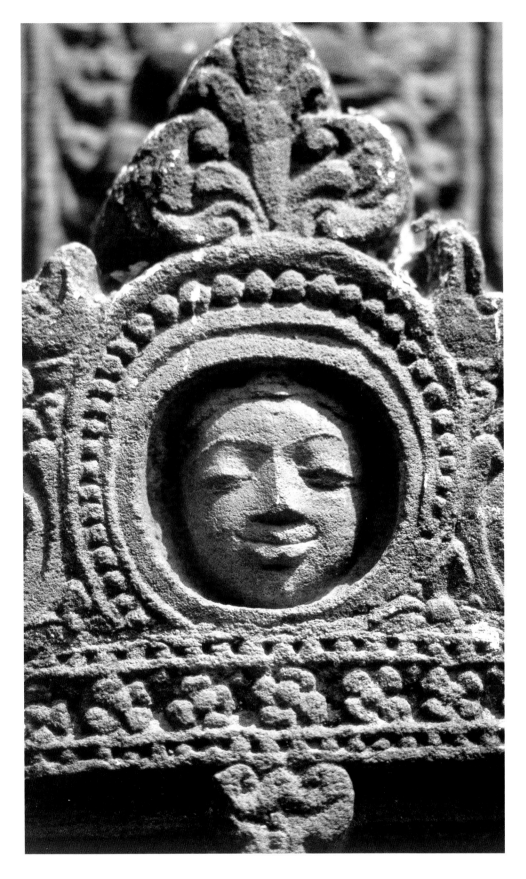

GETTING PHYSICAL

The properties of frankincense to treat physical disorders are defined as analgesic, antiseptic, anti-inflammatory, decongestant and expectorant. Historically frankincense was used to treat serious conditions from leprosy to meningitis, with a lengthy list between. Nowadays in the West complementary health professionals employ it as a clearly effective remedy for a range of physiological problems. With its soothing ability to relax a patient, and to slow down and deepen and the breath, it is used to treat chest complaints such as asthma, bronchitis, influenza and colds; and its expectorant aspect clears up mucous conditions such as catarrh. Its antiseptic qualities treat laryngitis and sinusitis, and have a beneficial effect on ulcers, abscesses, wounds, cracked, weeping and inflamed skin. The essential oil has deeply skin-regenerative properties, helping sufferers from eczema, acne scarring, stretch marks, and poor or ageing skin tone. Excretory complaints and haemorrhoids are treated with frankincense, as well as haemorrhaging, heavy periods, nosebleeds, and urinary-tract conditions such as cystitis.

Alternative therapist and Reiki Master, Krishni Borang, uses undiluted essential oil of frankincense: 'It is one hundred per cent organic and therapeutic, as I am aware that the skin is the biggest organ of the body and the oil goes directly into the bloodstream. Frankincense is a very high vibrating oil with sesquiterpenes, which stimulate the limbic system, hypothalamus, pineal and pituitary glands. The hypothalamus governs the production of various hormones in the body including the thyroid hormone. As my thyroid gland does not produce enough thyroxin, I put it on my throat (as well as taking extra thyroxin). I gave it to my mother to put directly on her heart when she had high blood pressure, since it is a muscle-relaxing oil. She was depressed too, and I noticed it had an uplifting effect, and she appreciated the fact that it was a medication that she did not have to

Above: Blissful face at Parasuravesvara Temple, Bhubaneshwar, Orissa, India

Right: Native American Tewan ceremony using copal incense, similar in fragrance and appearance to frankincense, New Mexico, USA

swallow. I also recommend my patients who have breast cancer to apply it to the breast, since it is known to be anti-tumoral. I put it on my forehead for meditation—the scent is divine!'

As we have seen in Arabia, frankincense is safe to use in pregnancy and childbirth. In fact there are no known contra-indications, nor is there any risk of overdosing. It is thus extraordinary, considering its extensive medical history, that frankincense has disappeared from conventional allopathic practice in the West.

SOURCING THE SUBLIME

Modern aromatherapy, following its ancient antecedents, is founded on holistic consciousness, encouraging health on every level, for the mind and the spirit, as well as the body. It involves a subtle process of self-empowerment, in which the individual begins to take responsibility for his or her sense of well-being, including leading a balanced life-style and tackling stress.

Why, of all the essential oils at the disposal of an aroma-therapist, is frankincense so often chosen to alleviate anxiety? Fundamental to its power to ground, relax and deeply uplift, is the fact that it is associated with the element of Earth. As Gabriel Mojay writes: 'Frankincense oil's most important sphere of action must be the nervous system. Here, its ability to relax yet revitalise makes it excellent for treating both nervous tension and nervous exhaustion. It smoothes the flow of stagnant *Qi-energy* (the vital force of the body and mind)

whenever an accumulation of stress has led to irritability, restlessness, and insomnia. As a mild tonic, it can also help to uplift, and so is an important antidepressant essential oil… It may be called upon for states of mental agitation and worry, or whenever the mind is distracted and overwhelmed by a cacophony of thoughts…. Whenever we have allowed ourselves to become oppressed by the mundane or tied to the past—indeed, restricted or weighed down by any form of over-attachment—frankincense can help us to break free'.[3]

Inhaling the warm, woody, balsamic fragrance of frankincense, one senses its element—earth—with its stabilising, balancing effect. Negative states of mind start to dissolve; insecurity, even fear, fade away. The grief of the bereaved begins to dispel; nightmares and claustrophobia recede; panic attacks and paranoia diminish. Constant self-criticism dissolves away; faith returns. The undisciplined begin to feel a sense of self-worth as frankincense restores their equilibrium and sense of purpose.

Frankincense is also associated with the Yogic *chakra* or centre of energy in the middle of the forehead, symbolised by the third eye. In Hinduism and Buddhism, this *chakra* opens the doors of perception to transcendence. Frankincense accesses a higher state of consciousness, connecting the individual to universal spirituality. On a practical level, with its ability to still the mind and deepen the breath, it is the perfect aid to contemplation and meditation. Frankincense, the ancient pathway to prayer, still has the potential to enable the soul to soar.

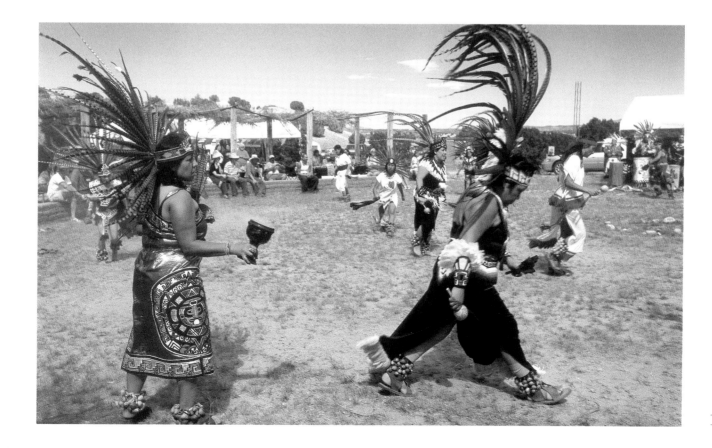

My land is bare of chattering folk;
The clouds are low along the ridges,
And sweet's the air with curly smoke
From all my burning bridges.

Dorothy Parker, *Sanctuary*, c. 1931

USING FRANKINCENSE AT HOME

Essential oils may be administered in a number of ways, all of them extremely pleasant, as well as therapeutic. The two primary methods are by inhalation or application to the skin. MASSAGE is the most effective home treatment, relaxing muscles when exhausted, or after sport or gardening. You can massage your own hands and feet, stimulating all the reflex zones of the body.

Blend two to three drops of frankincense essential oil with 15 ml/1 tbsp. of good quality carrier oil (almond, grape-seed, or calendula are all fine). Babies love being massaged, though the essential oil should be further diluted. The added advantage about using frankincense is its skin-conditioning benefits. This makes frankincense useful if the baby develops eczema or other skin complaints such as nappy rash.

A warm BATH scented with frankincense oil is one of life's epiphanies. It provides an ideal environment in which to relax and relieve tension, and a treatment for dry, damaged, sore or irritated skin. Afterwards sleep will be profound. Add eight to ten drops of oil, lower the light level, light a candle and float away. The warm water assists absorption by your skin, after which you can further nourish it by applying a SKINCARE product. Proprietary oils and creams containing frankincense are listed on pp. 166–168, but you can also blend your own. Add three to four drops of essential oil to an un-perfumed moisturising product.

Another quick remedy for tired, aching legs or swollen feet is a frankincense FOOTBATH. Fill a bowl with warm water, and six to eight drops of oil; then soak for at least ten minutes. COMPRESSES are excellent first aids: cool ones for acute pain in joints, stomach and head; warm ones to reduce inflammation and swelling from injuries and insect bites. Add three to five drops of frankincense oil to a bowl of hot or cold water and gently place a piece of soft cotton fabric onto the surface so that it soaks up the film of oil.

It is tempting to use the essential oil of frankincense directly on the skin as a perfume or inhalant or to staunch a bleeding wound and prevent infection. Opinions of aromatherapists are divided about the wisdom of applying the undiluted oil; it

Below: Prayers with incense at Polin monastry, Lantau Island, Hong Kong

Right: Ceremony at Emerald Buddha Temple, Bangkok

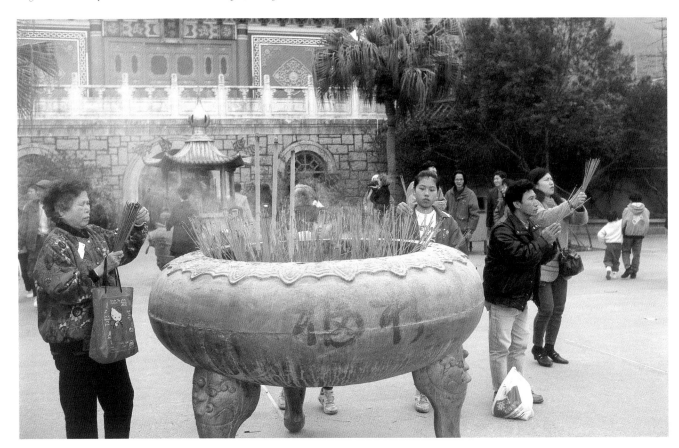

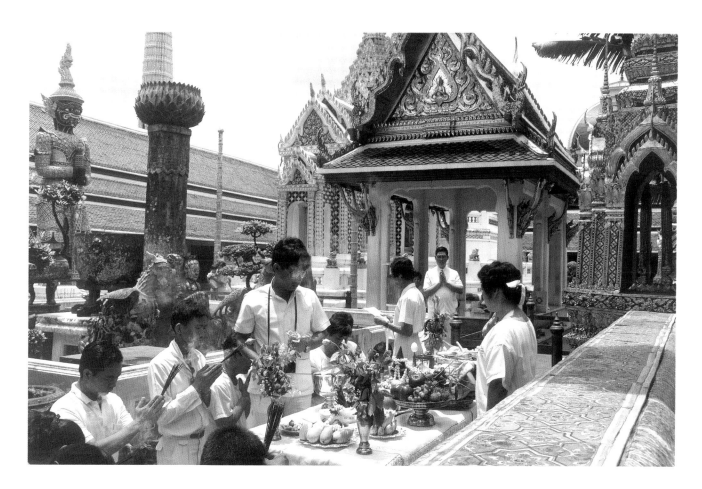

is after all the concentrated *essence* of the resin, and should be treated with respect. Some practitioners promote daily ingestion of essential oil, so if you propose to take frankincense internally, you could follow the traditional Middle Eastern practice of drinking a glass of water in which a few resin crystals have been steeped, or to which you have added a few drops of oil with a dash of honey, to counteract any bitterness. After aromatherapy massage, or any other skin treatment, don't wash for around eight hours, to ensure maximum absorption. Essential oils are volatile, and their containers should be kept tightly stoppered, as they are sensitive to light. They should be on sale in dark bottles, which, when stored in a cool, dark place, will last at least three years. Ensure that the label states 'pure essential oil' of frankincense.

Inhalation of frankincense is the fast track to all its benefits. Using STEAM INHALATION will relieve congestion and asthma, clear blocked sinuses and catarrh. Add ten drops of frankincense to a bowl of steaming water, lean over it, covering your head and the bowl to form a little tent, close your eyes and inhale the vapours deeply for up to ten minutes. Carry your therapy around with you by TISSUE INHALATION. A few drops on a tissue placed in a small plastic bag can be sniffed at stressful times at work, or if you have a cold. DIRECT INHALATION is even simpler, though again, not every aromatherapist would recommend this method, as it

involves placing several drops of undiluted frankincense essential oil into your hands. Cup them over your nose and mouth and breathe in steadily and deeply.

ROOM FRAGRANCES come in several forms. Vaporisers or essential oil burners are marvellous sickroom aids, charging the atmosphere with healing energy and helping to inhibit the spread of infection. They consist of a small bowl of water heated by the flame of a night-light in a burner beneath. The drops of frankincense added to the water gradually evaporate, filling the room with aromatherapy.

DIFFUSERS or SPRITZERS purify an environment, adding perfume and pleasure by spraying a fine mist of essential oil in water. Special attachments for LIGHT FITTINGS surround the bulb with scent, the oil diffusing as the bulb warms up; or simply sprinkle the cold bulb with a few drops of frankincense oil. Cardinal Wolsey is said to have always carried a POMANDER filled with frankincense resin. So could you, alternating the contents with POT-POURRI invigorated by the addition of a few drops of essential oil. SCENTING CLOTHES and BED LINEN is another delightful traditional way of adding fragrance to your life. Try sprinkling frankincense oil on drawer liners, or add a few drops to the fabric conditioner compartment of your washing machine.

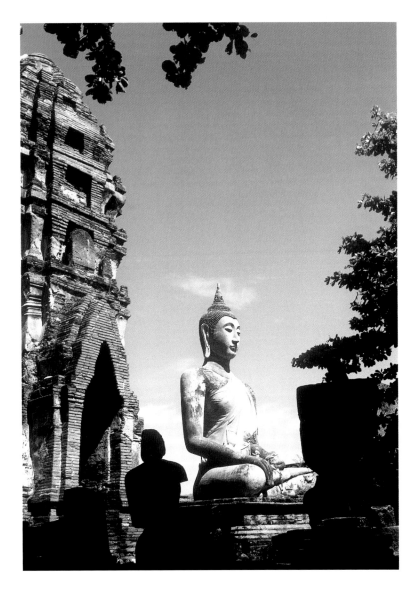

Accompany your prayer with a perfume and your words will reach God transported by an odorous exhalation telling Him of your gratitude and devotion.

The Vedas of India

Whether you call it meditation, contemplation or prayer, or just a time of being rather than doing, of stilling the chatter of the mind, devoting regular attention to your inner self will gradually seep into your everyday life and have a profoundly positive effect on every aspect of it. Frankincense, with its sacred aspect, and ability to calm the mind, is the ideal perfume to use.

Make sure that the room in which you are creating your sanctuary is pure: open the window if it is heavy with the dense vibrations of any other smoke than incense. It helps to have a warm, darkened environment, and a complete lack of distraction or extraneous noise. Try to go within at roughly the same time every day, and in the same position in the room. It may help to have your back against a wall, and to sit on a firm cushion with another at the base of your spine.

Now is the time to light your frankincense. As that extraordinary fragrance begins to pervade the room, you are embarking on your pathway to prayer. Open up to those infinitely generous emotions the Vedas suggest, of gratitude and devotion, generosity to your Self for being so *worthy*.

As the smoke ascends heavenwards, sit cross-legged, if that is comfortable, and check that there is no tension in your body, especially around the jaw and shoulders. Try to keep your back as straight as possible, so that the flow of sacred energy within you is unimpeded. Concentrate on the inhalation and exhalation of your breath. Trace its path as far inwards as you can, and rest there, in that most inner space for a second. Then trace the path of your breath outwards as far as you can imagine, and rest there. Inner and outer will gradually become a circle. You are already there, in meditation, here and now.

He saw that there was no mood of the mind that had not its counterpart in the sensuous life, and set himself to discover their true relations, wondering what there was in frankincense that made one mystical.

Oscar Wilde, *The Picture of Dorian Gray*, 1891

Whether creating a sensuous ambience, as the Syrians used to do, burning frankincense before and after sex; or encouraging a mystical environment, prior to Hatha Yoga or meditation, nothing is more powerful than lighting frankincense resin crystals. Prepare a fireproof surface such as a metal dish or bowl filled with sand; then, using tweezers or pliers, hold a good quality charcoal disk over a flame until it smoulders. Sprinkle the frankincense onto the disc, to ignite a heightened awareness of the spiritual realm.

The sense of smell is the sense of imagination.

Jean-Jacques Rousseau

Infuse the delights and benefits of frankincense into your life by creating inexpensive products and imaginative presents.

ESSENTIAL OIL BLENDS
Gabriel Mojay, Principal of the Institute of Traditional Herbal Medicine & Aromatherapy, London, suggests some blends of essential oils for emotional first aid (the numbers after each ingredient refer to the drops per 20 ml/1 tbsp. of carrier oil).
SUDDEN PSYCHOLOGICAL TRAUMA
Frankincense (2) + lavender (3) + spikenard (1)
OVER-PREOCCUPIED WITH DETAIL
Frankincense (3) + vetiver (2) + cypress
OPPRESSIVE OVER-ATTACHMENT
Frankincense (2) + myrrh (2) + cypress (2)

INCENSE BLEND
Showers of Gold is an incense created for this book by Helene Hodge of PeacockAngel Incense, formulated to bring about

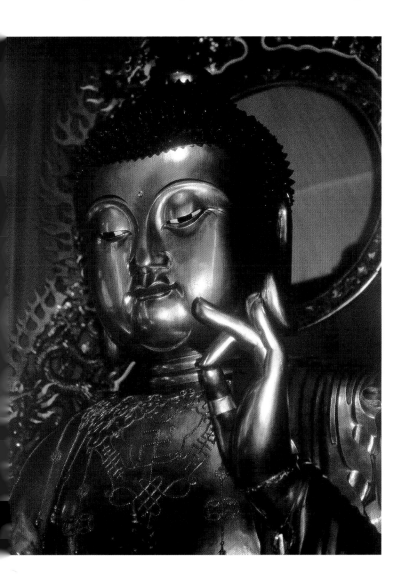

abundance. *Showers of Gold* addresses all matters pertaining to money and prosperity'. (The numbers refer to parts as a proportion of the whole blend).
Frankincense (4) + myrrh (1) + sandalwood ($\frac{1}{2}$) + benzoin ($\frac{1}{2}$) + bayberry herb ($\frac{1}{4}$).
Mix together well and store in an airtight jar out of the light. To use, sprinkle on a lighted charcoal disc.
Helen says: 'Just as a candle brightens up a darkened room, the aromatic effect of incense conveys tranquillity to the senses'.

NATURAL PERFUME
Christine Westwood, an acclaimed aromatherapist, seen in this chapter massaging clients, has created a simple but evocative essential oil blend. As a natural perfume it is tenacious, with its inclusion of frankincense, which is such an effective fixative, especially when applied to pulse points on the wrists and behind the ears.
5 ml of a light base oil such as apricot kernel, grape-seed or Jojoba + 2 drops of jasmine oil + 1 drop of frankincense oil.

NOURISHING NIGHT CREAM
Raje Airey is the author of books and articles on complementary health and spirituality. She writes: 'Frankincense helps reduce wrinkles and restores tone to slack muscles'.
50 g/2 oz jar of unperfumed base cream with a close-fitting lid + 2 drops frankincense essential oil + 3 drops rose essential oil + 3 drops jasmine essential oil.

Writers Lydia Eagle and Barbara Jackson contribute two recipes for skincare to which a few drops of frankincense essential oil may be added for fragrance and its regenerative effect:

HONEY CLEANSING LOTION
(FOR ANY SKIN TYPE)
1 tsp. honey + 2 tbsp. warm milk.
Blend together to make a lotion, then spread it over your face and neck with fingertips. Leave for 5 minutes, then rinse.

AVOCADO MOISTURISER (FOR ANY SKIN)
2 eggs + 1 tsp. glycerine (from a pharmacy) + $\frac{1}{2}$ tsp. lemon juice + 2 tsps. avocado oil + 2 egg yolks, beaten + $\frac{1}{2}$ tsp. cider vinegar + 2 tbsps. distilled water.
Mix the eggs, glycerine and lemon juice, and then slowly add enough avocado oil to thicken to a cream-like consistency. Stir in the vinegar. Add the beaten egg yolks and water, mixing slowly all the time. Keep refrigerated, for a short time only.

ADDRESS BOOK

11 Blade's Court, 1-1 Deodar Road, Putney, London,
SW15 2NU.
Tel: 020 8877 4524
For the rest of the world, check www.omantourism.gov.om

In Oman itself, at one of Salalah's five star hotels, I noticed
local tours advertised, visiting Job's Tomb (Nabi Ayoub),
where frankincense is burned around the clock, through
the spectacular Nejd mountains, to imbibe the evocative
atmosphere of the groves of *Boswellia sacra* trees. Another
tour, eastward-bound, takes in the splendour of Al-Balid, Taqa
with its fort and women creating *mejmar* incense burners,
then Sumhuram to look out over the inimitable Khor Rori
harbour, the old merchants' houses at Mirbat, ending up back
at Hafa Frankincense Souk. Zubair Travel is the one to catch,
or Al-Fawas Travel & Tourism. Much more ambitious safaris
are available too, following the old Incense Routes through
Oman and Yemen. Try searching The Frankincense Trail—
A Cultural Tour at www.bestway.com/itineraries/t25.html.

PROFESSOR JURIS ZARIN'S
ARCHAEOLOGICAL FUND

www.arabian-archaeology.com

MEDITATION

For further information, visit www.siddhayoga.org

ISIPCA AT UNIVERSITY OF VERSAILLES

www.efcm-master.com

INCENSE & OIL SUPPLIERS

PeacockAngel Incense offers frankincense resin and essential
oil, charcoal discs, and a range of blended incenses containing
frankincense which include Kyphi, Roman Sun and Helios; as
well as blended oils such as Anointing and Sekhmet.
www.peacockangel.com

Kindred Spirit supplies Omani Houjari Superior Frankincense
resin, and Frankincense & Myrrh Incense Sticks.
www.kindredspirit.co.uk

Scents of Earth, based in the US, sells resin and steam
distilled oil from Oman.
www.scents-of-earth/frankincense.com

Young Living Essential Oils offer frankincense as well as blends
including Twelve Oils of Ancient Scripture, Three Wise Men,
Exodus and Egyptian Gold, all containing frankincense,
as do other blends relating to emotions, such as Gratitude,
Forgiveness, Humility, Valour, Harmony, Abundance, and
Acceptance. A Boswellia Wrinkle Cream promises to 'build
collagen and minimise fine lines'.

Distribution is from Krishni Borang:
krishni@btopenworld.com

META-AROMATHERAPY™

This is a system of aromatherapy focusing on the wellbeing of
the mind and emotions as well as its physical benefits, offering
products and training courses for beginners through to advanced
practitioners. It was originated by Christine Westwood, whose
book *Aromatherapy: A Guide For Home Use*, lists a number of
conditions which may benefit from the use of frankincense
essential oil, such as cracked and weeping skin, and many
psychological states, including anxiety and fear.
www. meta-aromatherapy.com
www.christinewestwood.com

FURTHER READING

Aromatherapy: A Guide for Home Use, Amberwood 1991.
Aromatherapy: A Guide to Stress Management, Amberwood 1993.
Aromatherapy: Healthy Legs & Feet, Amberwood 1995.

PERFUMES CONTAINING FRANKINCENSE

The following two specialist shops in London stock unusual scents, many of them sourced directly from small companies, often owned by perfumers, who tend to use high concentrations of natural essences. Both are decorated like Marie Antoinette's boudoir and staffed by informed enthusiasts.

LES SENTEURS

71 Elizabeth Street, Belgravia, London, SW1W 9PJ.
Tel: 020 7730 2322.
www.lessenteurs.com
Apogee by Francis Robert (son of Guy Robert, creator of the first Amouage fragrance)
Serge by Serge Lutyens
Habanita by Molinard
No 9 by Cadolle
Parfum Sacré by Caron
Bal à Versailles by Jean Deprez
Abahna (body products only)

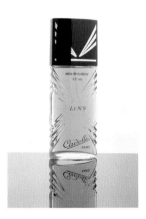

L'ARTISAN PARFUMEUR,

Created for this company, *Passage d'Enfer* is described as 'a haze of light incense to carry you up to cloud nine'. With three stores in London, you can also visit www.artisanparfumeur.com

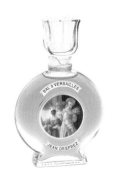

OTHER SPECIALIST OUTLETS

Harrods Perfume Hall, Knightsbridge; Selfridges, Oxford Street, London.

OTHER PERFUMES CONTAINING FRANKINCENSE

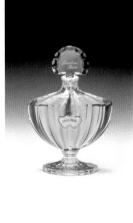

Jicky and *Shalimar* by Guerlain
Sacré Bleu and *Vanilla Tonka* by Parfums de Nicolai (Guerlain's granddaughter)
Ysatis by Givenchy
Ciara by Revlon
Cinnabar and *Youth Dew* by Estée Lauder
Opium by Yves Saint Laurent
Cuba and *Frankincense & Myrrh* by Czech & Speake
Frankincense & Myrrh by Jovan
Expression by Jacques Fath
J'ai Osé by Laroche
Scandale by Lanvin
Scherrer 2 by Jean-Louis Scherrer
Gem by Van Cleef & Arpel
Loulou by Cacherel
Coco and *L'Egoïste* (for men) by Chanel
Royal Secret by Monteil
Shaal Nur and *Messe de Minuit* by Etro
Ispalan by Rocher
Alessandro Dell'Acqua Parfum
Enigma by de Markoff
Kif by Lamborghini
1872 for Men and *Perfume X Creation* by Clive Christian
Giorgio by Giorgio Beverly Hills
Jules (for men) by Christian Dior
Old Spice (for men) by Shulton

AMOUAGE

Perfumes and *aatr* are available at Harrods, London; Ka De We, Berlin; Nordstrom, New Jersey and Bergdorf Goodman, New York, as well as 23 other selected international perfume outlets; duty-free shops in Abu Dhabi, Bahrain, Dubai, Kuwait, Oman, Qatar and Sharjah; and on the airlines of Gulf Air, Oman Air, Qatar Air and Saudia.

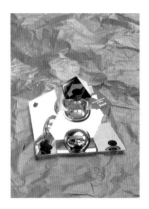

ARABIAN *OUDH*

The eponomously named shop stocks pure *oudh* as well as perfumes containing it. Their *1000 Flowers* is redolent with frankincense.

435–437 Oxford Street,
London, W1C 2PL.
Tel: 020 7491 3333.
www.arabianoud.uk.com

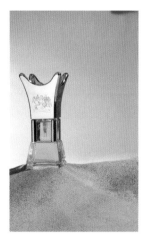

ARAB PERFUMES

Kato Aromatic has branches in Grasse, France; Giza, Egypt; New Jersey in the US; and the Crimea, Russia.
www.katoaromatic.com

Yas, The Royal Name of Perfume.
www.yas-perfume.com

Al Haramain Perfumes.
www.alharamainperfumes.co.ae

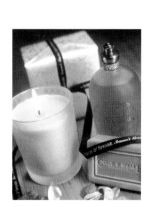

SKINCARE PRODUCTS

From Neal's Yard Remedies come Cleopatra's Secret Frankincense Nourishing Cream and Body Cream, described by *The Sunday Times* as 'the best moisturiser ever'.

Call 01483 454 444 for stockists, or visit Neal's Yard in London's Covent Garden.

E'Spa have a Concept range offering intensive care for maturing, stressed or distressed skins with Regenerating Face Treatment Oil, Firming Face Mask and 24-Hour Moisturising Complex, all containing frankincense.
www.espaonline.com

Czech & Speake offer 'Frankincense & Myrrh' in bath and bodylines, as well as personal and room fragrances at their elegant Jermyn Street, London shop and selected department stores.

One of Woodspirit Natural Soaps is 'Frankincense & Myrrh'.

Call 020 8293 4949 for stockists.

Top: *Les Larmes Sacrées de Thebes* by Baccarat

Middle: *Sahra*, a Gulf manufactured and marketed perfume, with a container in the form of an incense burner.

Bottom: *Frankincense & Myrrh* personal and room fragrances by Czech & Speake

A NOTE ON ETYMOLOGY

So synonymous with the concept of *incense* has frank*incense* become, that the words are often interchangeable. When detailing ingredients in the pyramid construction of both early and modern perfumes, the word incense designates frankincense, (as a long-lasting base note). In France, the foundation stone of the contemporary international industry, frankincense is known simply as *encens*. The English word is derived from the Old French *franc encens*, *franc* meaning 'true' or 'pure'.

Frankincense is also known as *olibanum* and *gum thus*. In Latin, it was known as *tus*; and in ancient Egypt as *neter-sent*, or *'nty w sntr*. It is an oleo-gum-resin, whose pseudonyms are *balsam* or *balm*, and is sometimes confused with *labdanum* (or amber), an oleo-resin obtained from the rockrose, found in Oman as well as the Mediterranean and North Africa. Misunderstanding may have arisen because of its shared location with frankincense, and also because the word *labdanum* might suggest *luban*. This really is the Arabic word for frankincense. Like the South Arabian *libnay*, *luban* derives from a Semitic root referring to 'milky whiteness', and inferring purity. Other variations on the *luban* theme are the Greek *libanos* or *libanotus*, the Hebrew *lebonah*, and the Akkadian *lebanatu*. Akkadian was one of the languages of Ancient Mesopotamia, whose form *lubbunu* for incense, lingers on in the name 'Lebanon'. Juris Zarins cites 2300 BCE as the date when the Akkadian term *kanaktum* began to be translated as frankincense. This may have survived in the later Arabic *qunnuq* or *kunnuk*, derived from the Persian *kunduruk*.

The Arabic scientific name for frankincense is *kundur* derived again, via Persia, from the Greek pharmaceutical term *khondros libanou* or 'grain of frankincense', very close to the Sanskrit term *kunduruka* used in India.

NOTES

INTRODUCTION

1 Nigel Groom, *The Perfume Handbook*, (London: Chapman & Hall, 1992), p. vi.
2 Quoted in Robert Tisserand, *Aromatherapy for Everyone*, (London: Arkana, 1988), p. 113.
3 Patrick Süskind, *Perfume*, (London: Penguin, 1987), p. 92.

CHAPTER ONE

1 Research carried out by Professor Juris Zarins of Southwest Missouri State University.
2 Juris Zarins, *The Land of Incense*, (Sultan Qaboos University Publications, Sultanate of Oman, 2001), pp. 56–57.
3 Nigel Groom, *Frankincense and Myrrh*, (London: Longman, 1981), p. 206. It should be noted that this book was written in 1981, before much of the archaeological work in southern Arabia had begun. Even now, these excavations are in their infancy.
4 *The Gilgamesh Epic & Old Testament Parallels*, (Chicago: University of Chicago Press, 1963), p. 87.
5 Edwin T. Morris, *Scents of Time*, (New York: Prestel/Metropolitan Museum of Art, 1999), p. 18.
6 Groom, *Frankincense and Myrrh*, p. 16.
7 Walter de la Mare, *Collected Poems*, (New York: Henry Holt, 1920), vol. 1, p. 135.
8 Strabo, *The Geography of Strabo*, (Loeb Classical Library, Heinemann & Harvard University Press, 1930), book 16, chapter 4, section 19.
9 Tisserand, *Aromatherapy for Everyone*, p. 5.
10 Wanda Sellar and Martin Watt, *Frankincense and Myrrh*, (Saffron Walden: The C.W. Daniel Company, 1996), p. 37.
11 Nicholas Clapp, *The Road to Wubar*, (London: Souvenir Press, 1999), p. 232.
12 Numbers 16:17, 32, 35.
13 Numbers 16: 46, 48.
14 Leviticus 2: 14–16.
15 St Luke 1:9–13.
16 Quoted in Caroline Stone, *We Three Kings of Orient Were*, (Texas: *Saudi Aramco World*, November/December 1980), p. 2.
17 Wilfred Thesiger, *Arabian Sands*, (Harmondsworth: Penguin, 1991), p. 190.
18 Edward H. Schafer, *The Golden Peaches of Samarkand*, (Los Angeles: University of California Press, 1963), p. 170.
19 Ibid., p. 163.

CHAPTER TWO

1 A. G. Miller and M. Morris, *The Plants of Dhofar*, (Royal Diwan, Government of Oman, Muscat, 1988), p. 78.
2 Freya Stark, *The Southern Gates of Arabia*, (London: John Murray, 1942), appendix.
3 H.A.R. Gibb (ed.), *The Travels of Ibn Battuta*, (Cambridge: CUP, 1962), vol. 2, p. 390.
4 Quoted in Groom, *Frankincense and Myrrh*, p. 105.
5 Quoted in Karen Pereczes, 'On the Frankincense Road' in *Kindred Spirit* magazine, November/December, 2005, p. 16.
6 Arthur O. Tucker, *Economic Botany* (1986), vol. 40, p. 425.
7 Gabriel Mojay, *Aromatherapy for Healing the Spirit* (London: Gaia, 1996), p. 156. Arthur Tucker in *Economic Botany* writes that it is 'a natural oleo-gum-resin composed of about 5–9% essential oil, 65–85% alcohol-soluble resins, and the remaining water-soluble gums'. Quoted in *Kindred Spirit* Shaima Ghazanfar adds that it 'contains oils, Sesquiterpenes, alcohols, esters, boswellia acids and ether-insoluble gum containing polysaccharides. The composition of the oil differs according to the climate and habitat'.
8 A. S. El Qassani, *Dhofar: The Land of Frankincense*, (Oman: Directorate General for Education, 1980), p. 3.
9 Pliny quoted in Groom, *Frankincense and Myrrh*, p. 137.
10 Pliny quoted in Groom, *Frankincense and Myrrh*, p. 144.
11 Thesiger, *Arabian Sands*, p. 45.
12 John Bostock and H. T. Riley (trans.), *The Natural History of Pliny* (Henry G. Bohn: London, 1855), vol. 3, p. 125.
13 Quoted in Nicholas Clapp, *The Road to Wubar* (London: Souvenir Press, 1999), p. 138.
14 El Qassani, *Dhofar: The Land of Frankincense*, p. 36.
15 Tim Macintosh-Smith, 'Scents of Place: Frankincense in Oman' in *Saudi Aramco World*, (Houston, Texas, May/June 2000), vol. 51, no. 3, p. 20.

CHAPTER THREE

1 Quoted in Groom, *Frankincense and Myrrh*, p. 202.
2 Wilfred H. Schoff (trans.), *The Periplus of the Erythraean Sea*, (New York: Longmans Green, 1912).
3 Groom, *Frankincense and Myrrh*, p. 33.
4 Pliny, *Natural History* (book 6, chapter 32, section 162).
5 Zarins, *The Land of Incense*, p. 154.
6 Ibid., p. 59.
7 Ibid., p. 93.
8 Clapp, *The Road to Wubar*, p. 207.
9 Thesiger, *Arabian Sands*, p. 191.
10 Clapp, *The Road to Wubar*, p. 203.
11 Zarins, *The Land of Incense*, p. 138.
12 Michael Jansen, *The Frankincense Trail*, (Paris: World Heritage Review, no. 38, 2004), p. 62.

13 Gibb, *Ibn Battuta—Travels in Asia and Africa—1325–1354*, p. 198.
14 Qur'an, sura 34:15
15 Strabo, *The Geography of Strabo*, chapter 4, sections 18–26.
16 El Qassani, *Dhofar The Land of Frankincense*, p. 52.
17 WHC Nomination Documentation: Decision of the World Heritage Committee. File Name: 1010.pdf. UNESCO Region: Arab States.

CHAPTER FOUR

1 Groom, *The Perfume Handbook*, p. vi.
2 Michael Edwards, *Fragrances of the World*, (Sydney: Fragrance Editions, 2004), p. 13.
3 Steven Arctander, *Perfume and Flavour Materials of Natural Origin*, (Copenhagen: Hoffenbergske Etablissement, 1960), p. 465.

CHAPTER FIVE

1 Karen Pereczes, *On the Frankincense Road Kindred Spirit* magazine, November/December 2005, p.19.
2 Sellar and Watt, *Frankincense and Myrrh*, p. 42.
3 Gabriel Mojay, *Aromatherapy for Healing the Spirit* (London: Gaia Books, 1996), p. 74.

SELECTED BIBLIOGRAPHY

ABERCROMBIE, Thomas J. 'Arabia's Frankincense Trail' in *National Geographic*. Washington, October 1985.

AIREY, Raje. *Scent Therapy*. London: Lorenz, 2001.

ARCTANDER, Steven. *Perfume & Flavour Materials of Natural Origin*, Copenhagen: Hoffenbergske Etablissement, 1960.

BARRAULT, Michèle. *Regards Dhofar*. Paris: Editions Michel Hetier, 1999.

BOSTOCK, John and H. T. RILEY (trans.) *The Natural History of Pliny*, Vol. 3. London: Henry G. Bishr, 1885.

CALLAN, Lou and Gordon ROBINSON. *Oman & the UAE*. Lonely Planet Guide, 2000.

CLAPP, Nicholas. *The Road to Wubar*. London: Souvenir Press, 1998.

'Dhofar, Land of Frankincense' in *Oman Daily Observer*, Ruwi 1997.

EDWARDS, Michael. *Fragrances of the World*. Paris and Sydney: Fragrance Editions, 2003/4.

EL QASSANI, A. S. *Dhofar The Land of Frankincense*. South Province Oman: Directorate General for Education, 1980.

FARIS, Nabih Amin. *The Antiquities of South Arabia*. Princeton: Princeton University Press, 1938.

GIBB, H.A.R. (ed.) *Ibn Battuta—Travels in Asia and Africa—1325–1354*. London: Routledge Kegan Paul, 1929.

GIBB, H.A.R. (ed.) *The Travels of Ibn Battuta*. Cambridge: CUP, 1962.

Gilgamesh Epic & Old Testament Parallels. Chicago: University of Chicago Press, 1963.

GROOM, Nigel. *Frankincense & Myrrh*. London: Longman, 1981.

GROOM, Nigel. *The Perfume Handbook*. London: Chapman & Hall, 1992.

HANSEN, Eric. 'The Hidden History of a Scented Wood' in *Saudi Aramco World*, November/December 2000.

HAWLEY, Sir Donald. *Oman & Its Renaissance*. London: Stacey International, 1982.

IRVINE, Susan. *Perfume*. London: Aurum 1996.

JANSEN, Michael. 'The Frankincense Trail', *World Heritage Review* no. 38. Paris: UNESCO, 2004.

KAY, Shirley. *Enchanting Oman*. Dubai: Motivate Publishing, 1999.

KING, Jamie. *Chic Simple: Scents*. London: Thames & Hudson, 1993.

LAWTON, John. *Silk, Scents & Spice*. Paris: UNESCO, 2004.

MACINTOSH-SMITH, Tim. 'Scents of Place: Frankincense in Oman' in *Saudi Aramco World*, May/June 2000.

MILLER, A. G. and M. MORRIS. *The Plants of Dhofar*. Royal Diwan, Government of Oman, Muscat, 1988.

MOJAY, Gabriel. *Aromatherapy for Healing the Spirit*. London: Gaia, 1996.

MORRIS, Edwin T., *Scents of Time*. Prestel/Metropolitan Museum of Art, New York, 1999.

MUKHOPAPHYAY, Sounick. *Perfume Passion*. Muscat: Tribute, Apex Publishing, 2001.

MÜLLER, Walter W. 'Notes on the Use of Frankincense in South Arabia' in *Proceedings of the 9th Seminar for Arabian Studies*. London Seminar for Arabian Studies, 1976.

PERECZES, Karen. 'On the Frankincense Road' in *Kindred Spirit* magazine, November/December 2005.

PRABHU, Conrad. *The Oman Visitor*. Ruwi, Oman: First Publishing, n.d.

PRICE, Shirley, *Practical Aromatherapy*. Wellingborough: Thorsons, 1987.

SCHAFER, Edward H. *The Golden Peaches of Samarkand*. Los Angeles: University of California Press, 1963.

SELLAR, Wanda and WATT, Martin. *Frankincense & Myrrh*. Saffron Walden: The C.W. Daniel Company, 1996.

STONE, Caroline. 'We Three Kings of Orient Were' in *Saudi Aramco World*. November/December 1980.

STRABO. *The Geography of Strabo*. London and Cambridge, MA: Heinemann & Harvard University Press/Loeb Classical Library, 1930.

TISSERAND, Robert. *Aromatherapy for Everyone*. Harmondsworth: Arkana (Penguin), 1998.

TUCKER, Arthur O. 'Frankincense & Myrrh' in *Economic Botany*. New York: New York Botanical Garden, 1986.

VAUGHAN, Carolyn. *The Gifts of the Magi*. New York: Bulfinch/Metropolitan Museum of Art, 1998.

WESTWOOD, Christine. *Aromatherapy: A Guide for Home Use*. Christchurch: Kerbina, 1991.

ZARINS, Juris. *The Land of Incense*. Muscat: Sultan Qaboos University Publications, 2001.

INDEX OF NAMES

AUTHOR'S ACKNOWLEDGEMENTS

Najeeb Rajab Al-Awadh, Director of Public Relations, Ministry of Information, Salalah, for introducing me to frankincense 15 years ago; Ghanim al-Shanfari, instrumental to the book for his 'insider' information; Kenneth Campbell, for publishing consultancy and constant support; Rosemary Hector, Media Coordinator, Ministry of Information, Muscat, for her efficiency and helpfulness for 15 years; H.E. Abdul Aziz Mohamed Al-Rowas, Advisor to His Majesty the Sultan for Cultural Affairs, for inspiring insight into frankincense; H.E. Sheikh Ghassan Shaker, for making the book possible and my 'dream come true'; Wendy Hewitson, Amouage Europe, for unswerving support; Philippa Hurd, Commissioning Editor, Prestel London, for pushing forward my boundaries as a writer; Basma Irsheid, Chief of Unit for UNESCO Goodwill Ambassadors for obtaining UNESCO support; Remi Kapo, for editing and constant creative encouragement; my children, Bambo and Madhuri, for putting up with me; Laila Shawa, for introducing me to H.E Sheikh Ghassan Shaker; Barbara Stickler, UNESCO, for her enthusiastic and efficient participation; Carolinda Tolstoy, for being so patient.

PICTURE CREDITS

All photographs © Juliet Highet with the exception of:

p. 12: Courtesy of Amouage

p. 26: Courtesy of Spink

p. 28: Copyright © The Trustees of the British Museum

p. 29: akg-images / Erich Lessing

p. 35: Copyright © The Trustees of the British Museum

p. 36: akg-images / Erich Lessing

p. 37: Louvre, Paris, France, Peter Willi / The Bridgeman Art Library

p. 41: akg-images / Cameraphoto

p. 42: © Coram Family in the care of the Foundling Museum, London / The Bridgeman Art Library

p. 44: Courtesy of Roger Keverne Ltd.

p. 45: Copyright © The Trustees of the British Museum

p. 46: © Photo RMN – © Martine Beck-Coppola

p. 47: © Guimet, Dist. RMN – © Richard Lambert

p. 52: Private Collection / The Bridgeman Art Library

pp. 54–55: Private Collection © Whitford Fine Art, London, UK / The Bridgeman Art Library

p. 56: akg-images / Cameraphoto

p. 61: © Christie's Images Limited, 2005

p. 151: Bottom photograph by Clive Arrowsmith for Harper's & Queen

p. 154: Courtesy of Guerlain

© for the text by Juliet Highet 2006
© for design and layout by Prestel Verlag,
Munich Berlin London New York 2006
© for illustrations see Picture Credits, page 175

The right of Juliet Highet to be identified as author of this work has
been asserted in accordance with the Copyright, Designs and
Patents Act 1988.

Prestel Verlag
Königinstrasse 9, D-80539 Munich
Tel. +49 (89) 38 17 09-0
Fax +49 (89) 38 17 09-35
www.prestel.de

Prestel Publishing Ltd.
4, Bloomsbury Place, London WC1A 2QA
Tel. +44 (020) 7323-5004
Fax +44 (020) 7636-8004

Prestel Publishing
900 Broadway, Suite 603
New York, N.Y. 10003
Tel. +1 (212) 995-2720
Fax +1 (212) 995-2733

www.prestel.com

Library of Congress Control Number: 2006928913

The Deutsche Bibliothek holds a record of this publication in the
Deutsche Nationalbibliographie; detailed bibliographical data can be
found under: http://dnb.dde.de

Prestel books are available worldwide. Please contact
your nearest bookseller or one of the above addresses for
information concerning your local distributor.

The information contained in this book was correct at the time of
going to press. However the Author and Publisher accept no liability
for any damage caused by the use of any information contained in
this book.

Editorial direction: Philippa Hurd
Picture research: Anja Besserer
Design, layout and typesetting: WIGEL, Munich
Cartography: Anneli Nau, Munich
Origination: Repro Ludwig, Zell am See, Austria
Printing and binding: Druckerei Uhl, Radolfzell

Printed in Germany on acid-free paper

ISBN 3-7913-3695-9
978-3-7913-3695-4